Wildflowers *of the* West

AN ARTIST'S GUIDE   MOLLY HASHIMOTO

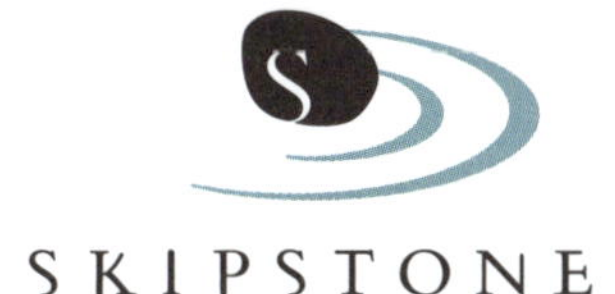

Published by Skipstone, an imprint of Mountaineers Books—an independent, nonprofit publisher

Skipstone and its colophon are registered trademarks of The Mountaineers organization.

Printed in China

28 27 26 25   1 2 3 4 5

Design: Kate Basart/Union Pageworks
Cover illustration: *Paintbrush and lupine, Rocky Mountains*
Frontispiece: *Balsamroot and lupine, Methow Valley, Washington*
The following poems are included with permission from the writers: "All Taxa Biological Inventory" by Saul Weisberg (from *Headwaters: Poem & Field Notes*, published by Pleasure Boat Studio, 2015); "Pasqueflower" by Jane Graham George; "Trillium" by Tim McNulty; excerpt from "This apron is Goodlow Rim" by John Daniel; "Yarrow" by Kim Stafford (from *Earth Elements*, self-published, 2024).
Art permissions: *Bamboo and Poppies* courtesy of Seattle Art Museum (Access no. 61.79.2; Kano Shigenobu; Japanese, early 17th century; pair of six-panel screens, 62⅛ × 140¼"; ink, color and gold on paper; Margaret E. Fuller Purchase Fund; photographed by Paul Macapia)
Alcea rosea L. Malvaceae, *Historia Plantarum*, Conrad Gesner (1516-1565), courtesy of Universtäbibliothek Erlangen-Nürnberg
Paintbrush by Sara Plummer Lemmon, courtesy of Wynne Brown, *The Forgotten Botanist: Sara Plummer Lemmon's Life of Science and Art*

Library of Congress Control Number: 2025933445

Printed on FSC®-certified materials

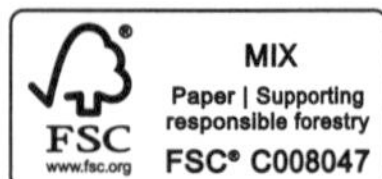

ISBN (hardcover): 978-1-68051-693-7

Skipstone books may be purchased for corporate, educational, or other promotional sales, and our authors are available for a wide range of events. For information on special discounts or booking an author, contact our customer service at 800.553.4453 or mbooks@mountaineersbooks.org.

Skipstone
1001 SW Klickitat Way
Suite 201
Seattle, Washington 98134
206.223.6303
www.skipstonebooks.org
www.mountaineersbooks.org

LIVE LIFE. MAKE RIPPLES.

Wildflowers *of the* West

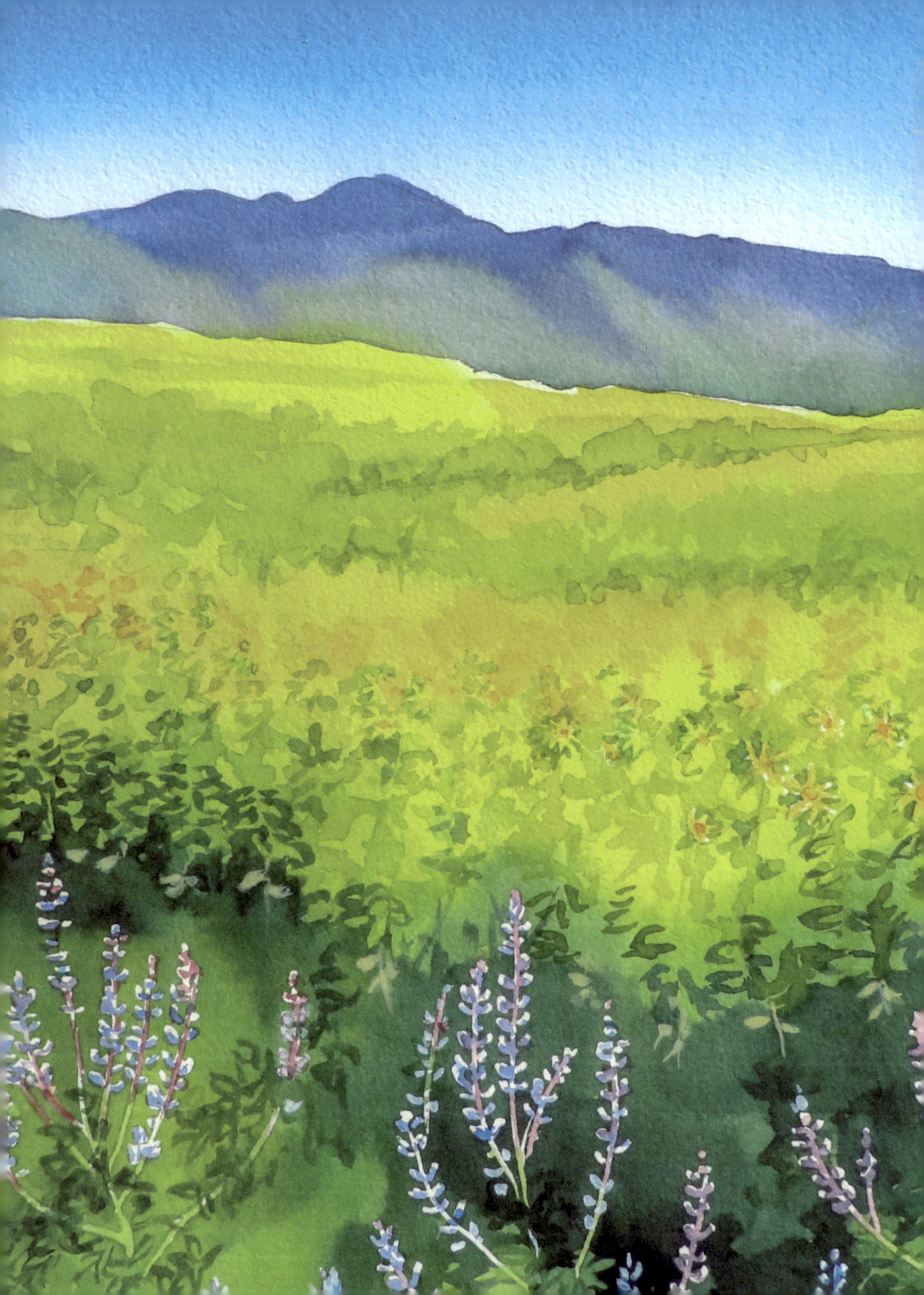

To Paul, best friend and

fellow adventurer, and to my family:

Tom, Rose, Jane, and Julie

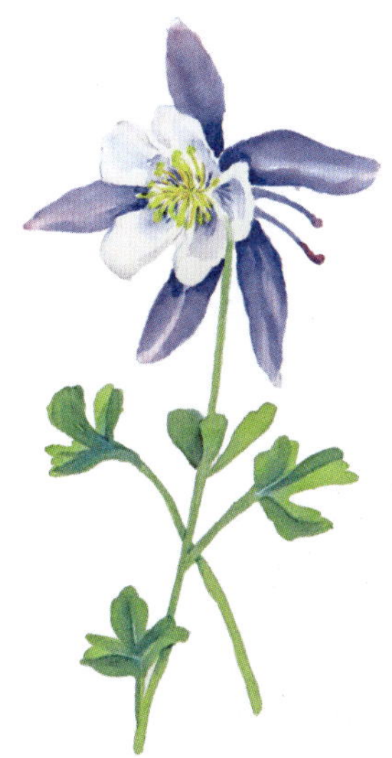

Contents

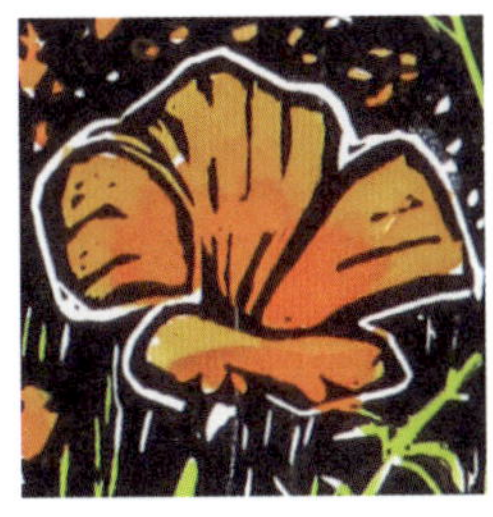

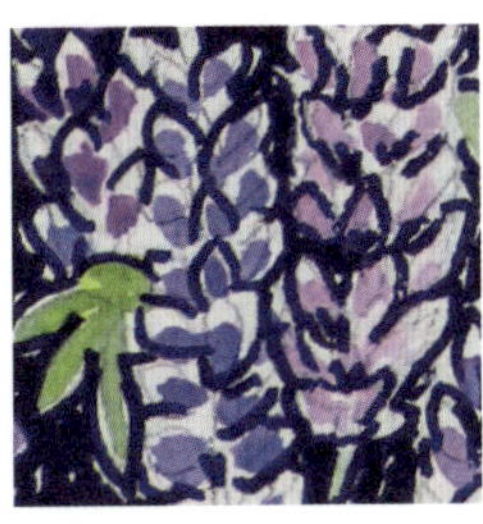

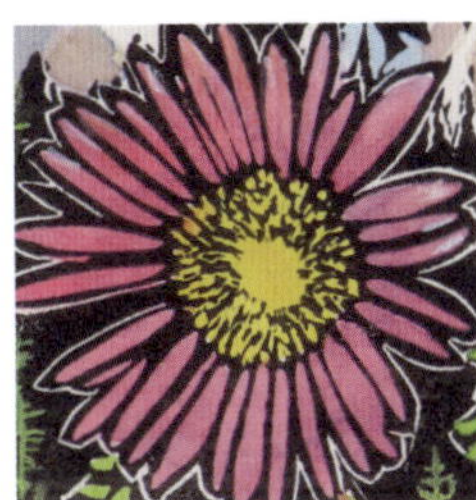

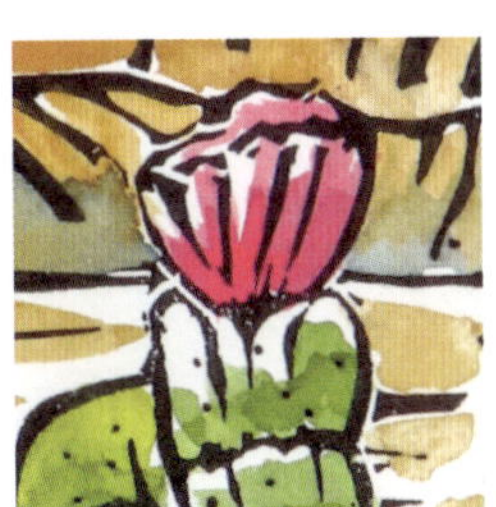

Introduction: First Flowers

My first garden was on Laurel Avenue in St. Paul, Minnesota. I grew up in a military family and we moved every couple of years, living on bases in housing that was a tight fit for my big family. When I was twelve years old, we moved off base to the big house on Laurel, built in the 1880s, with wood trim and box-beam ceilings, never updated, and with rooms papered in giant roses. Laurel Avenue was two blocks away from the fancier homes on Summit Avenue, where F. Scott Fitzgerald spent a lot of time in his youth. He wrote his first novel while living on Summit, which he later called a place of "architectural monstrosities." Houses on our street had narrow backyards that went down to garages and an alley. The former owners, the Niemeyer sisters, had left a lot of stuff in the basement, mostly useless, but we found old Red Wing pottery crocks there, and my mother suggested that I plant petunias in them to decorate the front porch. After that success, I started a small garden along the fence in the backyard. I bought some seed packets and grew bachelor's buttons, morning glories, and watermelons. I was entranced, watching them sprout and grow.

The house had a third floor with a dormer attic that looked out through a small window onto the backyard. A broken-down 1950s chaise longue that had been very stylish in that era sat beside the window; upholstered in gray, curly lamb's wool, it was a favorite of my mother's until we jumped on it and broke one of its legs. The attic was the first place where I experienced being alone, and I delighted in the dark silence of the room, peering down at the backyard. I don't remember my thoughts there, except that I felt a freedom to be quiet and daydream about anything that occurred to me. Maybe I thought about my garden and what I should plant in it. Or perhaps I considered what I might draw or write. It was a realm of the imagination, just like the woods and backyards we'd played in when we were younger—the difference was this was indoors and adventures took place wholly in my mind. Nowadays my home studio looks out on my backyard garden, and the connection I have with the outdoors remains the same as when I was a child. I wish every young person could have such a room, like the one—both metaphorical and real—described by Virginia Woolf in *A Room of One's Own*. I know that attic room was the beginning of my creative life.

A few years later, I wrote a story about our house, the first thing I had written aside from my diary. My father was stationed in Saigon at the time, and we frequently exchanged letters—I decided to send the story to him. He replied and told me it was very good writing. As the sports editor of his college newspaper, he had once dreamed of a career in journalism. I saved his letter, and the story, and as I read it now, I find it somewhat interesting, though far from brilliant—not the work of a future Chekhov:

> *The houses on Laurel Avenue were old. They were not slums, but they were not well-kept Victorian museums either. The homes did not have much width, nor did the yards, but they were long, elegantly long, with fences determining property boundaries. The flowers grew mostly in the backyards, which had narrow sidewalks creeping down to the garages. The*

The story I proceeded to tell was about my elderly neighbor, Mr. Ritt, who talked to me over the fence now and then, kindly giving advice. I remember he had some magnificent tall bearded irises, and the scent of them now reminds me of those early days—the iris, my own Proustian madeleine.

In every apartment and home that I have lived in over many decades, I have cared for plants, flowers in pots, or small vegetable plots. After I moved to Seattle in my early twenties, hiking in the Cascades thrilled me with alpine wildflower displays; the meadows at Mount Rainier were visual spectacles I could never have envisioned in my early gardening days. Through all my hikes and travels over the years, I kept records of the blooms and trees I saw, photographing and identifying them with field guides. After most of these outings, I maintained a very clear mental map of where I'd seen the trees and flowers, my memories of those specific locations seemingly more important to me than the geographic coordinates. On subsequent trips, I always sought those places out, quite possibly boring some of my hiking companions with gushing exclamations like "That's where I saw the Columbia lily! Let's see if it's as tall this time!" On one very memorable hike on Sahale Arm, just above Cascade Pass in the North Cascades, I saw two older women bending down to examine a wildflower, a copy of Stephen Whitney's *A Field Guide to the Cascades and Olympics* in hand. I remember admiring them intensely and hoping that one day, decades in the future, I might be like them.

Nowadays, conifers and other trees and shrubs enjoy the steeply sloping front yard of my current home, while the backyard is the domain of the flowers. There has been an evolution: even though I am still quite fond of roses, I have given over more of the garden to native wildflowers. Together, my gardens and my art bring the plant world closer to me. By painting and drawing plants, I commit them and their places in the landscape to lasting memory. And in tending native species in my small backyard garden, I continue to call up those memories from the wild and uncultivated world.

Western Wildflower Ecoregions

Plant geography and distribution in the West depend on latitude and longitude and weather, as well as geology, soils, and taxonomy. Global weather systems are created by moist hot air over the equator. When this air rises, it cools in the upper atmosphere and rain falls. The rising air is forced to roughly 30 degrees north and south of the equator, where the hot desert regions of the world are located; then the colder, drier air sinks to the surface of the earth and spreads out, resulting in less rain.

In the western United States, there are local weather effects, too, based on proximity to the Pacific Ocean and mountain ranges. When the moist ocean air moves up the west side of a mountain, it cools and then rains. When it goes over the top of a mountain, it is colder and drier. As it sinks on the lee side, the air warms up and since the moisture has all been released to the west, it is relatively or extremely dry on the eastern slopes of mountains. These conditions create the Great Basin Desert.

A "floristic province" is another way of looking at plant life in a region and can be distinct from a geographic location; it depends on the taxonomy (classification) and genetic makeup of a plant or group of plants. An example is western Utah and the Colorado Plateau, hydrographically not part of the Great Basin Desert, yet the plant life is associated with Great Basin flora (as well as Mojave and Great Plains species).

The chapters in this book explore wildflowers in the following biogeographic regions of the West: forests; chaparral and woodlands; wetlands and riparian habitats, including vernal pools and seasonally moist meadows; coasts and shorelines, encompassing the entire West Coast of the contiguous United States; shrub-steppe, grasslands, and prairie; subalpine and alpine zones, including the Cascades, Sierra Nevada, and Rockies; and deserts, including the Great Basin Desert (in which I also cover the red rock country of the Colorado Plateau), the Mojave Desert, the Sonoran Desert, and the Chihuahuan Desert. Some species are so widespread that you might find them in almost every location. In those instances, I have chosen places where I have seen them or where they are most common.

Plant Families and Identification

Because identifying plants involves observing common patterns or features, learning just a few will help you identify the family. Take a look at the mint, parsley, mustard, pea, lily, rose, and aster families, for example (see the Glossary for definitions of common flower and plant terminology):

- The mint family has square stalks and opposite leaves, and is usually aromatic.

All Taxa Biological Inventory

*And when we have learned
the names of all the ten thousand beings,
what then?*

Now, can we begin to talk about love?

—Saul Weisberg

from *Headwaters: Poems and Field Notes*

- The parsley family has compound umbels. Individual stems of the flower head branch out from a single point—think of the spokes of an umbrella.

- The mustard family has four petals with six stamens, four tall and two short. Look inside a four-petaled flower and you'll discover whether it's a member of the mustard family.

- The pea family has irregular or asymmetrical flowers with banner, wing, and keel petals not found in other flowers. The big upper petal is the banner, the two petals on the sides are the wings, and the last two petals are fused together, making the keel.

- The lily family has three sepals and three petals, usually identical in size and color. On a member of the lily family, you will see two distinct layers: three colored sepals and three colored petals.

- The rose family has five petals and numerous stamens; leaves are often oval and serrated. There are other families with five-petaled flowers, but in the rose family the petals are separate, and the numerous stamens are distinctive. The fuzzy center of the flower consists of partially fused pistils.

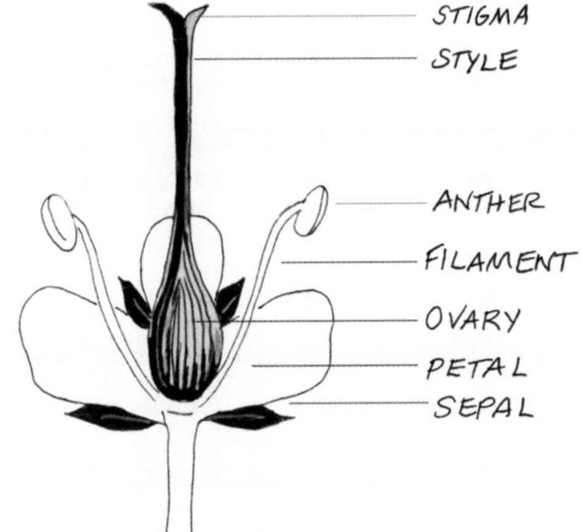

PARTS OF A FLOWER

- The aster family has unique composite flower heads. One flower head is made up of many smaller flowers, each attached to a pitted disk. In a sunflower, each sunflower seed is produced by an individual flower within the larger flower head. The flowers in the middle are called disk flowers, while the big petals around the outside are called ray flowers.

For each individual flower in this book, I provide the the common name, binomial name (genus and species), and plant family (appears in all capital letters following the genus and species).

Best Times to See Wildflowers

Looking for wildflowers is not so very different from bird-watching. Birds don't always show up when and where you want to see them. Sometimes the best you can hope for is to hear them, as they remain invisible in the upper stories of forests and woods. Many factors determine when, where, and for how long you'll see specific wildflowers. Most wildflowers have a short blooming season and then go dormant. Some habitats support many months of wildflowers, whereas others are limited to only a few months.

In any given year, wildflower bloom times will vary, depending on the amount of moisture that has fallen over the fall and winter, as well as on temperature—colder temperatures will delay the blooming, as I found on several trips where I expected to see wildflowers. In an especially good year, a superbloom will occur (see the sidebar). The concept of "superbloom" applies more to California and Arizona; Pacific Northwest flowering is more consistent, as are alpine blooms in the Sierra Nevada and Rocky Mountains.

The best spring desert wildflower displays can actually start in the fall if there is a good autumn rain. Generally, wildflower seeds sprout and stay close to the ground, waiting for warmer temperatures, which can occur at various times, depending on which of the deserts they inhabit. (Wildflowers, which seed, predominate in desert locations because perennials would wither and die in the extreme heat.) When temperatures warm, the flowers begin to bloom.

In any location, a sudden rise in temperature or inadequate rainfall can adversely affect flowering plants. I witnessed this one year at Mount Rainier National Park near Sunrise. Many of the explorer's gentian blooms were brown, due to the extremely dry summer.

Although every location has its prime bloom season, many different species continue to bloom throughout spring and summer. Timing is very important; yet disappointments and happy surprises are part of the experience of seeking wildflowers. Getting out and hiking even a short distance away from highways can yield unexpected sights. Often, you'll see a large number of a few species, but if you pay attention, you may discover a rare find in their midst—whether botanically significant or simply new to you. It is deeply refreshing to leave the world of houses, businesses, and paved streets behind and immerse yourself in the world of flowers in every possible season.

For each species listing in this book, I provide its bloom time: early spring, summer, or spring to summer, or a specific month or range of months. For flowers that are more widespread, the region and elevation should be taken into account when planning a visit. The best guides for year-to-year accuracy about what's blooming in specific locations can be found online: see Further Reading & Resources for a list of helpful websites. Another good bet is to call a local hotel or chamber of commerce in the area you want to visit, since they often know what's blooming. Finally, most complete field guides (also see Further Reading & Resources) provide very specific information.

Superblooms

The word *superbloom* describes a rare and special bloom event—one with a higher-than-average number of spring wildflowers—that can occur when conditions are just right, on average once a decade. Typically associated with desert regions, this phenomenon requires a complex matrix of events: There needs to be a series of soaking rains, beginning in October and continuing through February, following several years of drought and few flowers. If there is too much rain, resulting in flash floods, the growing plants will wash away. Winds can also uproot the young plants. After the rains, the desert floor must have enough cloud cover to protect the soil from the intense heat as well as the overnight freezes. Although superblooms are mostly limited to desert lands in state and national parks in California, they can take place where vernal pools in a wet year create the right conditions. An example of the latter is the Carrizo Plain in San Luis Obispo County, not technically a desert.

The origin of the word *superbloom* is unclear, but the media has apparently been responsible for its proliferation—ecologists and botanists don't use it. Richard Minnich, professor of geography at the University of California, Riverside, remarked to UC Riverside News in 2019 that a superbloom is "all in the eye of the beholder." When the Coachella Valley burst into flower in 1991, scientists called it the "March Miracle." Both the Coachella Valley and Death Valley experienced intense blooms in 2005, and it happened again in Death Valley in 2016 and 2024. A huge burst of desert wildflowers in Arizona in 2023 was also called a superbloom.

Unlike scientists, the media is in the business of stirring up excitement. It concerns many that news of a superbloom spreads rapidly whenever one occurs, because the crowds that arrive can turn an extraordinary and precious natural occurrence into a theme-park-type experience, complete with the trampling of flowers and pollinators. In 2023, the city officials of Lake Elsinore, California, closed local trails preemptively to prevent the mayhem that occurred in 2019 when people tried to view the California poppy bloom in nearby Walker Canyon. The bloom in 2023, which extended from the Central Valley to Southern California, was so spectacular that the entire world was able to view it remotely by way of NASA satellite images—a crowd-free experience possibly just as beautiful as being there in person.

There is a more positive way to look at the attention generated by the media. Aside from the benefit of tourism to small towns adjacent to the deserts, it can help bring awareness of the beauty of the desert to a wider population, along with an understanding of what makes a superbloom happen: the miracle of millions of seeds lying dormant, awaiting these perfect conditions. In an April 2024 *Washington Post* interview, Naomi Fraga, director of conservation programs at the California Botanic Garden, said, "The thing about a superbloom is it forces you to realize the abundance of life that's actually here. Because all of a sudden you have all these annuals that are everywhere and it's amazing. It just feels magical, beautiful."

A Year of Wildflower Hunting

One recent year, my friend Paul and I dedicated ourselves to being wildflower hunters—to finding common and rare plants, many of them at different stages in their life cycles. Living in the Pacific Northwest, where we have such a variety of ecoregions, made it easy to take last-minute trips from Seattle to the east side of the Cascades and to the Columbia River Gorge that divides Washington and Oregon. We also ventured away from our home turf to California, Arizona, and Utah. Due to scheduling difficulties, we often arrived at places just a little before or after the most impressive bloom times—a telling demonstration that timing is everything when it comes to seeing wildflowers. But the great consolation, always, is that blooms are successive. If every flower bloomed at the same time, they couldn't all find pollinators, so each plant thrives in its own niche and proper time of year. Our journeys throughout the year were rich in wildflower experiences.

February: We visited friends on the central California coast, where a cool, rainy winter delayed the wildflower bloom, though a few California poppies braved the cold winds at Montaña de Oro State Park. Driving farther south and across the state, we stopped at Joshua Tree National Park, where temperatures were in the thirties, but we still got to see the remarkable teddy-bear cholla in the Cholla Cactus Garden, where the cacti were not yet flowering but still held on to their very decorative yellow fruits. Across the state line, in Arizona, I saw my very first saguaro cactus. Brittlebush was flowering reliably at the Desert Botanical Garden in Phoenix, and at Saguaro National Park, fairy dusters were abloom beside the strange desert forest of barrel cactus and giant saguaros.

April: Early in the month, a visit to Cowiche Canyon Conservancy lands near Yakima, Washington, introduced us to miniature jewels of the shrub-steppe—grass widows, sagebrush violets, and yellow bells. Mid-April took us to Wenatchee's Sage Hills, where the arrowleaf balsamroot was just coming into flower, the lupine still a bit behind, though there were individual plants ahead of the major bloom. On the same weekend, we visited the Beezley Hills Preserve near Ephrata, discovering Hooker's balsamroot as well as a big surprise: the hedgehog cactus, holding off flowering in April when we discovered it, but still startling—its plump shape completely out of place in the northern steppe of Washington, or so I thought. It had once been quite common there, before the Columbia Basin Reclamation Project. Later that month, we traveled to Utah's national parks and monuments on the edge of the Colorado Plateau: Zion, Bryce Canyon, and Grand Staircase–Escalante. Brilliant blooms decorated the red rock, and rare moist hanging gardens in the canyons nurtured flowering alcove columbine and shooting stars.

GRASS WIDOWS

May: In the first part of the month, we visited the Columbia River Gorge to see camas and bit-terroot. At the bookstore in Hood River, I bought a used copy of *Wildflowers of the Columbia Gorge*, a wonderful field guide that maps out where to find species, which helped to direct a few of our trips. Along the Washington side of the Columbia, we spotted rose-violet Barrett's penstemon growing in lush bouquets atop tiny ledges on the basalt cliffs above us—an abundance of blooms that seemed so improbable in such an inhospitable place. But I learned that penstemon love dry, rocky soils. What better than a cliff face? Later in the month I taught a class for Yosemite Conservancy. Driving up from Fresno, we saw pink and magenta clarkia and blue and white sky lupine decorating the oak foothills, and once we entered the national park, white dogwoods dappled the pine forests everywhere.

June: We headed to the Methow Valley in north-central Washington, on the east side of the Cascades, to see the wildflowers in the first week of June. We knew that the balsamroot would be at the end of its peak there since it was very warm and the snow had melted weeks earlier. But we weren't disappointed. On the Cedar Creek Trail, just west of Early Winters Campground, I saw one of the most spectacular Columbia lilies I'd ever seen. They don't tend to grow in large groups—rather, an individual will stake out a place in a sunny spot, showing off its amazing Turk's-cap-shaped flowers. On the same trail, the arnica had finished blooming in most areas, but there were small-flowered penstemon, large swaths of birchleaf spiraea—the shrubs festooned with huge, white, airy blooms—and a lot of paint-brush, including a very tall variety I'd never seen, with reddish-pink flowers. The next morning, we visited Pearrygin Lake State Park and the Rex Derr Trail. It was early, about 8:30. The light was perfect, and all the balsamroot were still glori-

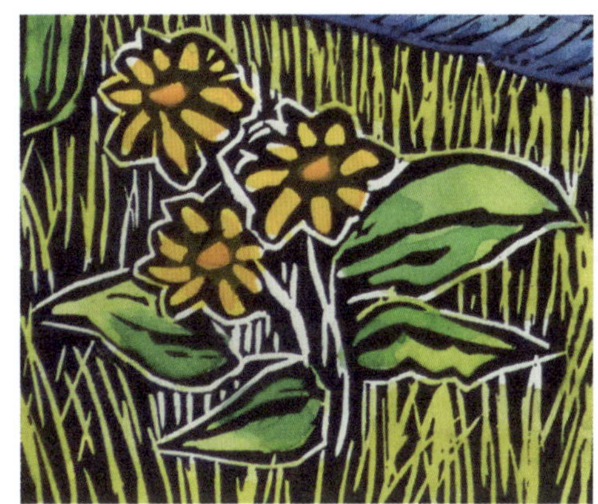

BALSAMROOT

ously in bloom—no doubt because of a cooler microclimate there, unlike other balsamroot areas. Very small things can make a huge difference.

August: A family wedding brought us to San Francisco, where we visited the San Francisco Botanical Garden and saw the late blooms of clarkia and flannelbush in the Arthur L. Menzies Garden of California Native Plants. These plants had bloomed much earlier in the chaparral, but delayed their flowering in the cool, foggy climate of the western Bay Area. We made a special outing to Muir Woods, north of the city, where the tall California hedge nettle soared skyward, dwarfed by the redwoods.

September: Our last trip was to Sunrise, in Mount Rainier National Park, with perhaps the most beautiful wildflower of all: the explorer's gentian. Cascade asters were hanging on, though many were dying back, and the bees and butterflies desper-ately sought out the remaining ones. We were like the pollinators, grasping at one last chance to visit the wildflowers.

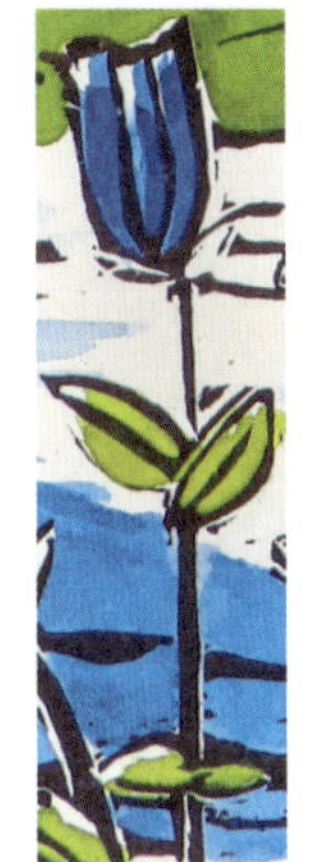

GENTIAN

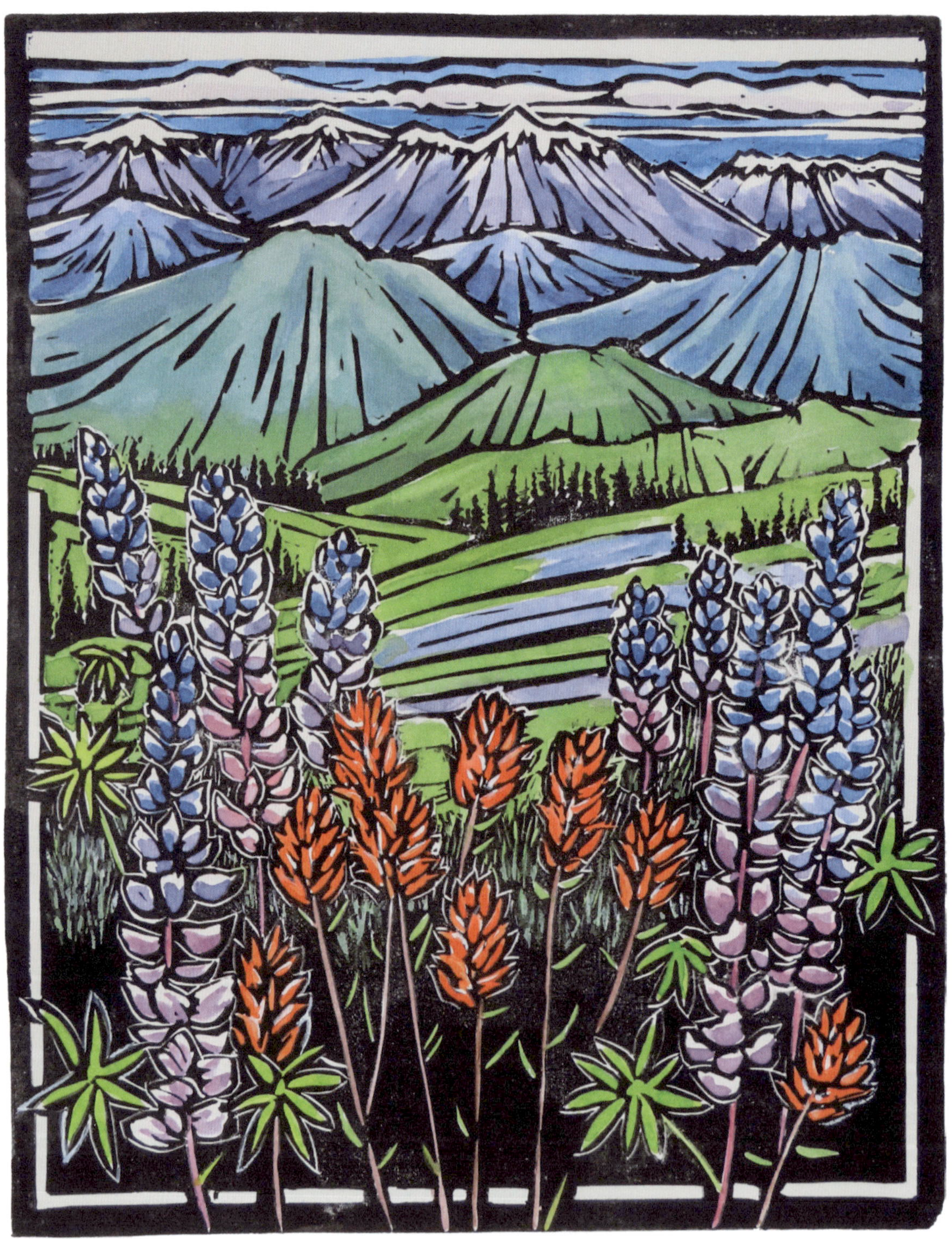

PAINTBRUSH AND LUPINE, ROCKY MOUNTAINS

Artists and Flowers

For . . . art is embedded in nature; whoever can draw her out, has her.

—Albrecht Dürer

The earliest cave art is around 64,000 years old and depicts animals. Plants were not the subject of art until the invention of agriculture in the Middle East, a mere 10,000 years ago. The first flower to be shown in art was the lotus, revered by ancient Egyptians as a symbol of the sun. It can be found on amulets, ceramics, and papyrus paintings. In *The Cabaret of Plants*, Richard Mabey writes that much of the early artistic representation of plants occurred in "spaces that have a sense of enclosure and possession," implying that until human beings had tamed plants by domesticating them, they had not seemed important enough to represent artistically.

Artists in the Far East, inspired by Shinto animism and Buddhism, valued nature far earlier than any Western culture; flowers, birds, insects, and trees formed an important part of their repertoire. These were popular subjects in China from the early Tang dynasty (618–907) onward. As China's influence extended along trade routes across Asia, its artistic styles spread to Persia, Japan, and other far-flung regions. Artists in Persia adopted Chinese techniques for bird and rose paintings and literature beginning in the eleventh century, taking gardens as a worthy subject for art.

During the Heian period (794–1185) in Japan, many floral motifs appeared on textiles and in herbals (books about the medicinal properties of plants). Flowers became increasingly realistic during the artistically rich Edo period (1615–1868). Despite Japan's policy of isolationism at the time, Japanese artists continued to feel the influence of China. They also began to appreciate the European art tradition, which exposed them to Western botanical and zoological subjects. In many paintings and prints from this era, it is clear how a growing understanding of perspective changed the traditional representation of space. The Seattle Asian Art Museum collection includes a magnificent pair of screens from the early Edo period: *Bamboo and Poppies*, by the seventeenth-century artist Kano Shigenobu. In the screens, Shigenobu has achieved a beautiful synthesis of traditional composition and realistic representation of the plants. The bamboo frames the screens on either side with graceful extended trunks, while the poppies are painted precisely, demonstrating their growth habit of tall stems, ragged leaves, and lush blooms.

The Japanese artist Hokusai, working in the late Edo period and famous for the woodblock print *The Great Wave Off Kanagawa*, introduced both landscape and bird-and-flower imagery as worthy subjects of art; previously, these subjects had been a minor genre. Hokusai's influence on subsequent artists—in both the East and the West—cannot be exaggerated. Once Japan reopened to foreign trade in the late 1850s, an entire European genre called "Japonisme" took off, with Western artists imitating Hokusai, Hiroshige, and other nineteenth-century Japanese woodblock printmakers.

Early plant art in western Europe can be traced to around 700 CE, when extremely stylized, even distorted, images were reproduced in herbals, used primarily for medical purposes. These crude

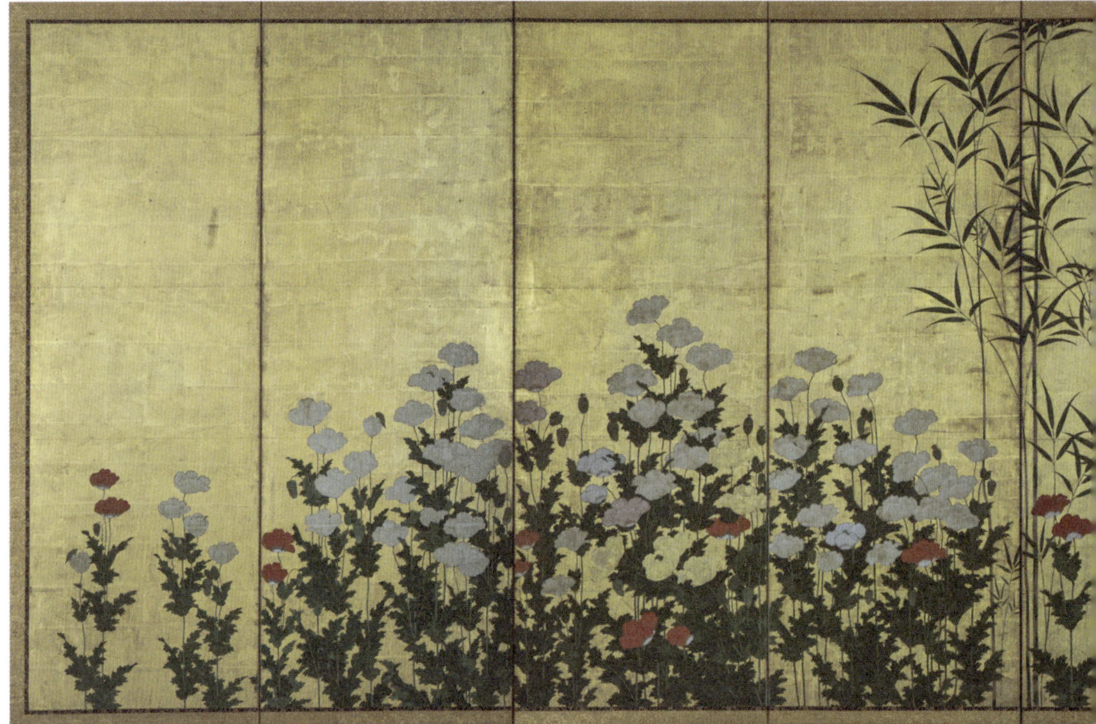

BAMBOO AND POPPIES, KANO SHIGENOBU (SEATTLE ASIAN ART MUSEUM)

woodcut images were often derived from classical manuscript illustrations and were not meant to help identify plants, but simply decorated the much more authoritative texts. Many of these texts were handed down and had little foundation in any type of empiricism or direct observation. In the late Middle Ages and Renaissance, words and text, rather than images, were esteemed as the primary source and conveyer of knowledge.

One remarkable exception is found in the art of Conrad Gesner, a sixteenth-century Swiss physician who trained in Paris and Basel. In addition to practicing medicine in Zurich, Gesner was a scholar of ancient languages—he created an index of Greek, Latin, and Hebrew writers—and an avid natural historian. Rather than rely on classical texts, he sought to observe, collect, and describe specimens himself. To that end, he traveled to see flora and fauna in many parts of Europe, including the South of France, and in his own backyard, the Alps, where he viewed and sketched some of the beauties of the timberline. His sketchbook page of a fritillaria is a wonderful predecessor of more modern natural history sketchbooks.

From the fifteenth through the seventeenth centuries, the European voyages of discovery brought back many exotic flowering plants. Collectors and wealthy patrons coveted the live plants for their gardens, as well as opulent books that described and illustrated these specimens in great detail and in

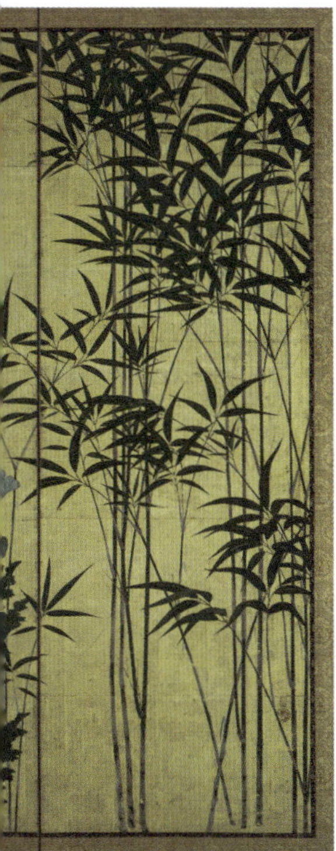

color. Florilegia—literally, "books of flowers"—arose as an entirely new genre of plant description, featuring both text and art, where the art was as important as, or more important than, the text.

During this period, the Swedish biologist and physician Carl Linnaeus, perhaps largely in response to all the new plants being discovered, came up with a revolutionary way to categorize flora: the binomial system of nomenclature, which he applied consistently for the first time in his 1753 compendium of plant species. Prior to his system, plants had been classified according to their utility for human beings: aromatics, vegetables, and medicinal plants. Linnaeus traveled in search of new plants and animals and may have been inspired by an early insight on a trip to Lapland, where his observations of teeth had him ponder the possibility of a natural system for arranging mammals. In binomial nomenclature, the two-part Latinized names consist of the genus and the species. The first is the genus, always capitalized, and the second is the species name, always lowercase; both are italicized. With each new discovery, botanists learned more about the relationships of plants, and as their knowledge deepened, so too did the realism of botanical illustrations. The art itself became increasingly significant as a means of identification. This can be seen in Linnaeus's *Hortus Cliffortianus*, illustrated by botanical artist G. D. Ehret and published in 1738. It was an effort financed by George Clifford, a wealthy Dutch collector, to catalog and categorize the plants in his extensive garden.

The rise of amateur naturalists in the nineteenth century, many of them women, fueled a demand for illustrated field guides. These were incredibly popular and remain so to this day. (See the "Women and Early Wildflower Exploration" sidebar.) Although photographic guides are now more ubiquitous, an illustrated guide can be superior since important structures and seasonal variations in plants can be much more easily rendered by an artist than by a photographer.

Beyond the realm of books, the flower as an artistic subject evolved as well. The still-life painters of seventeenth-century Holland often painted vases of

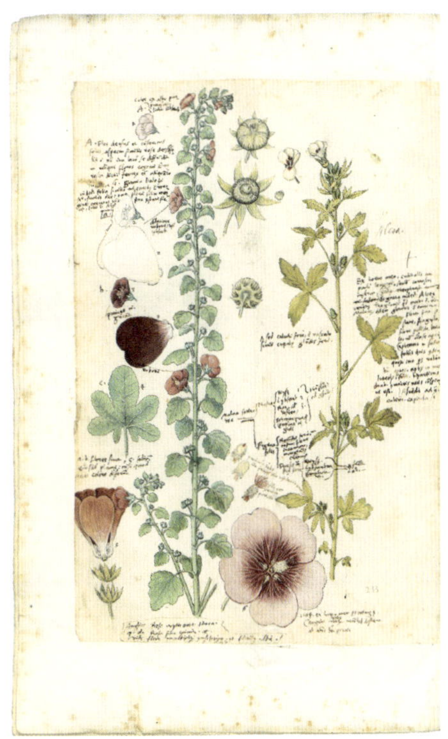

ALCEA ROSEA L. MALVACEAE, **CONRAD GESNER**

Women and Early Wildflower Exploration

Every walk into the fields is transformed from an aimless ramble into a joyous, eager quest, and every journey . . . becomes a rare opportunity for making new plant-acquaintances—a season of exhilarating excitement.

—**Mary Elizabeth Parsons,** from *The Wild Flowers of California: Their Names, Haunts, and Habits*

Some of the West's earliest plant and flower hunters were women—intrepid hikers, botanists, artists, and later, photographers.

In the latter nineteenth century, much of the American botanical world was in constant communication with Asa Gray, who taught botany at Harvard and, after retiring, became the full-time curator of the Harvard Herbarium (known today as the Gray Herbarium). He supported a large network of collectors, among them numerous women. This is evident in a note in *Botany*, the two-volume book he wrote with W. H. Brewer and Sereno Watson cataloging the flora of California. At the end of the second volume (1880), Watson—Gray's assistant in the herbarium at the time—highlights several women who worked as botanical collectors in the West: "It is a pleasure here to make especial acknowledgement of those who by their contributions have aided essentially in the preparation of this Botany of the State. As the frequent recurrence of their names through the two volumes shows, there are several ladies to whom very much is due."

One of these women was botanist Sara Plummer, who had spent many hours exploring the flora around Santa Barbara. She'd settled there in 1870, looking for a warmer climate after years of ill health on the East Coast. In 1880, she wed another prominent botanist, JG Lemmon. Once married—both rather late, in their forties—she and JG traveled extensively throughout California, Arizona, and Mexico, discovering and classifying new species. Plummer Lemmon was an excellent illustrator who paid close attention to all aspects of the wildflowers they encountered. Several plants are named after her, including *Penstemon plummerae* and *Baccharis plummerae*.

In honor of her work, Plummer Lemmon was one of the first two women invited to join the California Academy of Sciences, and in 1881 she was the first woman allowed to speak to the members. Over the years, she and JG donated illustrations, specimens, and photographs to the Academy's botanical collection. Unfortunately, the fires that devastated San Francisco in the aftermath of the 1906 earthquake destroyed the Academy building that housed the collection, which at the time was the largest in the western United States. Alice Eastwood, the collection's curator, managed with a volunteer to lower almost 1,500 of the herbarium's most important specimens by rope, strings, and her work apron—even as her own home eventually burned down in the fires. (Born in 1859, Eastwood began her exploration of the plant kingdom in the mountains of Colorado; she moved to California in her early thirties, eventually rising to her curatorial role

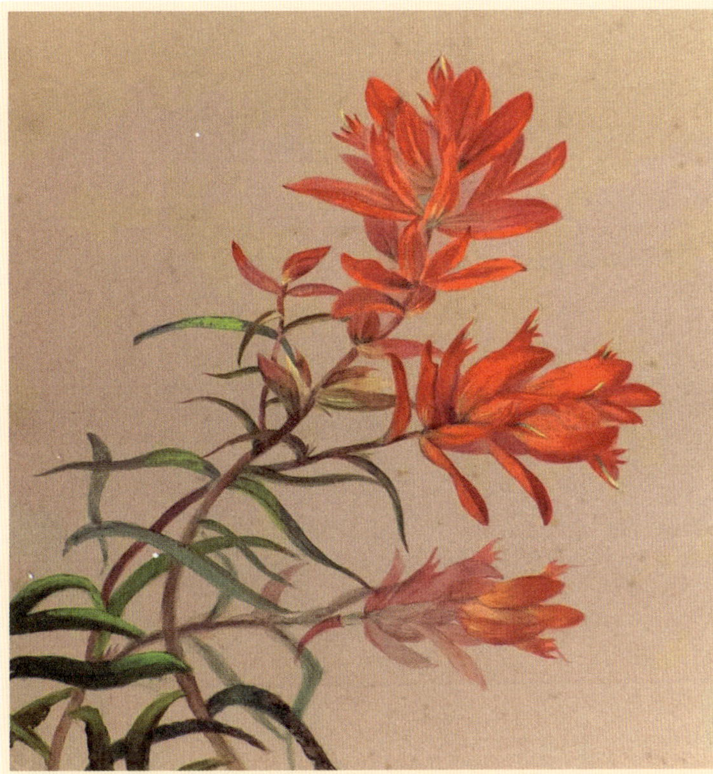

PAINTBRUSH BY SARA PLUMMER LEMMON

in 1897 in a style more like a typical field guide. She asked Margaret Warriner Buck to illustrate the book. Buck drew simple pen-and-ink drawings in the field as she explored alongside Parsons.

Also notable was Margaret Armstrong's 1915 *Field Book of Western Wild Flowers*. Armstrong may have been the first woman of European descent to travel to the floor of the Grand Canyon, where she found and illustrated several new plant species. A trained artist and amateur botanist, she illustrated more than three hundred book covers and collected and pressed about a thousand herbarium specimens, some of which remain in the New York Botanical Garden Herbarium.

Julia W. Henshaw's *Mountain Wild Flowers of America* was published in 1906, focused mostly on Canadian species, as Henshaw lived in Vancouver, British Columbia. Unlike most artists of the time, she employed photography, taking pictures of her plants in a studio setting.

Edith Clements was one of the most significant wildflower explorers in the western United States. She studied at the University of Nebraska, receiving a PhD in botanical ecology in 1904. Her husband, Frederic Clements, was also a plant ecologist. Together, they published *Rocky Mountain Flowers* in 1914—more notable as a beautifully illustrated book, rather than a field guide. The following year, in 1915, Edith

at the Academy.) Despite Eastwood's heroic efforts, none of Plummer Lemmon's illustrations held at the Academy survived. Some of her work is still preserved at the University of California, Berkeley, in the Jepson Herbarium.

Emma Homan Thayer, another botanical artist, wrote one of the earliest guides to flora of the West Coast, *Wild Flowers of the Pacific Coast* (1887). It wasn't really a field guide, but rather a series of short travel essays, each linked to a local wildflower. This, along with her earlier book on the wildflowers of the Rocky Mountains, served to interest East Coast audiences in the flora of the West Coast.

Another early guide was *The Wild Flowers of California: Their Names, Haunts, and Habits*, by Mary Elizabeth Parsons, which was published

published *Flowers of Mountain and Plain* on her own. Willa Cather, the twentieth-century novelist, was a good friend of Edith and Frederic's, and it's probable that her accurate and beautiful descriptions of the landscapes and plants of the West were influenced by that friendship. In an interview for the November 6, 1921, edition of the *Lincoln Sunday Star*, Cather spoke of her love for Nebraska wildflowers and paid homage to Edith and Frederic: "There is one book that I would rather have produced than all my novels. That is the Clements' botany dealing with the wild flowers of the west." Some of Edith's finest work appears in *Flowers of Coast and Sierra* (1928), which covers the mountain ranges of Oregon and Washington as well. She was a self-taught artist and sought in-person encounters with wildflowers by driving herself throughout the West to paint from life.

For more on these and other remarkable women, see Wynne Brown's *The Forgotten Botanist* (a biography of Sara Plummer Lemmon) and Brian R. Thompson's "Women Botanists and Botanical Artists," a series of articles for the *Washington Park Arboretum Bulletin* (Winter issues 2019–25).

flowers (many of which were newly discovered exotic species), depicting them at times as *memento mori*, reminders of the shortness of life, and at others as a celebration of the riches of the Dutch empire. Flowers from different seasons were often painted together, artistic fantasies that appealed to the wealthy merchants who displayed the opulent paintings.

By the nineteenth century, artists found flowers sufficient in and of themselves as subjects and painted them without explicit moral messages. The French artist Édouard Manet claimed that the still life was "the touchstone of painting." Near the end of his life, from his sickbed, he painted a moving series of sixteen canvases that illustrated the bouquets that his friends brought him. He was so enchanted by flowers that he decorated his private letters with watercolors of roses and irises. Other painters claimed different species as their own; the Dutch painter Vincent van Gogh told his brother Theo in a letter that "the sunflower is mine in a way."

In the twentieth century, American painter Georgia O'Keeffe wrote, "When you take a flower in your hand and really look at it, it's your world for the moment. I want to give that world to someone else." O'Keeffe's intense close-ups of flowers allow the viewer to see details and forms that are not apparent when casually observing a flower. Like O'Keeffe, contemporary artists continue to express their vision through the world of flowers. In the botanical tradition, American artist Natalie Levine creates paintings of flowers with elements of fantasy. Rosalind Wise, a British painter, describes her 4-by-5-foot canvases as paintings of garden, field, and meadow. They capture the joy of multiple blooms side by side. Japanese artist Takashi Murakami, inspired early in his life by manga and anime art, fuses elements of Japanese pop culture with traditional themes and methods of representation found in textiles and other Japanese crafts. Stylized daisies can cover an entire painting, multiplied dozens of times; the result is playful and downright funny.

The Art of Flowers: Methods and Materials

Art is the flower—life is the green leaf. Let every artist strive to make his flower a beautiful living thing . . .

—Charles Rennie Mackintosh, from "Seemliness"

To re-create the essence of a flower brings forth a different response from every artist, and even botanical illustrations that strive for close representation are unique. Each flower and meadow I've seen has called on me to respect its distinctive character and to honor its beauty. There are challenges inherent in some flowers—they might be dainty, miniature, fabulously hued, or structurally complex. In seeking the best medium for each species, including meadow landscapes, I'm constantly experimenting, at times attempting work beyond my comfort zone. But that is always good for an artist. Begin with the medium you feel most at home with, then try out something new. I hope you find it as much fun as I do!

MANY GARDENS MIX WILDFLOWERS WITH CULTIVARS.

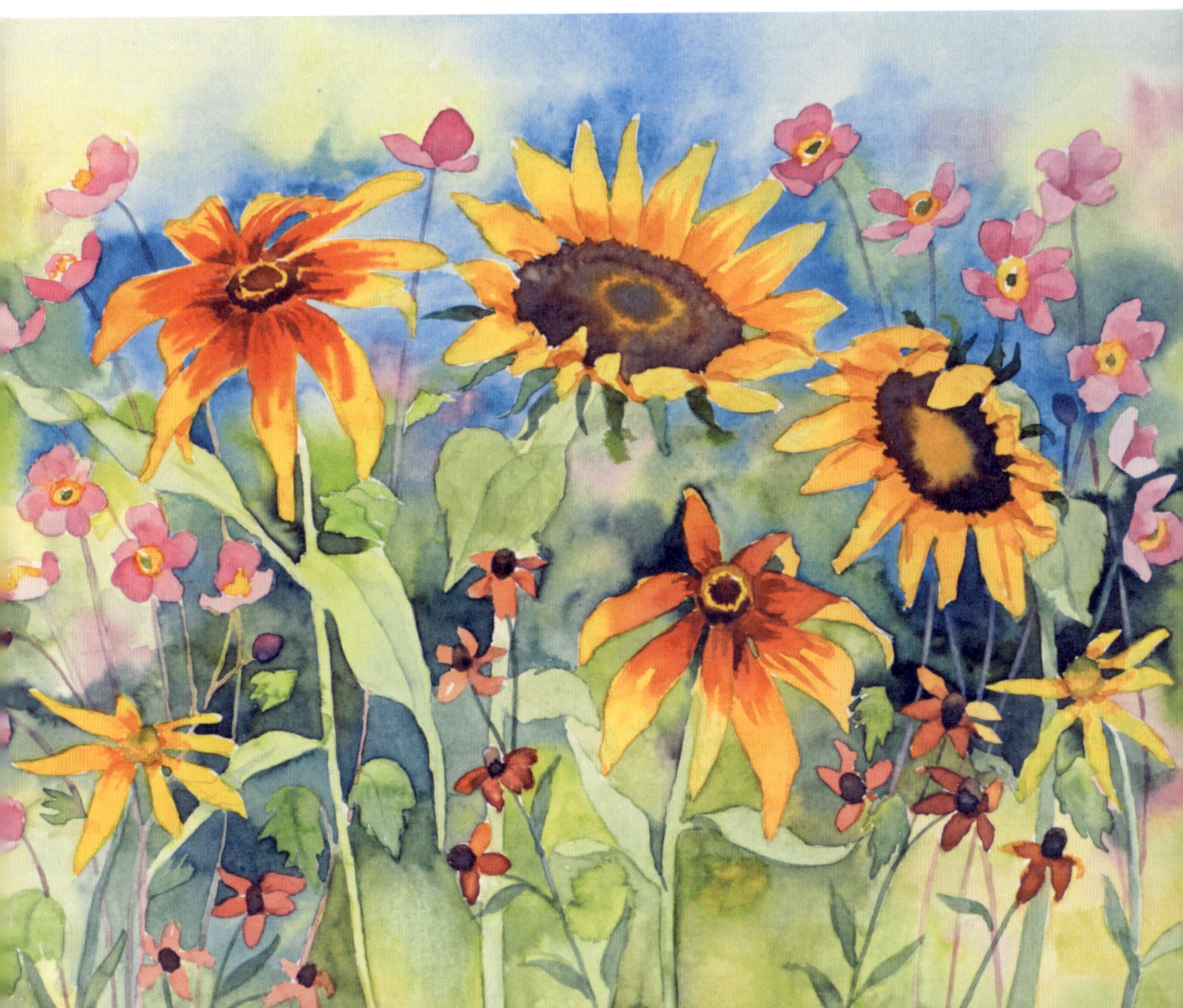

Watercolor is the quickest painting medium to execute: you can make a speedy pencil sketch of the major shapes and fill them in as your time outdoors allows. If you are fitting flowers into a larger landscape, you can wet the entire paper first and then fill in all the colors you see, beginning with the purest floral hues and surrounding them with greens and other colors. Edges won't be defined because you're using a wet-into-wet method, but the colors will be accurate because you're outdoors doing this. No other medium affords this possibility. Watercolor can express mist, rain, and fog, as well as the greens and flowery hues of a meadow. It's a great way to try out ideas and sample colors. In the European tradition, artists have been using it for studies since the late fifteenth century, when Albrecht Dürer demonstrated the potential of the medium, producing small yet detailed landscape vignettes and plant and animal studies. But you don't need to be as precise as Dürer to use watercolor. I think of it as being a very democratic medium—accessible, inexpensive, easy to try out, and easy to set up. It doesn't have to be done in a studio—outdoors or a kitchen table works just fine—and extensive technical training is not a prerequisite.

One of my favorite things about watercolor is its nontoxicity. Even though it's now becoming more common to clean up oil paints with oil—a practice of Renaissance painters—solvents are usually used for the task. This dates to the eighteenth century, when painters quickly switched to these new inventions, a by-product of the Industrial Revolution, since they made cleaning so easy. But solvents are very hard on the environment and painters alike. Watercolor, on the other hand, rinses clean in water and cleans up in minutes.

I generally make my own watercolor sketchbooks, which can be more versatile. I cut Arches paper into a 10-by-13-inch size, then I take the cut paper to a copy store and have a spiral binding and plastic cover added. The spiral binding and heavyweight paper together mean that the sketchbook can be

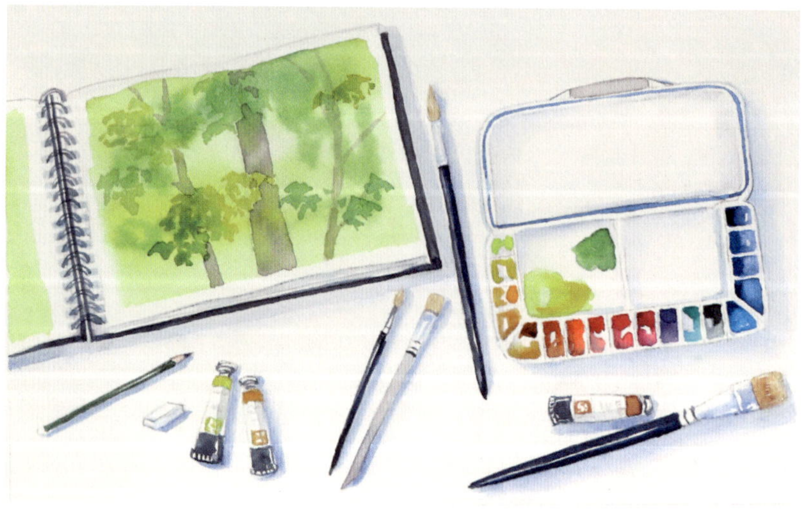

Drawing Flower Shapes with Graphite Pencils

These are four common flower shapes:

- **Campanulate**: bell-shaped, like bellflowers
- **Crateriform**: shallowly bowl-shaped, like poppies
- **Ligulate**: with strap-like rays and central disks, like daisies and asters
- **Funnelform**: funnel-shaped or trumpet-shaped, like desert morning glories

To draw them, begin with a 2H pencil to create the outside dimensions of the flowers. Feel free to erase until you have the outside lines drawn accurately. Then draw the inside shapes, like the inside of a bell, or trumpet, including stamens and pistils when they are visible. Next, decide where your light is coming from. In the Western painting and drawing tradition, it is usually pouring down from the upper left when work is created in the studio. That means that the right side of your flower is going to be shaded, as well as the inside of the bell, tube, or bowl. On a ligulate flower, the outside rays are probably lighter, and where they meet the disk, you can add some shading. I use a 5B pencil for this stage of the drawing, beginning with short strokes, usually parallel to the shape's longest side. Finally, sharpen your pencil and darken a few lines and selected shaded areas.

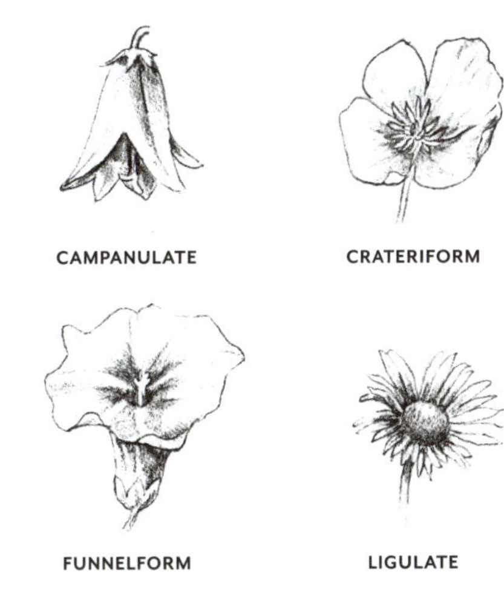

opened out in the field with no support—for plein air drawing and painting on one page, or spread out to two pages for a large panoramic landscape. Arches 140-pound watercolor paper is 100 percent rag and is double-sized with gelatin, which means you can scrub it without destroying the paper surface. So I don't fret too much if I make a mistake, knowing I can easily correct it. (Contrary to what many assume, it is possible to fix watercolor once you've laid down the wash. Just remember, this works only with heavy papers that are well sized.) The Arches paper allows me to paint in the field using wet-into-wet washes, as well as in the studio once I get home. I can add pen or other water-based media, knowing that the sturdy paper can stand up to repeated washes and applications of other materials.

Mixing Colors

You can do a multitude of things with watercolor—make quick sketches, create finished paintings, add it to pen and acrylic drawings, and tint prints with it. Just knowing a few basics about color mixing will equip you with enough knowledge to use it for your sketches and prints. In the color wheel you see two of each primary color:

YELLOW: Hansa yellow deep and Hansa yellow medium

BLUE: phthalo blue (green shade) and phthalo blue (red shade)

RED: permanent alizarin crimson and pyrrol scarlet

With these you can mix secondary colors. For a warm orange, mix Hansa yellow deep and pyrrol scarlet. For a violet, mix permanent alizarin crimson and phthalo blue (red shade). For a very bright green, mix Hansa yellow medium and phthalo blue (green shade).

Notice on the color wheel just how many possibilities there are within each third of the wheel. Some lean more toward one color. You can also see this on the green mixture chart. I often add a bit of quinacridone burnt orange to my green mixtures. Most greens in nature are not quite as vivid as pure secondary hues and need to be neutralized just a bit. Another way to achieve neutrals is to cross the line on the color wheel—any time you mix by using a color across the line, you

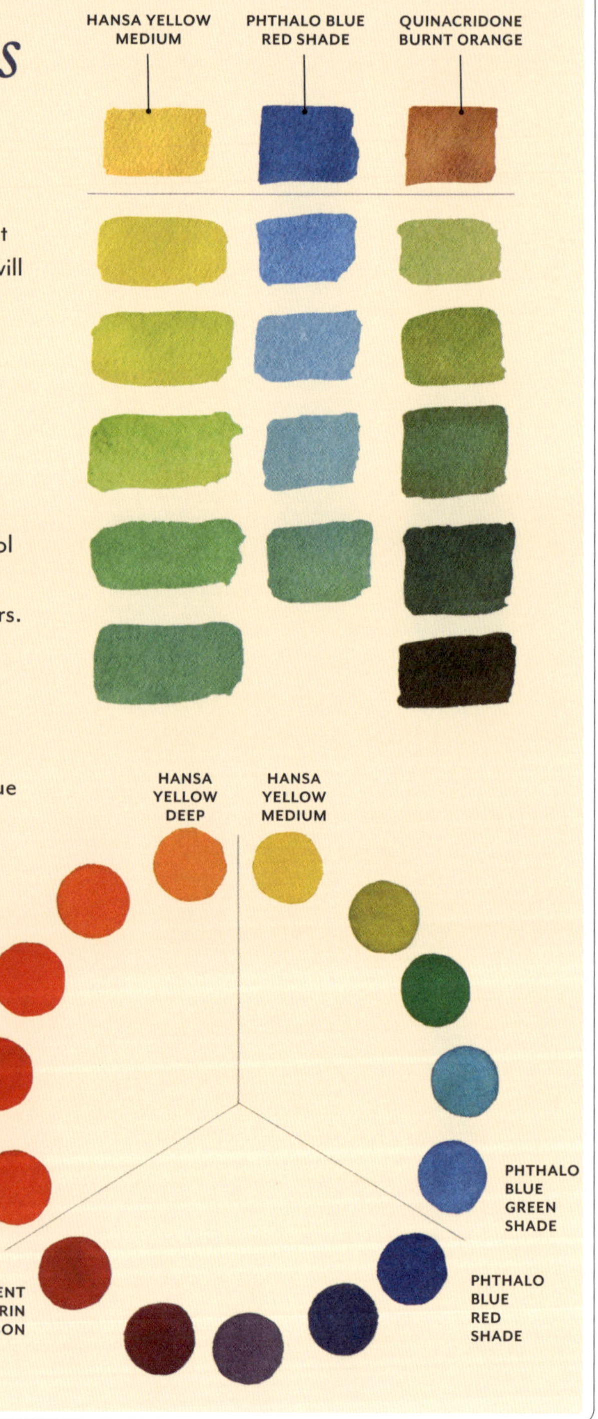

get something a bit more neutral. So, I use Hansa yellow medium and phthalo blue (red shade), rather than phthalo blue (green shade), which would get me a much brighter green. Another way to get a neutral green is to add a very small amount of permanent alizarin crimson to your mixture of Hansa yellow medium and phthalo blue. Some annual and perennial wildflowers have brighter green leaves; for them, don't add quite so much of the neutralizing color. Desert foliage is often grayer and bluer, so you might lean your green mixtures more toward phthalo blue (red shade) and quinacridone burnt orange.

Colors that are adjacent to each other on the color wheel are called harmonious or analogous colors. Mixing them gives you clean, bright mixtures that are very useful for the pure and intense colors of flowers. Colors opposite each other are called complementary colors, and as described above, mixing them gives you some very interesting neutral hues—try this, and you'll discover intriguing greens with hints of gray, brown, and blue. These can be very useful for annual and perennial leaves and cactus flesh colors. There are no rights and wrongs in color mixing. Try everything and make notes about which colors you used; those notes will come in handy for future painting sessions.

Note: You may want to add a few extra colors to your paint box or palette for flowers. Mixing colors works well enough for sketches, and almost always is successful for the greens of foliage, but sometimes you want a hue right out of a tube of paint to achieve the most vibrant, lifelike flower colors. I suggest taking a look at all the quinacridone, pyrrol, and perylene colors in the ranges of violet, red, pink, and orange. Penstemons, paintbrushes, and poppies all demand eye-popping color.

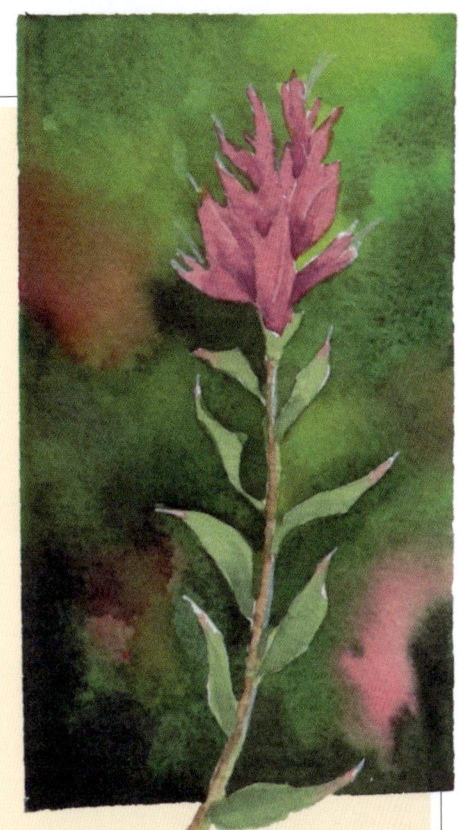

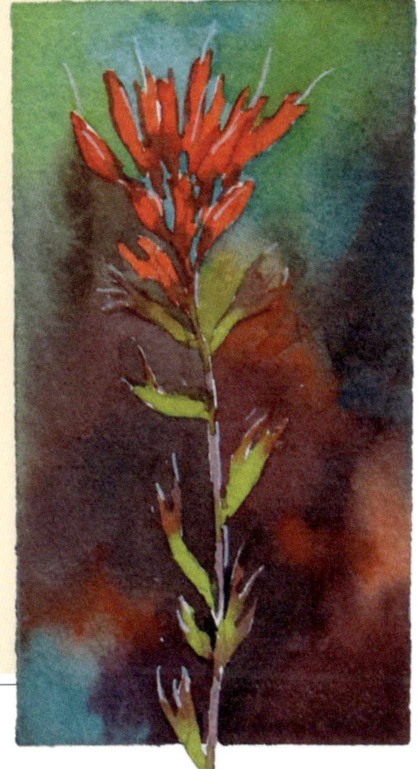

MAGENTA AND SCARLET PAINTBRUSH WITH DARK AND
NETURAL-HUED BACKGROUNDS

Since writing my previous books, I've sampled other sketchbooks and found that they are also useful; some, being a little smaller, are more portable for plein air work and travel. I like a 7½-by-10-inch spiral-bound sketchbook with heavyweight, hot-press (smooth) paper. Smooth-paper sketchbooks can be very nice for pen-and-wash sketches. I appreciate how quickly you can work in them, as well as the fresh and unlabored look of the sketches. I also use various sizes of a sketchbook I recently discovered, a handsome bound book made by Hahnemühle with 100 percent cotton fibers, not dipped in sizing (as Arches paper is) but still excellent.

When I look at my bookshelf filled with my sketchbooks, I find myself believing that there is a semblance of structure to my life and to my studio. I label them so I know where to find sketches, and they rest on a shelf together in chronological order, giving me a sense of accomplishment (however illusory!). Once you begin keeping sketchbooks or journals, you realize the importance of recording experiences and ideas—it is a very personal endeavor, but one that makes you a more thoughtful participant in the landscapes you venture to see.

Here's what I bring when I have time to paint outdoors for half an hour or more: an HB pencil, a plastic eraser, a sketchbook, a ¾-inch flat sable watercolor brush, a ½-inch flat synthetic brush, numbers 4 and 6 round sable watercolor brushes, and a lightweight plastic palette loaded with the list of colors that follows. (It's safest to squeeze them into the plastic palette a few days before heading out so they have a chance to dry, otherwise they can leak out while still runny.) I put them on the uphill side of the slanted palette wells, and then when I use them, I add water and let the wash of color float down to the bottom of the well. The paints start with yellow and go counterclockwise around the palette: Hansa yellow light, Hansa yellow medium, Hansa yellow deep, yellow ochre, quinacridone gold, quinacridone burnt orange, pyrrol scarlet, perylene red, permanent alizarin crimson, quinacridone magenta, carbazole violet, phthalo green, perylene green, phthalo blue (green shade), phthalo blue (red shade), French ultramarine blue, cobalt blue, indanthrone blue. On longer outings I also bring some tubes of colors I use a lot such as Hansa yellow medium and deep and quinacridone burnt orange.

It's not always possible to finish a sketch when you are out in the field. Light and weather conditions change rapidly. Or you might have a hiking companion who has no interest in stopping while you sketch for an hour. Pencil notes as well as photographs can help you with color that you're not able to complete outdoors. It's important to make good color notes while you're in the field. I often record light direction by drawing a small pencil sun in the appropriate corner of the sketch. The camera can be a very good aid too—I have a digital camera with excellent zoom capabilities and image stabilization. I make good use of my phone camera too since the technology for those has improved dramatically. I often take photographs from flower level, kneeling or squatting close to the bloom, rather than standing above and looking down. I also take photos of the surrounding landscape, in case I decide to place the plant in its larger habitat. With my photos, I can re-create the experiences I have outdoors once I'm back in the studio. I try not to wait too long to do that since the immediate sensations lose their intensity over time.

Plein Air Painting in a Backyard Pollinator Garden

When I'm not out exploring in parks, looking for birds, trees, and flowers, I spend much of my time in my backyard garden. It's quite small, but I've packed it with plants, most of them ones that are attractive to pollinators. Loving beauty gives us so much in common with bees and butterflies. I've planted dahlias, roses, clematis, salvias, asters, and agastaches, as well as native plants like sneezeweed and shrubby cinquefoil, both quite showy and full of bright, cheerful yellow flowers. It's difficult planning long trips in the summer when the garden is at its peak; I feel almost heartbroken as I bid farewell to the flowers. On my last August trip, I returned to an even fuller bloom than when I had left, and the flowers were buzzing with hundreds of bees—a welcome that made me feel happy about my absence. They'd had full run of the place while I was gone!

I sketched the flowers growing along my backyard retaining wall when I returned from my trip, when most of them were at their peak. I set up my chair and easel and began with a quick pencil sketch, outlining the major shapes. Luckily the bird-bath gave structure to an otherwise chaotic assemblage—the plants were so large that they concealed the retaining wall that might have provided an anchor. The pot could have given a solid form too, but the flowers overflowed, mostly hiding it. After drawing, I added water-color, beginning with the yellows and pinks, then moving to the greens. I mostly employed a dabbing brushstroke because I wanted individual leaves and flowers to stand out. Often, in a larger landscape, I start with a wet-into-wet method on wet paper. But here, with all the diverse colors, it wouldn't have made sense, as all the colors would have merged, muting their vibrancy. Continuing with the dabbing strokes, I added darker greens in the spaces between the leaves and flowers.

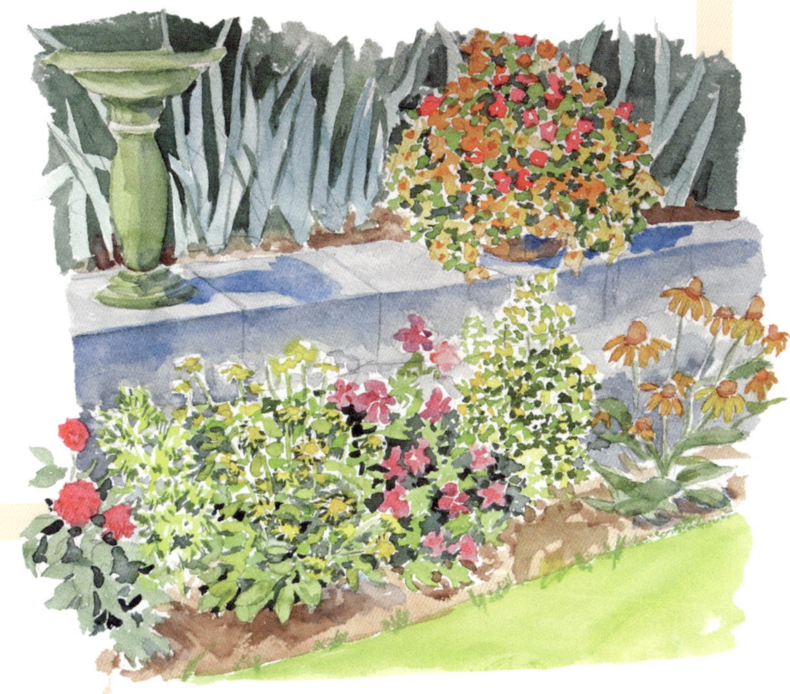

It's important to note that painting wildflower specimens is often more of a studio endeavor, even if you're not as exacting as a scientific illustrator. Much of the work in this book was done back at home with the help of photos I took in the field.

WATERCOLOR PENCILS

Watercolor pencils are indispensable for sketching multiple blooms, as you might find in a meadow. Watercolor alone is not the easiest medium for rendering a lot of small details; it's best for flower studies or larger landscapes with broader areas of color. Watercolor pencils, on the other hand, make it simple to quickly sketch in fairly representational individual blooms.

A meadow of intense blue camas blooms would be very difficult to achieve in watercolor, requiring hours of work. Instead, using just a few watercolor pencils to sketch in the flowers and stems, plus a watercolor wash behind them, I was able to quickly represent an entire meadow of the startlingly beautiful camas (see the Wetlands & Riparian Habitats chapter). I sketched them and added a little bit of clear water to most of the pencil marks to dissolve them into the various colors. It's a good idea to leave a few areas of white, as well as some pencil marks, since they add an energy to the masses of flower spikes, as well as help indicate the shape of the flowers. I used four colors of pencil—iris, bright blue, violet, and leaf—and then mixed a watercolor wash of Hansa yellow medium plus a very small amount of phthalo blue (red shade) and an even smaller amount of quinacridone burnt orange to establish the background color.

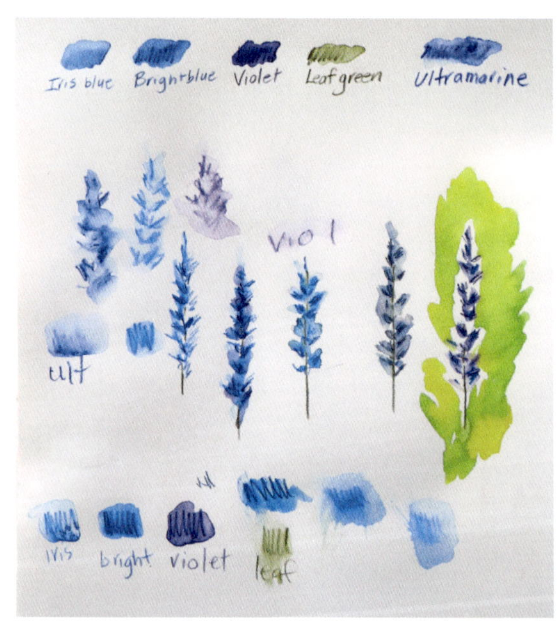

A TEST SHEET FOR CAMAS PAINTING

PRINTMAKING

When paper, invented in China, was introduced to Europe in the eleventh century—transmitted through the Islamic world, which had used it since the eighth century—woodcut printing became an economical way to reproduce multiple pictures, making images and texts affordable for a larger segment of the population. In this art form, images are drawn directly on or transferred onto a woodblock; then the wood surrounding the outline (imagine a pen line) is carved away. The outline of the figure or the letter remains raised, or in relief, so that a brayer or brush loaded with ink that is rolled or brushed across the block will leave a residue on the raised line. When paper is laid on the block, only the raised line prints. In the twenty-first century, images can be carved into linoleum (with the end print known as a linocut), wood, rubber, or any soft material—even a bar of soap. The resulting print is called a relief print. (The terms *block print* and *relief print* are interchangeable and can refer to any material.)

The earliest woodcut prints in Europe—images of saints and other religious figures—came from Germany and were sold as pilgrims' souvenirs at shrines and fairs; travelers collected mementos from their trips, very much as we do today. But early pilgrims also carried them as amulets on their journeys, to protect themselves from the plague or other misfortunes, and often kept them at home as well. Many of the earliest woodcut images have been found pasted into small travel chests. These simple figures were crudely carved, though full of strong line work, and contrasted notably with the high art achieved by later wood engravers such as Albrecht Dürer.

I draw inspiration in my own woodcuts from two of my favorite twentieth-century artists, Russian Wassily Kandinsky and German Ernst Ludwig Kirchner, who created many woodcuts early in their careers. Kandinsky, impressed by the folk art of the Vologda region of Russia, later produced art that was very decorative, featuring bright colors contrasting with dark backgrounds. Kirchner's

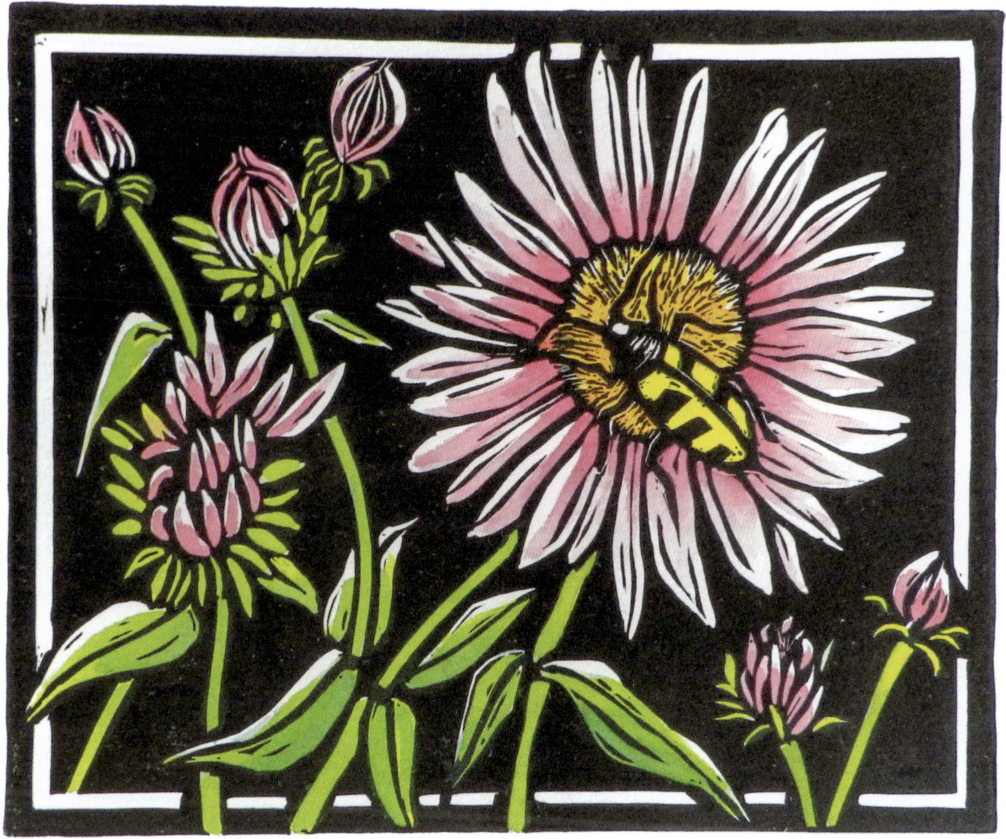

MOUNTAIN ASTER AND BEETLE

woodcuts employ dramatic, expressive line work that is deliberately rough and crude, calling to mind some of the earliest German woodcuts. Both artists were drawn to the dynamic interplay of dark and light, as well as to intense color. In my block prints, I try to capture something of what I admire in these two artists: the folk-art craftsmanship of Kandinsky and the energy of Kirchner's carved lines.

After working as a watercolor artist for years, I tried carving rubber blocks (a soft material very similar to linoleum but much easier to carve) as an introduction to printmaking and fell in love with it after my very first carving. I found it was a way to create art with high values contrast, something not easily achieved in watercolor. With watercolor, edges are blurred, much is based on subtle gradations, and colors can be somewhat weaker. With a block print, lines have clearly defined edges, and when black is used as one of the colors, the contrast between it and the other colors is even greater. I also appreciate the very tactile three dimensions of the carving block itself and the carving tools—it's as close to sculpting as I've come, and it's deeply satisfying. That said, block prints are more time-consuming to create, and some delicate details are much harder to capture than with watercolor or some of the other media demonstrated in this book.

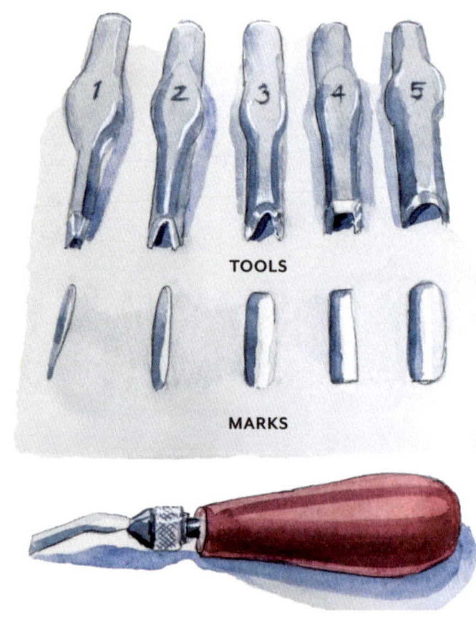

CARVING TOOLS AND THE MARKS THEY MAKE

CARVING TOOLS AND THE MARKS THEY MAKE

The tools used for making relief prints are called gouges, and they come in different shapes and numbered sizes. There are U-gouges and V-gouges (both big and small) and square gouges, all of which cut grooves of varying widths, depths, and angles in the wood, linoleum, or soft rubber block. The square gouge is the most effective for creating sharp corners, as you'll notice along the outside edges of many of the prints in this book.

In addition to easily carved rubber blocks, I've worked on wood and linoleum, though I stay away from the latter because it's very hard on the wrist and takes a lot more time. To color the prints, I've used both oil-based inks and watercolors in the Japanese *moku hanga* (*moku* means "wood"; *hanga*, "print") style, which typically relies on water-based media, though many *moku hanga* artists do use oil-based inks (see Woodland Blue Flax in the Chaparral & Woodlands chapter and the California poppy in the Coasts & Shorelines chapter for examples of water-based *moku hanga* prints). Because I've produced so many relief prints over the years for calendars and note cards, the easily carved rubber blocks have been my mainstay—I've probably made more than one hundred prints that way. There's always some new subject I want to try, and if I work only in the more labor-intensive media, such as woodblocks, I'll never get to experiment with new designs.

Making a Block Print

The process of creating a block print requires a number of steps but is relatively simple.

Quick sketch with marker and colored pencils: I often create a quick sketch on light-weight paper using a black marker because it makes bold lines that will simulate what the relief print will look like before color is added. Then I use colored pencils to explore the colors. I can't try out colors with watercolor on a thin paper, so if I want to do that, I use Bristol paper, a heavyweight smooth paper strong enough to absorb a light wash without disintegrating.

Drawing for the block print: The drawing refines the concept I explored in the quick sketch. I create the drawing with an HB pencil, and once I'm happy with it, I use a very dark pencil (5B) to draw over the lighter pencil lines. Then I flip the drawing onto the carving block and rub it with a heavyweight kitchen spoon to transfer the image onto the block.

Carved block: On the following page you see the finished block with the areas that will be painted, or will remain white, carved away. The shapes that remain in relief will help to model the landscape contours, the clouds, the butterfly, and the petal and leaf curves and veins. I carved out the paintbrush flower, leaves, and butterfly first, then the mountain peaks and cloud shapes, beginning with the outside contours before moving to the inside areas. For the flower, the inside shape was relatively easy since the bracts are large. On the fritillary butterfly, it was more difficult as I needed to preserve the spots and lines so they would print black. I made curving shapes to define the clouds, and for the sky around them, I kept my carved lines horizontal. I used a thin gouge to carve the outline of the foreground trees, then scooped out the branch shapes with a U-gouge.

Inking the block: In printing, I don't use relief inks, which I find don't come in the beautiful range of colors I typically like to choose from. Instead, I use high-quality oil-based etching ink (soft black, ivory black, or carbon black), which will resist—not bleed into—the

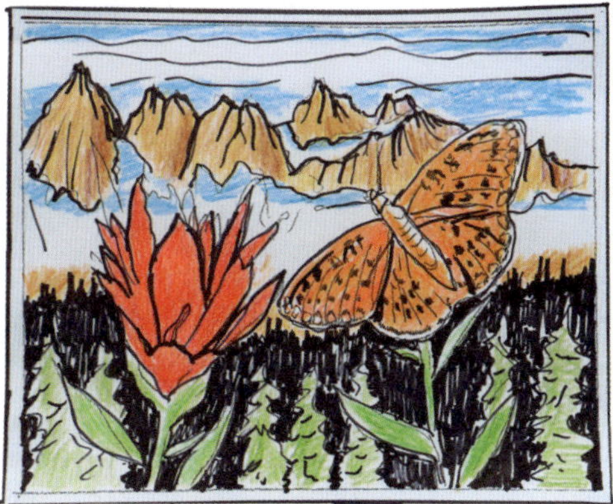

SKETCH WITH MARKER AND COLORED PENCILS

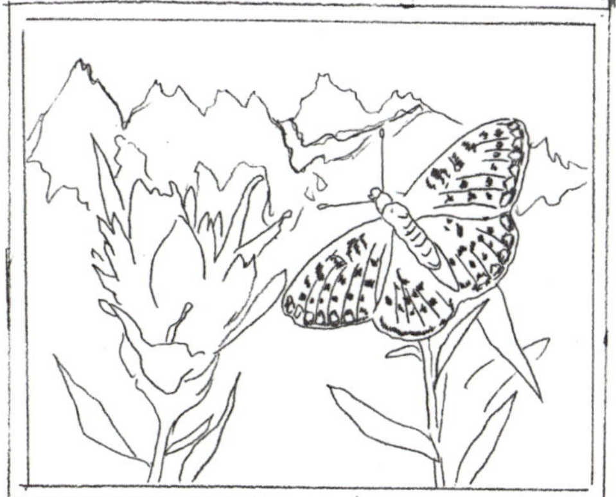

DRAWING WITH DARK PENCIL

watercolor I'll use later to tint the print; as the saying goes, oil and water don't mix! I roll out an ink that is fairly gooey, not stiff. If the ink is an etching ink (as opposed to a relief ink), I may need to thin it out a bit, depending on the color, as different colors have different degrees of viscosity, or tack. To thin the ink, or in print-making lingo, to "reduce the tack," I will add some burnt plate oil. I use this ratio: 1 table-spoon of burnt plate oil to 5 tablespoons of ink. Extremely dry conditions may require more burnt plate oil; warm, humid weather less.

Using an ink knife, I spread the ink on a piece of glass or plexiglass (plexiglass is nicer because you don't have to worry about it breaking) to about the width of the brayer. Then I roll the brayer back and forth on the plexiglass until I obtain a thin layer of ink sufficient to cover the brayer but not completely overload it. Next, I roll the brayer across the block, first horizontally and then vertically. Going in both directions ensures good coverage.

Printing: I place a good-quality hot-press (smooth, without any tooth) watercolor paper on the block and then rub vigorously with a heavyweight kitchen spoon. I gently lift up one corner of the print to see how well the image is transferring to the paper. If coverage is too light, I hold down the upper half of the print firmly, lift up the lower half, and reapply ink. I reverse this process for the upper half.

There's no need to clean the block between prints; you can leave the ink on and apply more ink with the brayer for each additional print. Successive prints achieve better coverage because of the residual ink that remains on the block, resulting in fewer gaps. (When printing by hand, you don't have the advantage of the solid drum pressure you get when using a mechanical press.)

Tinting the block print: There are different ways to introduce color into a print. The block can be printed with oil-based black ink and then tinted by applying watercolor with a brush. (See the "Watercolor" section on page 24.) Or the block can be printed with a colored ink. If only one color is chosen, then one block is sufficient, but if multiple areas with different colors are required, it's necessary to carve multiple blocks, with each block dedicated to a specific color,

CARVED BLOCK

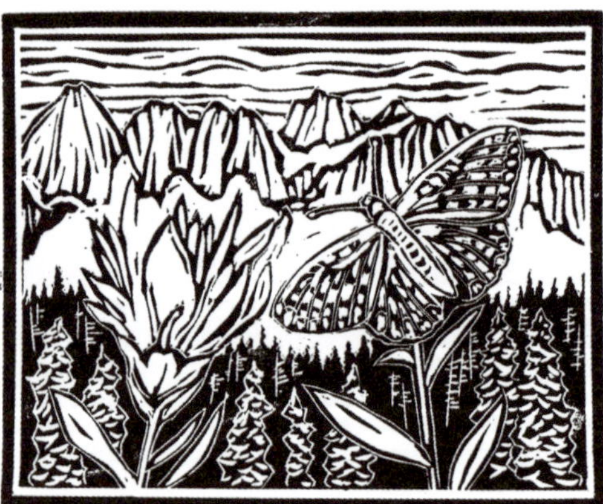

NOTICE HOW THE PRINT IS A MIRROR IMAGE OF THE CARVED BLOCK.

and each color "in register" (properly aligned) on the print. (See the "Multiblock Printmaking" sidebar in the Forests chapter.) When I tint with watercolor, I'm careful to accentuate the bright colors, since the strong blacks require intense color for balance. Often, leaving a few white, unpainted areas helps to dramatize the blacks and bright colors.

Cleanup of materials: Cooking oil removes the ink on all surfaces. I like to use a single-edge razor blade to remove the ink from the plexiglass before squirting it with oil to finish cleaning it. Unless you pay for a laundry service to clean your supplies, it's best to use paper towels; washing oil-soaked rags isn't good for your washing machine, and putting them in your dryer can cause a fire.

Editioning a print: Many printmakers do an entire edition, or set of prints, at once; twenty-five is considered a standard edition, but you can make anywhere from five to five hundred. Printmakers often label their prints below the actual artwork with the title, their signature, and a set of two numbers—for example, 1/25. The first number refers to the number of the print in an edition, the second to the total number of prints in that edition. If you make all twenty-five prints at once, you number them up to 25/25. If you're not sure what additional artistic touches you'll add to finish the print, you can label it AP, which stands for "artist's proof." Usually you make no more than five of those, as you eventually make your final artistic decisions. If you think the edition is going to be quite variable because of factors you can't really control, such as maintaining a consistent hue, you can label the print EV, which stands for "edition variable." You'll still need to number the prints.

Because my hand-tinted prints are so very handmade, I generally print only a few at a time. It can be wasteful to use twenty-five pieces of paper to make prints that may never sell, as you never know how the public will respond to a given print; I print only as many as I need. Many artists do the same—there's no rule that says you have to print an entire edition at once.

But I do decide at printing time how many I'll eventually be making, and I cannot increase that number later— even if the print proves to be very popular—for the sake of the collectors who buy my prints. It would be unfair to them to make more prints from a block after the fact; generally, the smaller the edition, the more valuable the print. Also, as prints in an edition sell, the remaining ones— those numbered closer to the end of the edition, as in 24/25 or 25/25— may be seen as worth more.

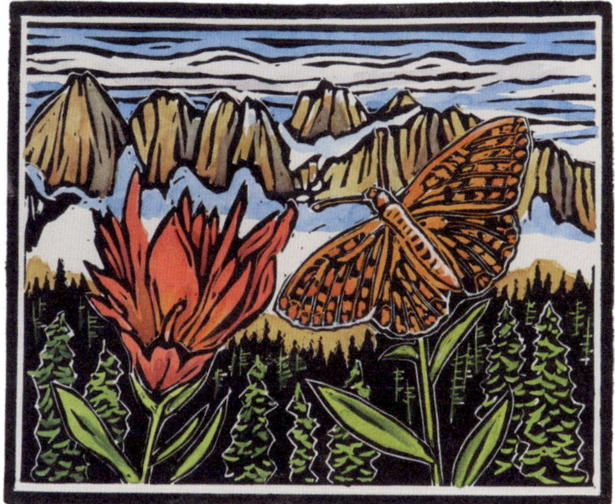

FINAL TINTED BLOCK PRINT

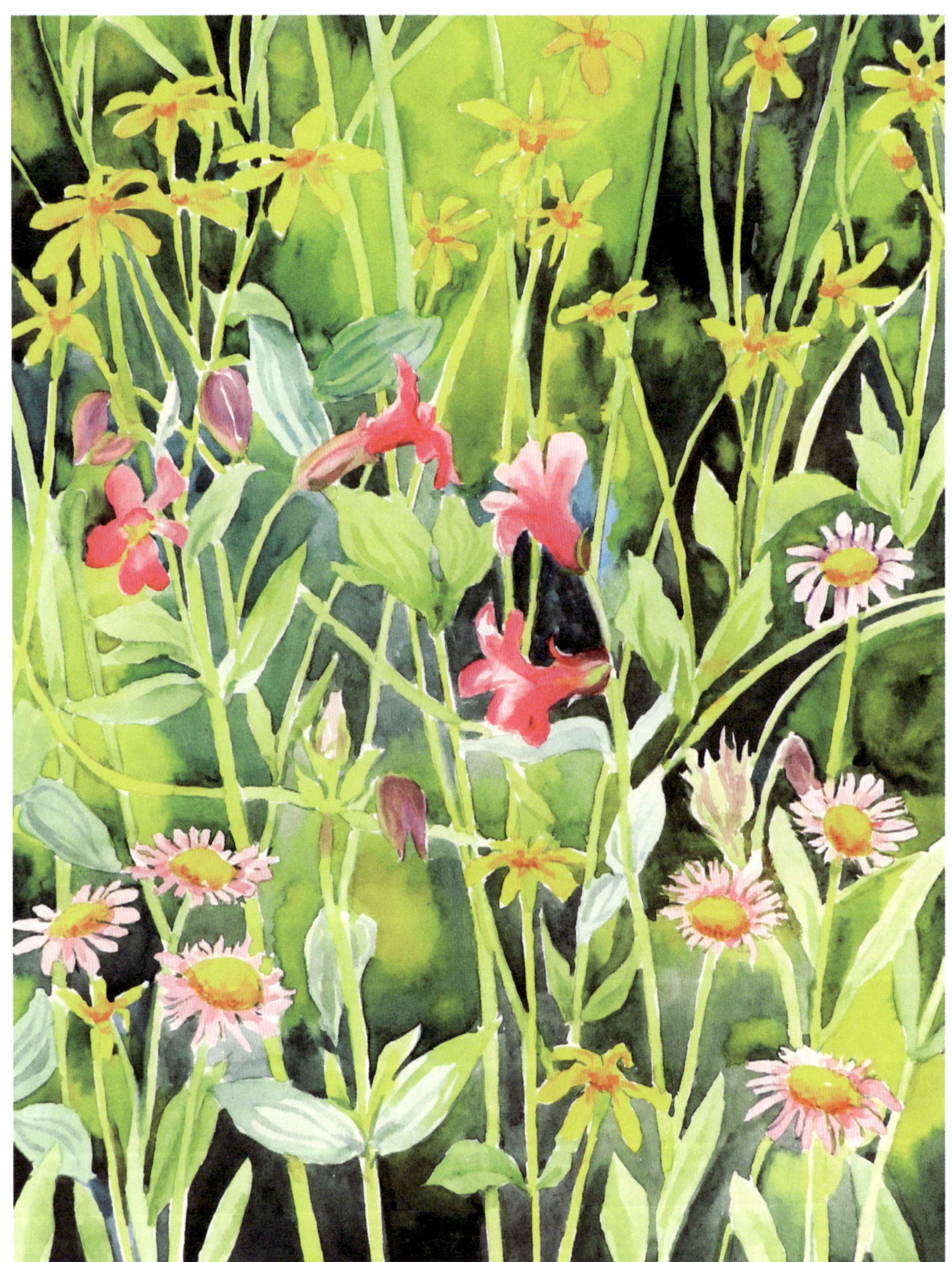

DAISIES, ARNICAS, AND MONKEYFLOWERS

Choosing a Flower to Draw or Paint

As you read this book and look at the illustrations, you'll see that my wildflower choices are not comprehensive. Some wildflowers are extremely dainty and not particularly suited to the styles and media that I enjoy. I'm not a scientific illustrator, and detail sometimes eludes me. Thus, this book isn't intended as a field guide; rather, it represents only common and recognizable species of a region, as well as others I've seen and ones that are my favorites—including a few rarer plants that demanded my attention.

You'll find that certain wildflower species appeal to you as well, and I hope that you'll be inspired to try to depict them using some of the media I demonstrate in this book. One of the most enjoyable aspects of the art of flowers is the diverse choice of media—not just watercolor, but also pencil, pen, and block print. Each flower seems to ask for a different interpretation. Perhaps you'll want to illustrate a flamboyant flower in full color, or a delicate white flower in black and white. You'll find examples of many possibilities in this book. My aim is to honor wildflowers and the great pleasure they give me, so rather than offer very strict interpretations, I try to let each flower express itself through my art.

CLIFF PAINTBRUSH

Forests

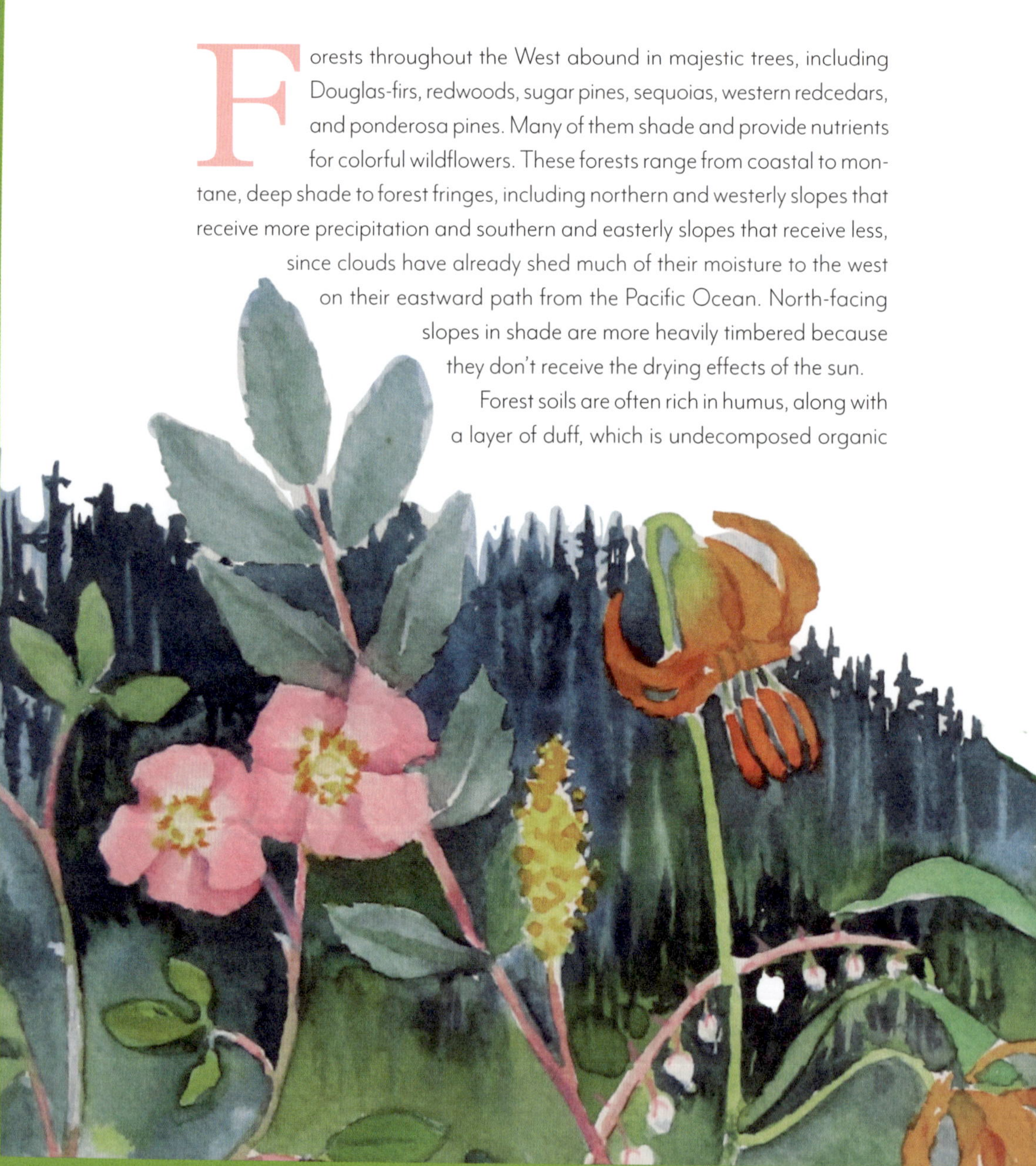

Forests throughout the West abound in majestic trees, including Douglas-firs, redwoods, sugar pines, sequoias, western redcedars, and ponderosa pines. Many of them shade and provide nutrients for colorful wildflowers. These forests range from coastal to montane, deep shade to forest fringes, including northern and westerly slopes that receive more precipitation and southern and easterly slopes that receive less, since clouds have already shed much of their moisture to the west on their eastward path from the Pacific Ocean. North-facing slopes in shade are more heavily timbered because they don't receive the drying effects of the sun.

Forest soils are often rich in humus, along with a layer of duff, which is undecomposed organic material. Forests with the heaviest canopies support members of the orchid and heath families, some of which are saprophytic (obtain their nutrients from organic decay), such as Indian pipe. There are many widespread species, like fireweed, that grow in forest openings or fringes. Shrubs are among the most beautiful of Northwest coastal forest flowers, including the Pacific dogwood, azaleas and rhododendrons, and various wild rose species; these can be found from Washington south to the Northern California redwood forests. Roses and Oregon grape are widespread in all the western forests, although their size will be smaller in drier areas.

East-slope ponderosa pine forests support many species. The area around Leavenworth, Washington, is a perfect spot for an April trip—you'll see bluebells, geraniums, queen's cup, and trillium in the understory of the ponderosa forests around the town. Some east-slope forest flowers are widespread elsewhere, including trillium, which can be found in city parks in Washington and Oregon and throughout the West. In Seattle, I've observed them in Schmitz Reserve Park and Carkeek Park, both heavily forested urban oases.

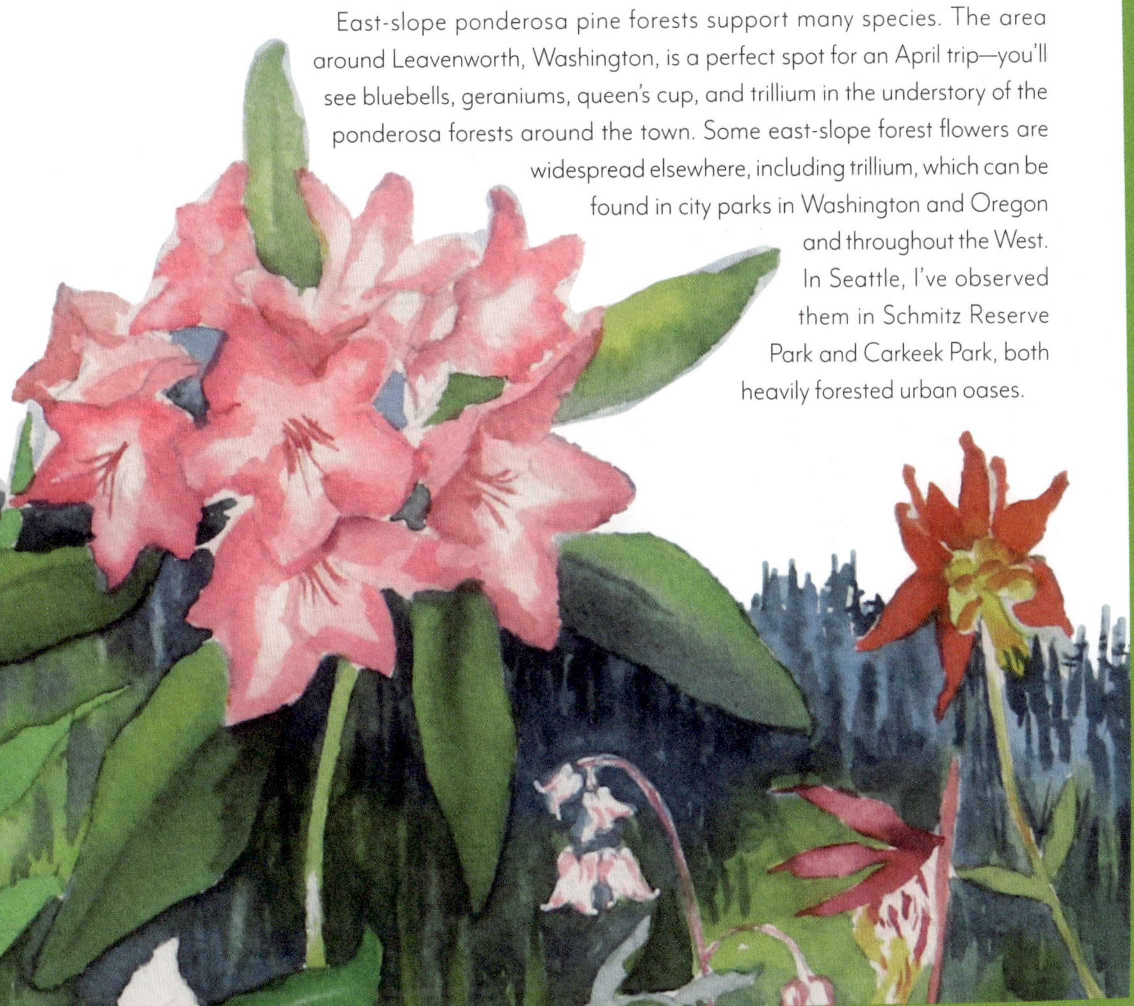

Nootka rose (*Rosa nutkana*, ROSACEAE)

I spotted this perennial shrub near Newhalem, Washington, just outside the boundaries of North Cascades National Park. It was growing in a forest opening in a moist meadow in June alongside other blooms, low to the ground and with grasses surrounding it. Nootka rose shrubs are common in moister forest habitats west of the Cascades and the Sierra Nevada, in low to mid-elevations, as well as in coastal areas.

The shrubs form loose thickets and reach from 3 to 6 feet in height. The toothed leaves have rounded tips and are slightly hairy. Solo pink flowers, blooming in late spring to early summer, are up to 3 inches across and have tips that are markedly notched. The stamens and pistils are a pale yellow. The block-print medium seemed the best way to express the large, bold petal shapes and the graceful grasses that grew beside it.

A similar plant, *Rosa woodsii*, or Woods' rose, can be found east of the Washington and Oregon Cascades—thus the name *Rosa woodsii* var. *ultramontana*—as well as in Yosemite, where it grows in moist forests.

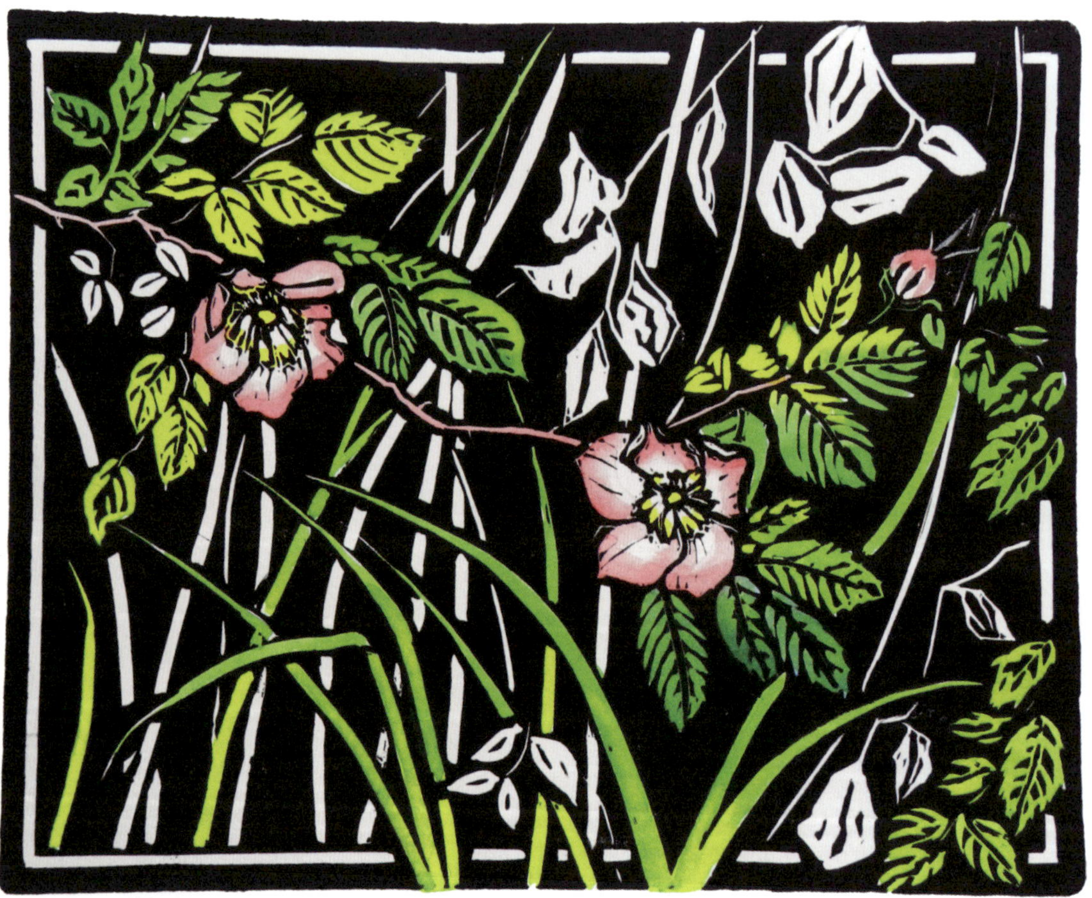

California hedge nettle (*Stachys bullata*, LAMIACEAE)

The California hedge nettle, a member of the mint family, is an evergreen perennial endemic to California, growing in coast ranges from the Bay Area southward and in the Transverse and Peninsular Ranges. It is 1 to 3 feet tall, with whorls of six two-lipped deep pink flowers. The upper lip can form a canopy. Despite its name, it doesn't form a hedge and doesn't sting like nettles! Its favored habitat is wet, boggy places from sea level to 1,600 feet, and depending on location and elevation, bloom times can extend throughout the summer into autumn.

At Muir Woods National Monument, north of San Francisco, where I saw this hedge nettle, I had just an hour and a half for my visit. It was a very short time, and I felt rushed, but no matter how long I had spent there, it would have been but a second compared to the lifespan of the redwoods. A sign in Cathedral Grove requested silence; yet it was hard for children to suppress their excitement as they ran along the path. One boy was a touching exception. He placed his face right next to a tree and talked about how the tree was exhaling as he was inhaling.

When I got back to my studio with photos, I decided to take a playful approach in my choice of medium. I began with a quick pencil sketch, positioning the hedge nettle against the looming pillar of one of the redwoods, as if I was looking up into the canopy. The elegant and very tall hedge nettle struck me as being a delightful counterpart to the height of the trees. I then applied a mixture of green and brown acrylic inks with a chopstick, to keep the sketch loose. After the ink dried, I applied watercolor. I found that I needed to intensify the dark wash on the redwood in order to bring out the delicacy and bright hue of the hedge nettle.

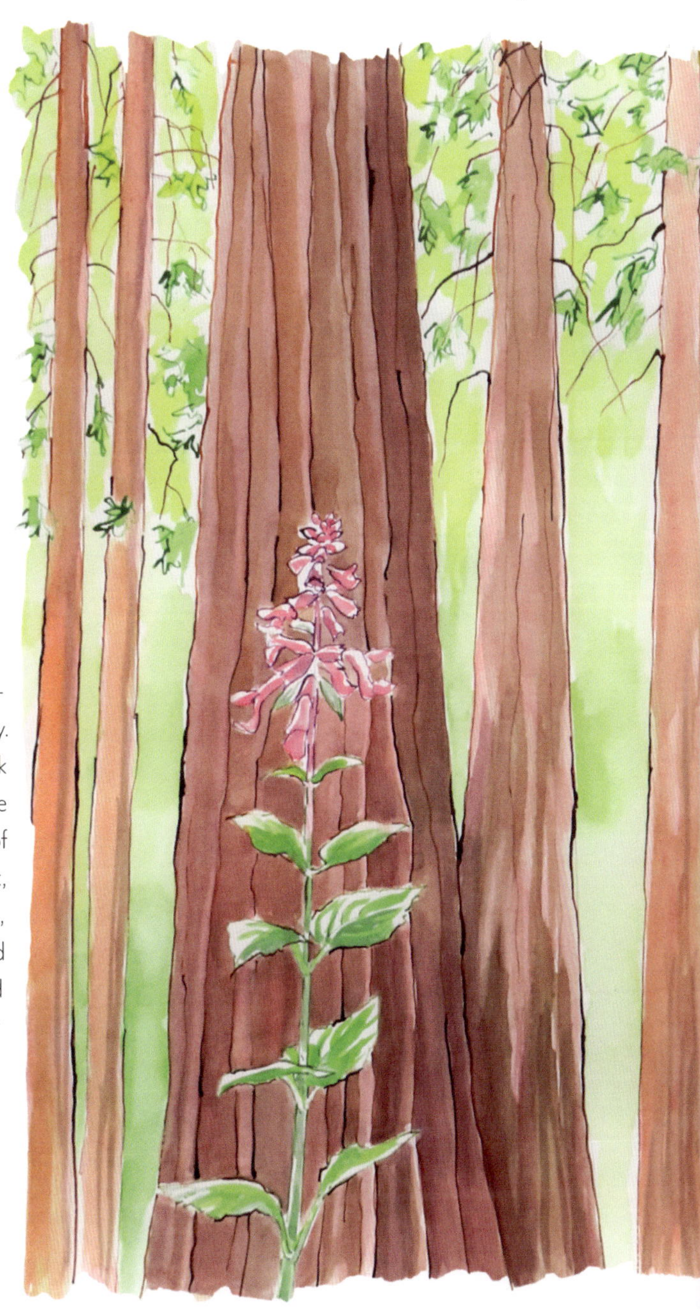

Golden columbine (*Aquilegia flavescens*, RANUNCULACEAE)

I have encountered golden columbine among talus boulders on the Pacific Crest Trail south of Stevens Pass, Washington, on each trip I've made to the area. This perennial plant can grow from 12 to 30 inches tall. Five petals are attached near their central points, with rounded lobes below; above are long spurs. Those spurs led to the name "columbine," which comes from the Italian word *colombo*, meaning "dove"; if you look closely, you may see that the spurs look like the heads of doves. The petals alternate with sepals of the same color, although most of the individuals I've seen have had red spurs and yellow sepals. Dozens of stamens emerge from the center of each flower. The leaves are basal, and the leaflets (smaller leaves emerging from higher up on the stems) are rounded and lobed.

The golden columbine is found in open woods and fringes of mid-to-higher-elevation forests, both along the Pacific coastal states and from Utah and western Colorado north to Canada. Bloom time is late spring and early summer. Although it is typically a forest flower, there are varieties of columbine more closely associated with other ecoregions (see Alcove Columbine in the Deserts chapter).

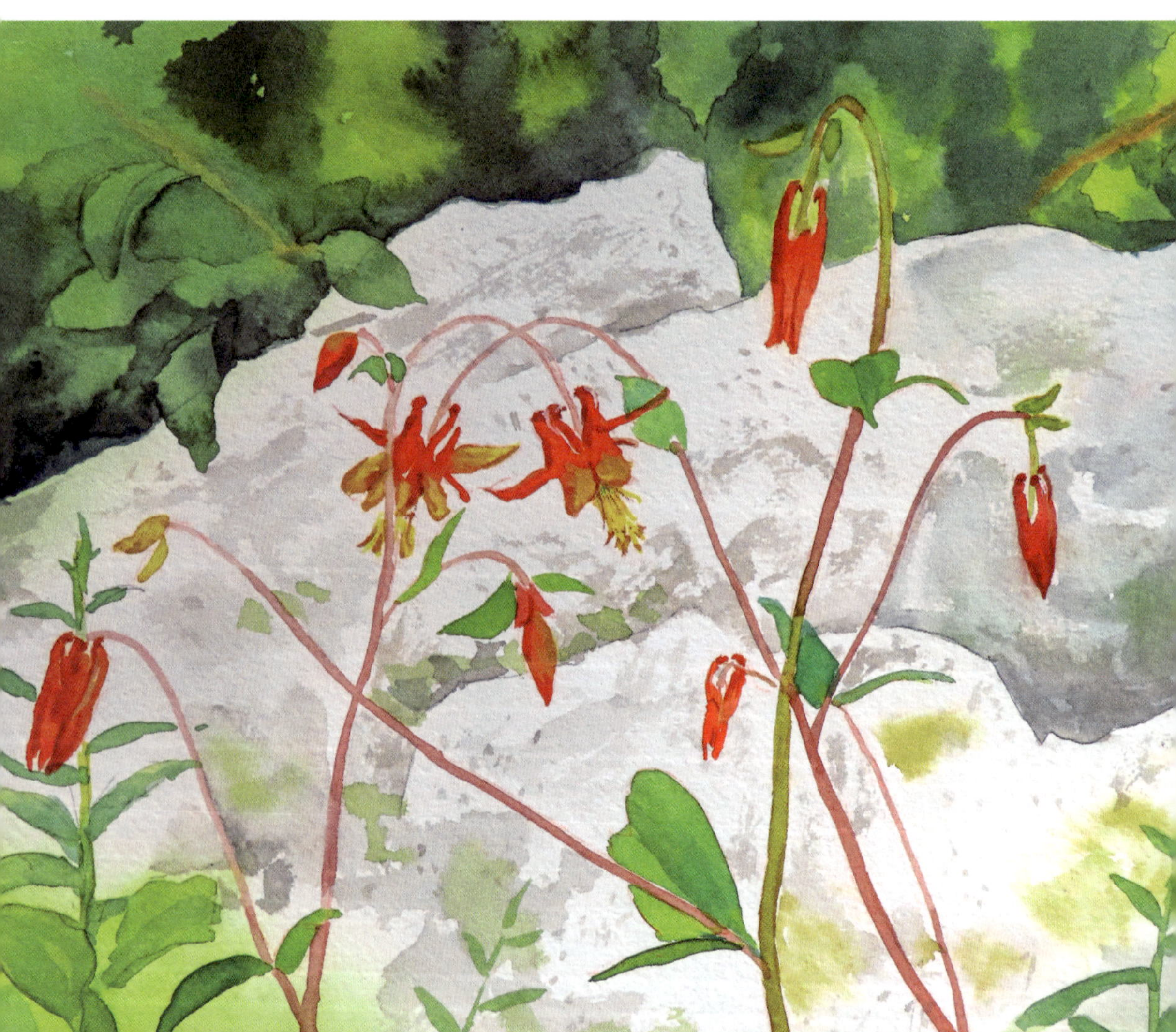

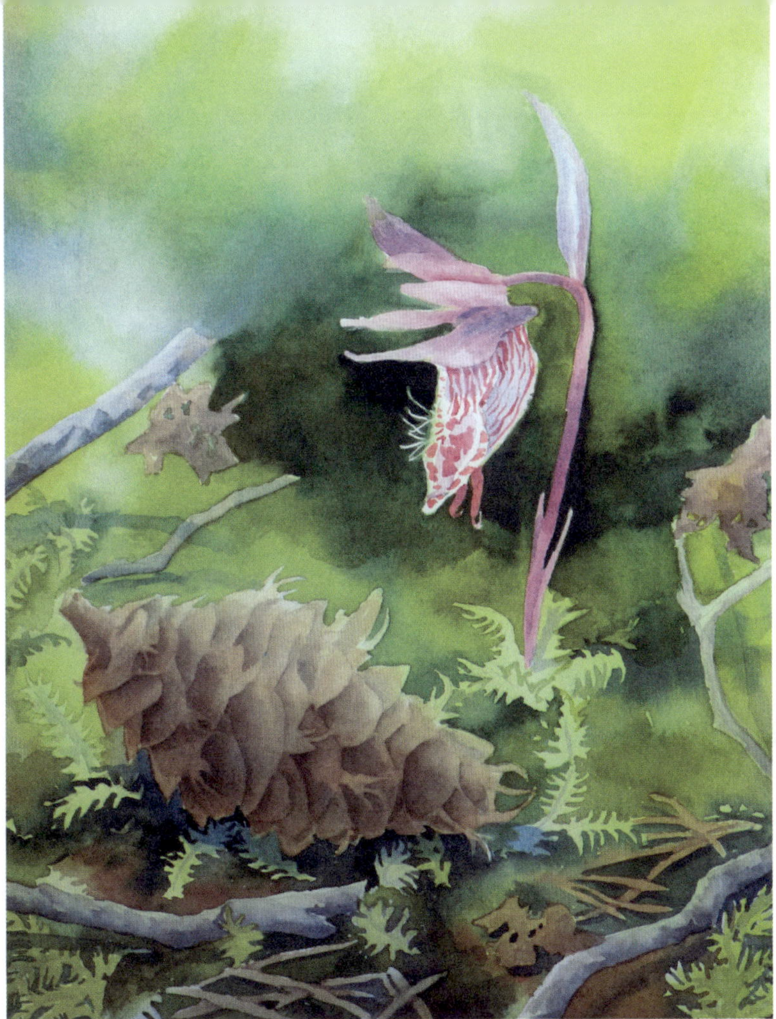

Fairy slipper (*Calypso bulbosa*, ORCHIDACEAE)

The fairy slipper, also called the calypso orchid, is a perennial that grows across the West, from coastal forests to east-slope forests up to 5,500 feet. Although it can be found in forests in many places worldwide, it isn't common where I live in the Pacific Northwest, nor elsewhere in the United States—it's endangered in some states and extinct in the Northeast. Once while hiking above Diablo Lake in North Cascades National Park, I found this small treasure mingled with the forest duff alongside a Douglas-fir cone. I thought watercolor was the best way to represent the lush quality of the flower and the surrounding forest.

The plant grows from 3 to 7 inches tall and features a parallel-veined leaf 1 to 2½ inches across that emerges in autumn, remains throughout the winter, and dies back in summer. Flowers appear in spring, soon after snowmelt. The flower displays three showy pink-to-magenta pointed sepals and two petals above a "slipper" (lower lip) that is paler pink or white, with some spotting at times. According to Mark Turner and Phyllis Gustafson's *Wildflowers of the Pacific Northwest*, albino fairy slippers are not rare, although I've never seen one.

Pacific dogwood (*Cornus nuttallii*, CORNACEAE)

Pacific dogwood shrubs grow in moist forests in the lowlands of Washington and Oregon. In California they grow both in moist lowland forests and at elevations up to 6,500 feet—everywhere except the northeast corner of the state and the deserts. The flowers take many forms, with the four to seven petals—which are actually bracts—sometimes twisting and sometimes forming more regular and flattened shapes 2 to 3 inches long. The true flowers are in the center, a sort of yellowish-green color, and they become berries in autumn. The leaves are pointed and deep green, 1½ to 4 inches long. This perennial shrub or small tree can grow to 50 feet but is more commonly shorter. It becomes insignificant to our eyes through the summer after the blossoms have fallen, but in autumn it startles once again with its beautiful russet and rose-colored leaves.

In May, Yosemite National Park sparkles with rushing water and white dogwood blooms. Over the years, I've taken my Yosemite Conservancy class to a favorite painting site, Cook's Meadow, just south of Yosemite Falls in the shade of incense cedars and oaks, where we sketch Half Dome. These spring sessions usually bring us beautiful sightings of flowering dogwood. Even though the dogwood I depicted here wasn't actually framing Half Dome, I took artistic license in creating such a scene, feeling that the dogwoods would dramatically set off the granite monolith. I have seen dogwood blossoms in the Pacific Northwest too. A few years ago, I painted the watercolor on page 46 of a tree in its earliest state of bloom.

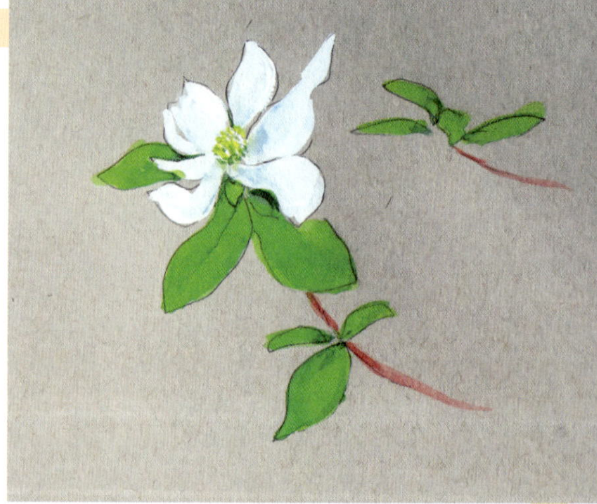

TECHNIQUE
Gouache on Toned Paper

I began this quick treatment of a dogwood bloom by drawing the sprig and stem with leaves. The Bristol paper has a surface that is quite smooth, which results in crisp edges and tolerates a little bit of reworking, but no removal of paint. I started with the white gouache and a pale green in the central disk of the bracts. After the white gouache dried, I added some pale blue—phthalo blue mixed with white—and used yellow, white, and green for the central disk. For the leaves, I added a small amount of white gouache paint to the green—a mixture of Hansa yellow medium and phthalo blue (red shade), leaning mostly toward yellow. When you are working on toned (or tinted) paper, it is important to adjust brights to even greater intensity and saturation, because the toned paper will mute your colors, causing them to appear more neutral in the final result.

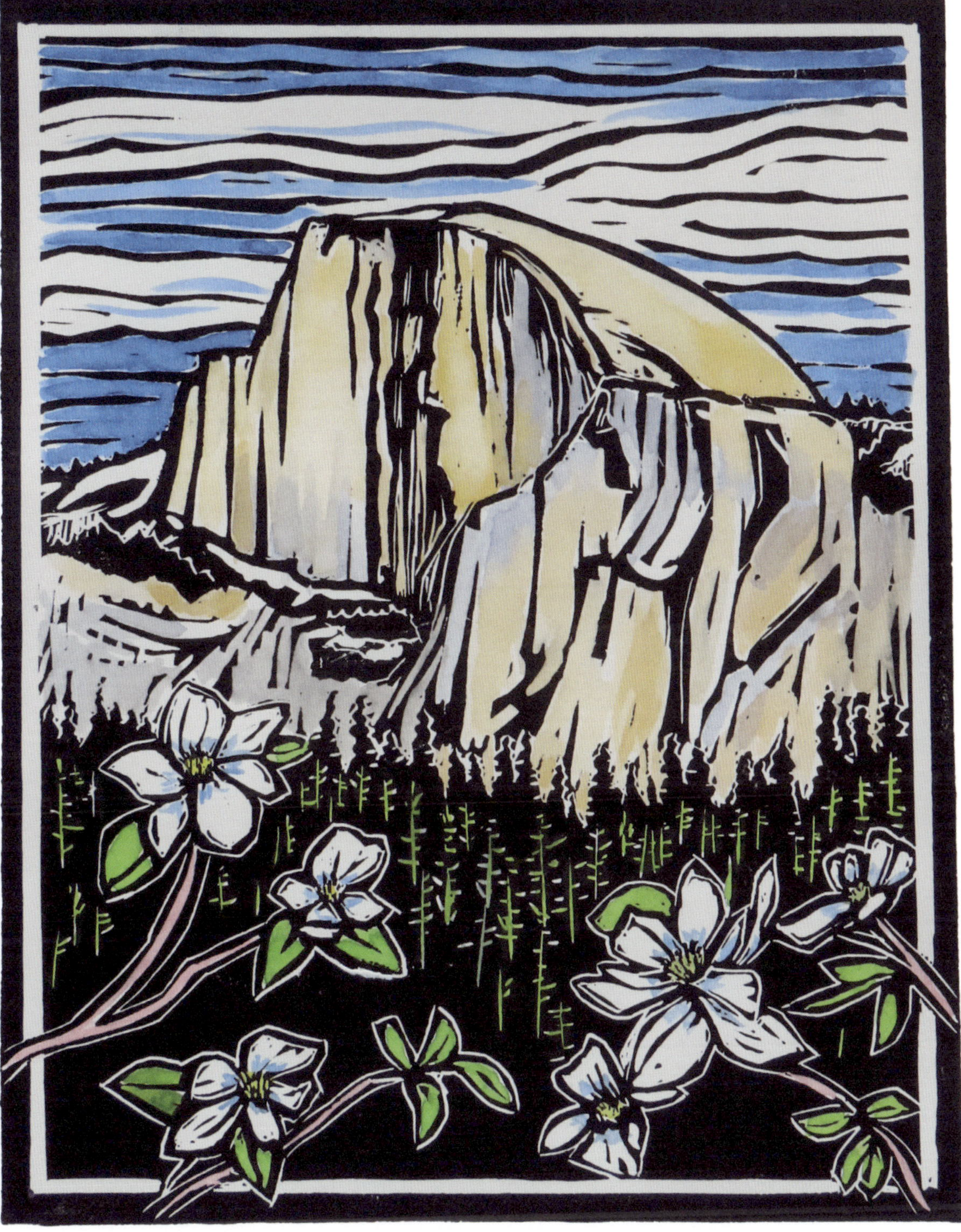

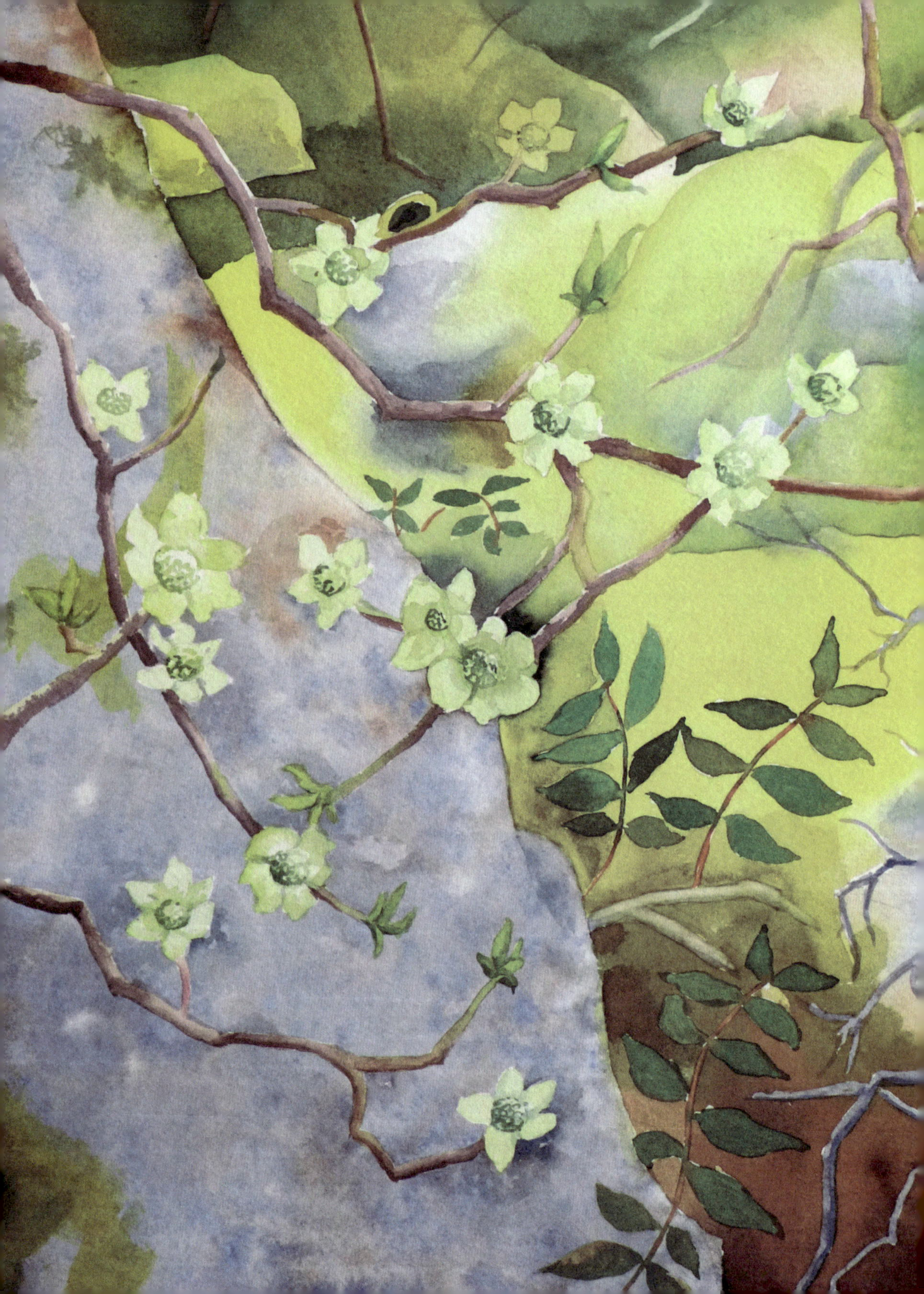

Indian pipe (*Monotropa uniflora*, ERICACEAE)

The perennial Indian pipe is also known as the ghost plant because of its star-tling white color, although it is occasionally pinkish. The fleshy stems, up to 10 inches tall, sprout in clumps but are not branched, and are decorated with scales. When the plant blooms in mid- to late summer, a single bell-shaped flower with five overlapping petals droops from the top of each stem. The plant is found in very dark, humus-rich conifer forests at lower elevations throughout North America; its survival depends on its underground connection through fungi to the nearby conifers.

Once when I was teaching for North Cascades Institute, my students and I observed a blooming plant beneath a towering Douglas-fir on the Sourdough Creek Trail. I was so surprised by it, having never seen an Indian pipe before, that I added a painting of it, shown here, to my water-color journal.

Eminent American poet Emily Dickinson referred to the Indian pipe as "the preferred flower of life" in an 1882 letter to her friend and eventual editor Mabel Loomis Todd. It had made a lasting impression on her in childhood when she first saw it in the woods: "I still cherish the clutch with which I bore it from the ground . . . ," she wrote, "an unearthly booty." The cover illustration on her first collection of poetry, *Poems by Emily Dickinson*, published posthumously in 1890, was a painting of an Indian pipe by Loomis Todd.

PACIFIC DOGWOOD BLOSSOMS

'Tis whiter than an Indian Pipe—
'Tis dimmer than a Lace—
No stature has it, like a Fog
When you approach the place.

—**Emily Dickinson,** poem ca. 1879, Amherst College Archives and Special Collections

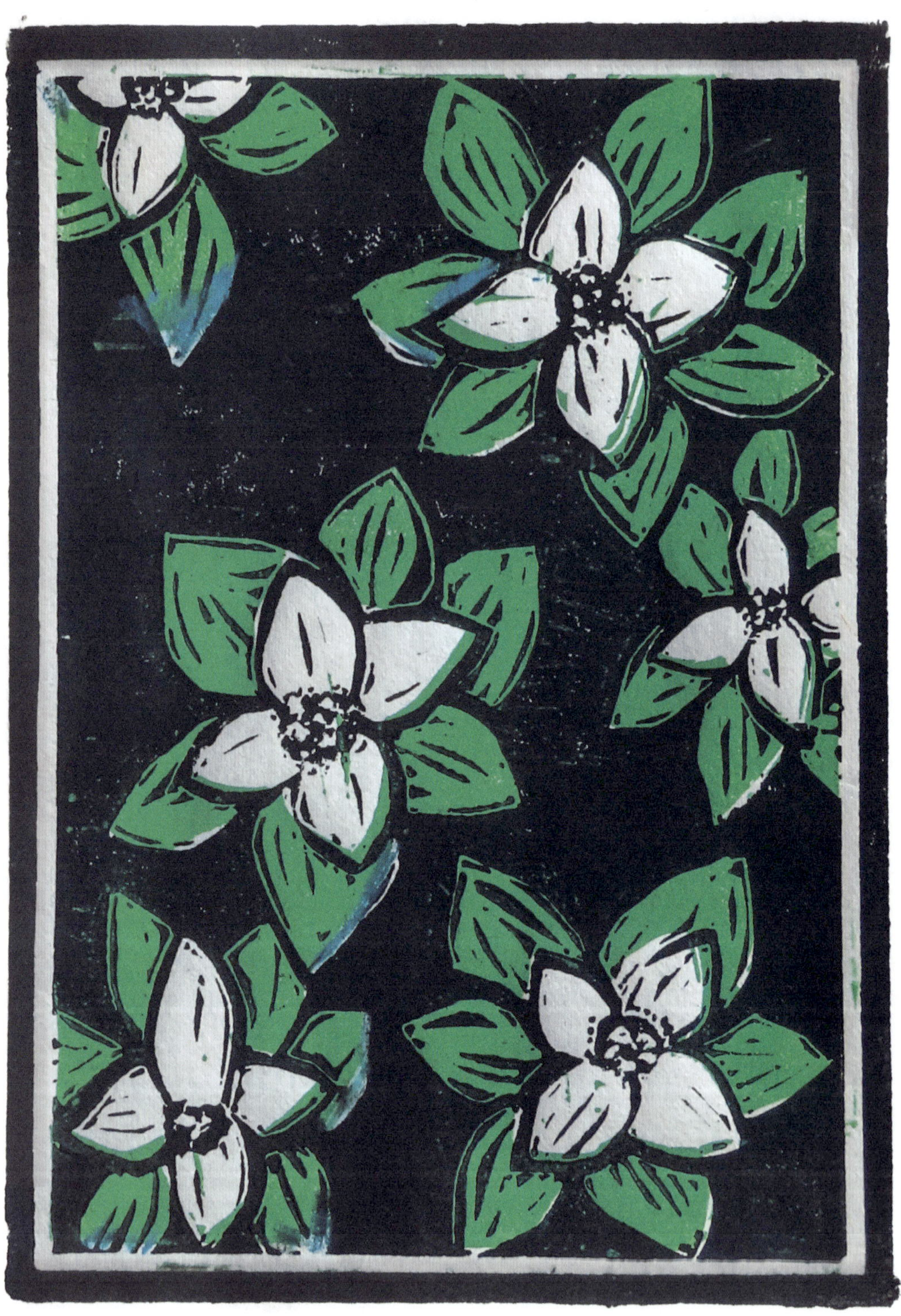

     Wildflowers of the West

Bunchberry (*Cornus canadensis*, CORNACEAE)

This perennial plant in the dogwood family is found in moist woods from low to mid-elevations throughout the Rockies and Cascades, blooming in late spring to early summer. It displays four white bracts of considerable size—almost 1 inch long, oval, and pointed at the ends. The tiny flowers are positioned in a dense cluster just above the bases of the bracts. If you look closely, you can see deep violet centers. The 2-inch leaves are about the same shape as the bracts and form a whorl of four to six below the bracts. Ripening in late summer, the bunchberry's fruits look like small berries; they are edible but don't have much flavor.

TECHNIQUE
Multiblock Printmaking

In looking at bunchberries growing on the forest floor—the random but natural arrangement, the simple yet expressive colors—I was reminded of the Finnish company Marimekko's bold designs. I felt a block print that employed two colors, a dark green and a bright green, would express the pristine beauty of the plants. To achieve this, I carved two blocks, one for each color. Here are the steps to creating a multicolored print:

1. Draw a design, planning the outside dimensions so that they are an even measurement—for example, 5 by 7 inches or 8 by 10 inches. At this design stage, for easy erasure, I use an HB pencil to draw. Before transferring the design to a block (see below), redraw with a 5B pencil so that it transfers well.

2. Cut each block to the exact size of your drawing's outside dimensions. If different color areas are far apart, you won't need to have a separate block for every color. But if the colors are adjacent or close, you'll need a separate block for each color.

3. Place the drawing on a registration board or a mat board cut into an L shape. Lay the drawing face down on the board so that the perimeter of the drawing fits into the L shape. Tape the left edge of the drawing securely to the board. Lift the paper up and place the block snugly into the L shape. Rub your drawing with the back of a spoon to transfer the drawing onto the block.

4. Repeat with each block.

5. For each block, use a marker or something similar to designate which color is being left in relief. Color only the areas that will be printed, and carve all others out. Use the same direction when you carve—there will always be a certain number of marks remaining (called chatter), and it's confusing if they go in many different directions. Often there is a logical direction—either horizontal or vertical—that seems best for a particular subject.

6. Use a brayer to roll out a thin layer of ink onto the block, first in a horizontal direction, then in a vertical direction—to ensure good coverage. Place the block on the registration board.

7. Measure your paper to at least 1½ inches outside the block's perimeter. Tape the left

edge to the registration board, as you did with the drawing when you transferred it to the block. Press firmly with a spoon, then lift the paper gently to see if you are getting a good transfer of ink.

8. Gently flip the paper back without dislodging the tape and remove the block from the registration board.

9. Ink the second block with a different color. Place the second block on the registration board.

10. Without removing the tape, lower the paper back onto the second block and press firmly with a spoon. Repeat the process for additional blocks/colors.

11. When satisfied with the print, remove the paper and the tape.

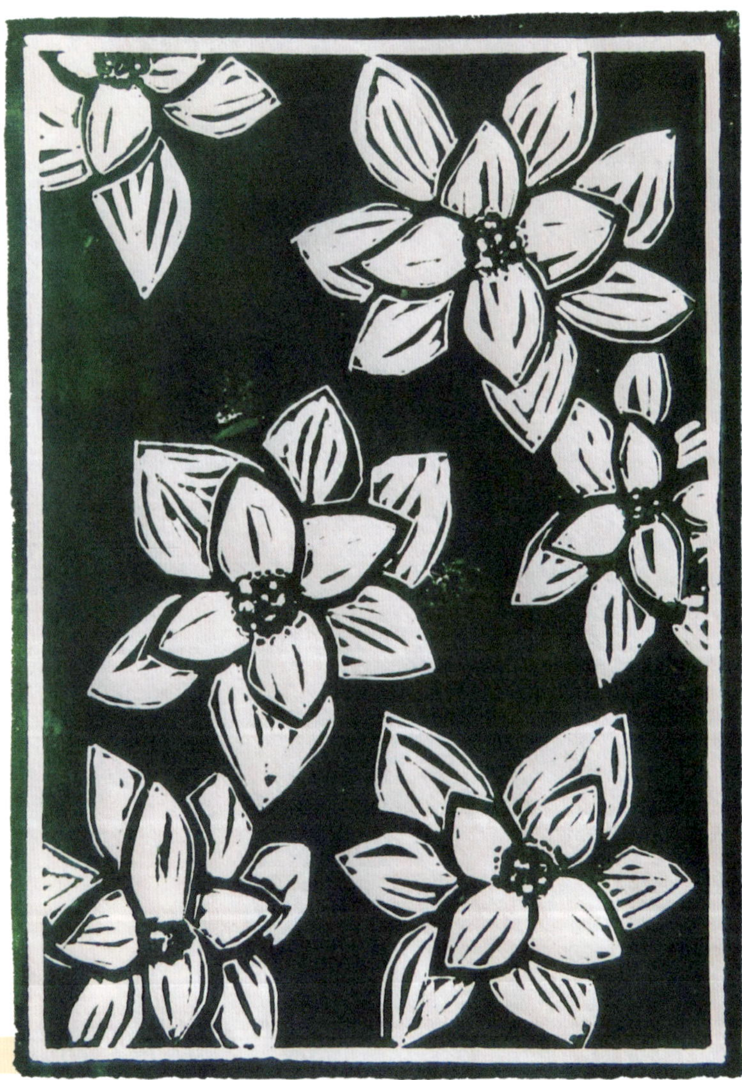

    Wildflowers of the West

Birchleaf spiraea (*Spiraea betulifolia* var. *lucida*, ROSACEAE)

Birchleaf spiraea is an erect perennial shrub that grows up to several feet tall. Although somewhat uncommon, it is more likely to be found on the east side of the Cascades in Washington and Oregon in early spring. I saw this one on the east slope of the North Cascades along the Cedar Creek Trail. The flow-ers, which present in clus-ters, both flat-topped and slightly rounded, are 2 to 5 inches across. The shrub is quite beautiful and one that I would welcome in my garden, though perhaps the wet west side would be unsuitable for it. I liked it enough to try rendering it in gouache on black paper, with the white flower clusters and bright green leaves standing out in bold contrast to the dark background. To bring out the intensity of the hues, I mixed white gouache with my watercolor paints, creating an opaque paint with good coverage.

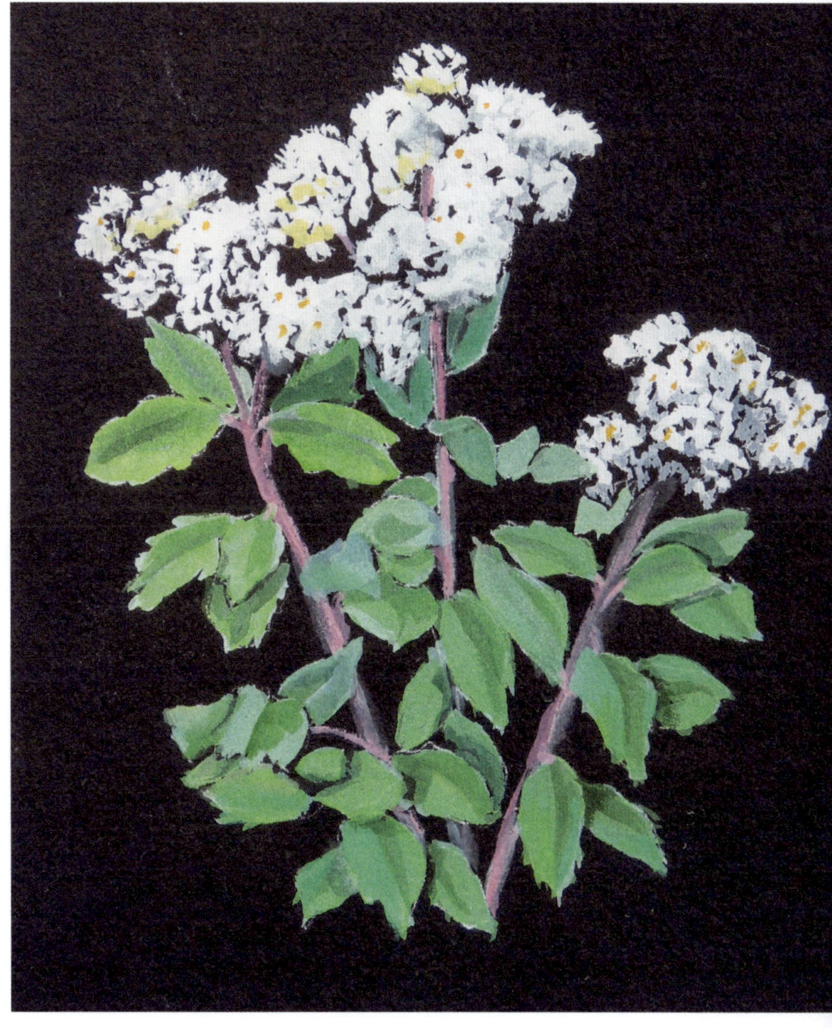

Trillium (*Trillium ovatum*, LILIACEAE)

Trillium, also picturesquely known as wake-robin, is often the first sign of spring in the forest. Living in the Pacific Northwest, I find this perennial a welcome sight after months of rainy, cloudy weather. I've seen it in many locations on both sides of the Cascades. When my children were younger, it was our family's ritual to let me decide what we'd do on Mother's Day, and hiking in a montane forest was almost always my first choice. One year, on the McClellan Butte Trail west of Snoqualmie Pass, we encountered dozens of huge trillium lighting up the dark forest on the lower reaches of the trail—one of our most memorable celebrations.

The flowers consist of three white petals, about 2 inches long, which turn pink and rose with age, surrounded by three green sepals. The seed capsule is a small green or white berry, which ants collect and take back to their nests, leaving the uneaten seeds to germinate once again in the forest. The stem is erect, with a bare lower stem; the leaves are 2 to 8 inches long, widening midway and then coming to an elegant point. Unlike most plants in the lily family, which tend to have narrow leaves, trillium features broad leaves and networked veins. It is abundant in western forests, from the coastal states east to Colorado and Wyoming; you'll encounter these flowers in lower elevations in April and at higher elevations in May. In the redwoods and on other forested slopes in California, the trillium can bloom as early as February.

I painted this trillium using a technique I employed for flowers throughout this book. To create the rectangular border, I taped down the four sides of my paper. After drawing the flower within the box shape, I painted it first and then added rich saturated color behind it, trying to harmonize with the flower's hue. In this case, with a white flower, it meant picking up some of the green in the leaves. Extending the stem beyond the border makes the study a little more playful.

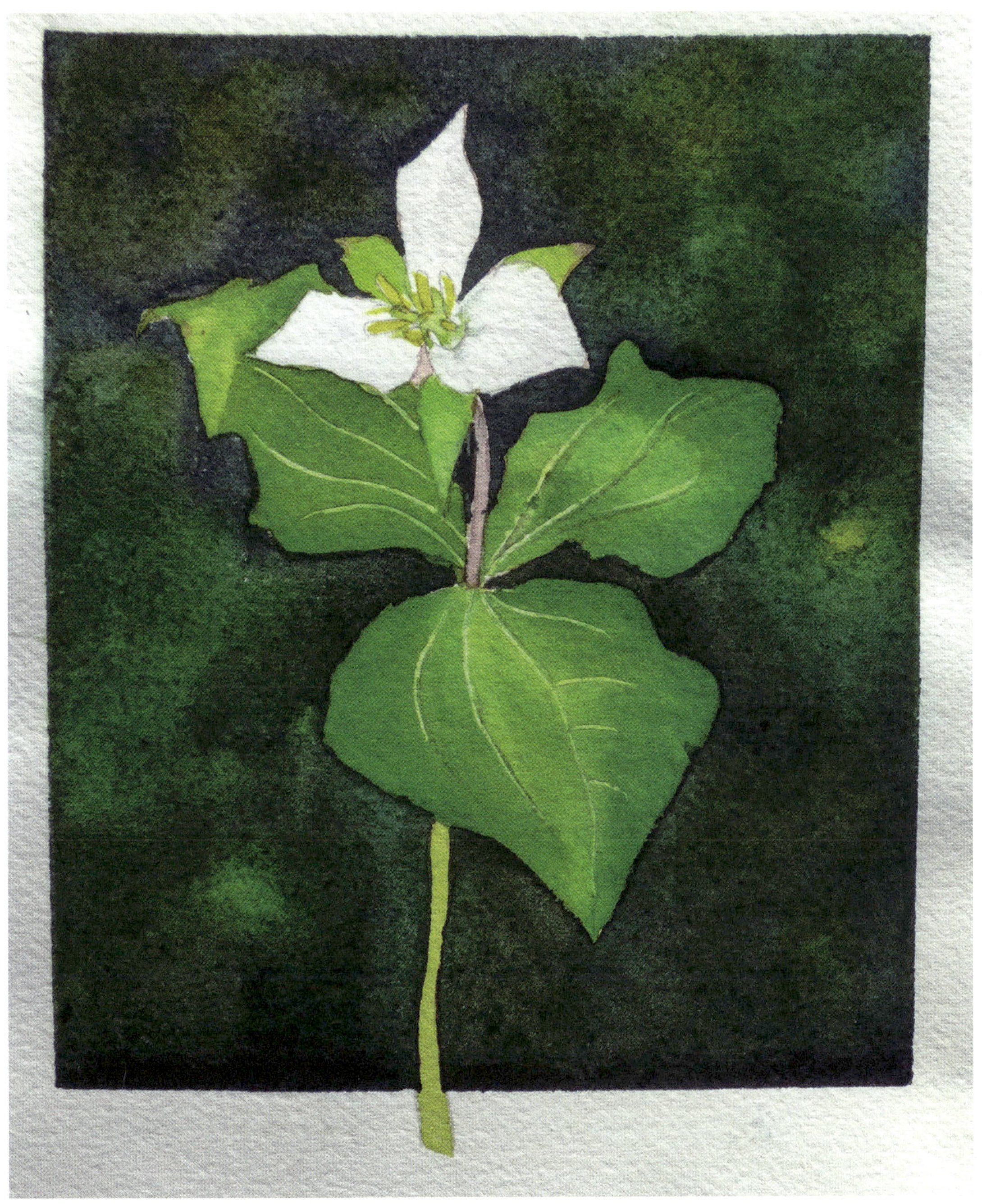

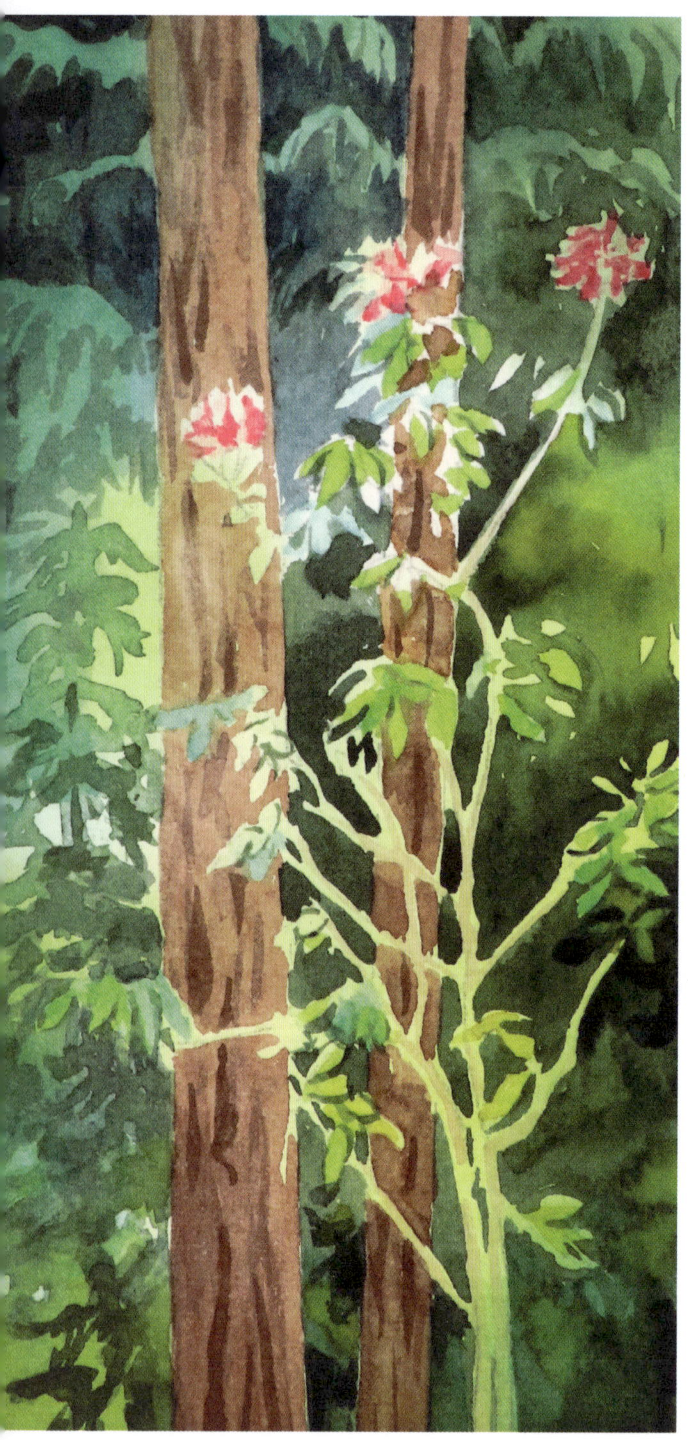

Rhododendron
(*Rhododendron macrophyllum*, ERICACEAE)

The perennial rhododendron grows in coastal and west-side forest areas from Washington through Northern California, from sea level to higher elevations. It ranges from 3 to 15 feet tall and has evergreen leaves that are 3 to 8 inches long, pointed and leathery with a sunken midvein. The upper side of the leaves is dark green, the underside a paler yellow-green. The clustered 1-to-1½-inch flowers are pink to rosy purple, with the five individual petals fused at the bottom to form an elegant shallow bell. The rhododendron is Washington's state flower, and once you've seen one flowering in the wild—from late spring to early June—you can understand why, as it looks more like a cultivated garden shrub with its huge, luxurious blooms. I've seen rhododendrons on Whidbey Island on Puget Sound, and while hiking at around 4,000 feet in a central Oregon forest one June. I still remember the surprise of finding this tall shrub among Douglas-firs high up in the mountains—a first for me in all my years of hiking in the Cascades.

Checker lily (*Fritillaria affinis*, LILIACEAE)

A perennial also known as mission bells, the checker lily is a small, graceful, and unusual member of the lily family. It is very common both east and west of the Cascades in Washington and Oregon, as well as in California foothills up to 6,000 feet. Blooming in mid-spring, it favors locations under shrubs and trees where conditions can remain moist, but is found even in drier locations. It can grow 1 to 3 feet tall, with

several nodding, bell-shaped flowers, remarkable in color and featuring a playful pattern you would imagine had been painted on: the base color, which appears yellow, is overlaid with violet-brown spots in a rough checkerboard array. The first time I saw one on Lopez Island, I was utterly charmed. The narrow leaves grow on stems and can be whorled below and opposite above. Some relatives are commonly grown in flower gardens—I have *Fritillaria meleagris*, also known as checkered lily, and it is one of my favorite spring-flowering bulbs.

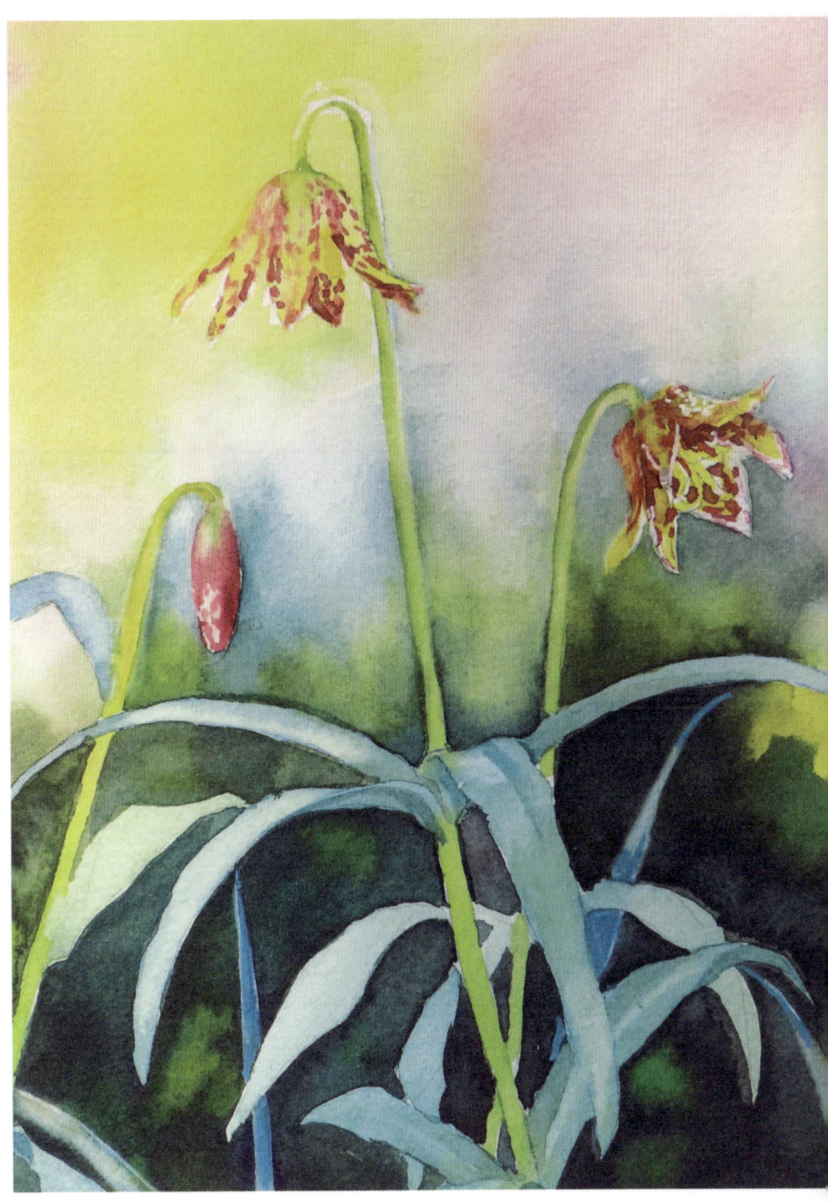

Columbia lily (*Lilium columbianum*, LILIACEAE)

The perennial Columbia lily is a common early summer sight for hikers in the Cascades of Washington and Oregon. It grows from coastal areas to forests to subalpine zones. I've photographed and sketched these wildflowers many times over the decades I've been hiking. I used to seek out a particular individual that grows just below Sourdough Creek Falls in the North Cascades. Over the years, I noticed how different winter conditions seemed to produce flowers of varying sizes. A wet winter encouraged tall growth and multiple flowers—thus the plant can vary from 1 to 4 feet in height. Leaves are lance-shaped, 2 to 4 inches long, and the flowers, 1 to 2½ inches across, hang chandelier-like from separate curved stems, facing downward. It's hard to miss these striking flowers, because their shape and golden-orange hue are both rather rare in the Pacific Northwest. The one I illustrated in the block print was growing beside Highway 20 just west of Newhalem, Washington.

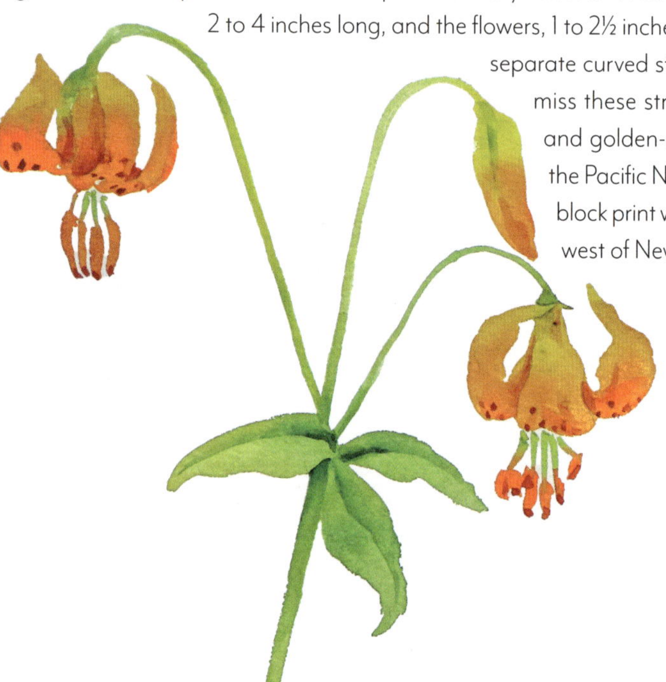

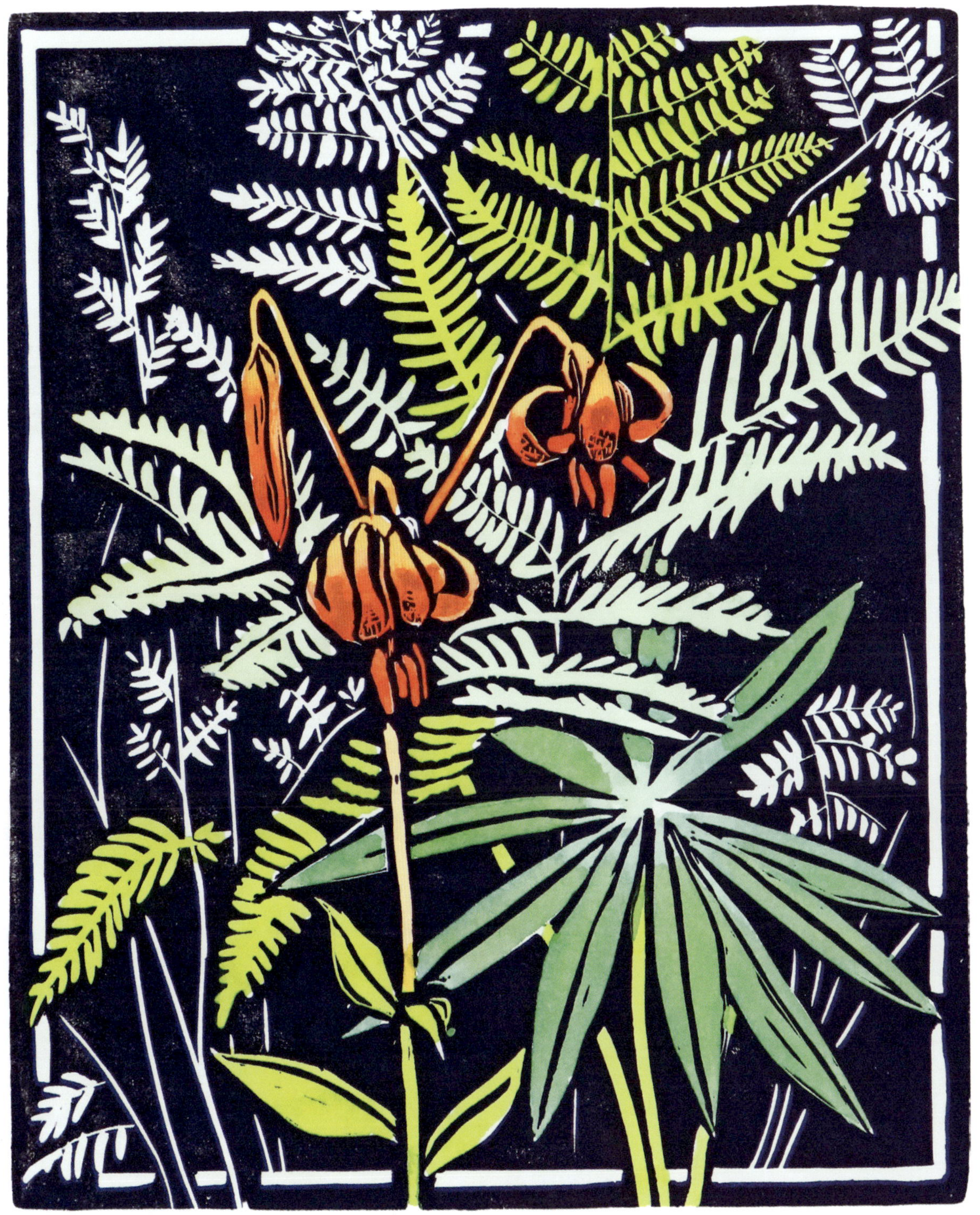

Chaparral & Woodlands

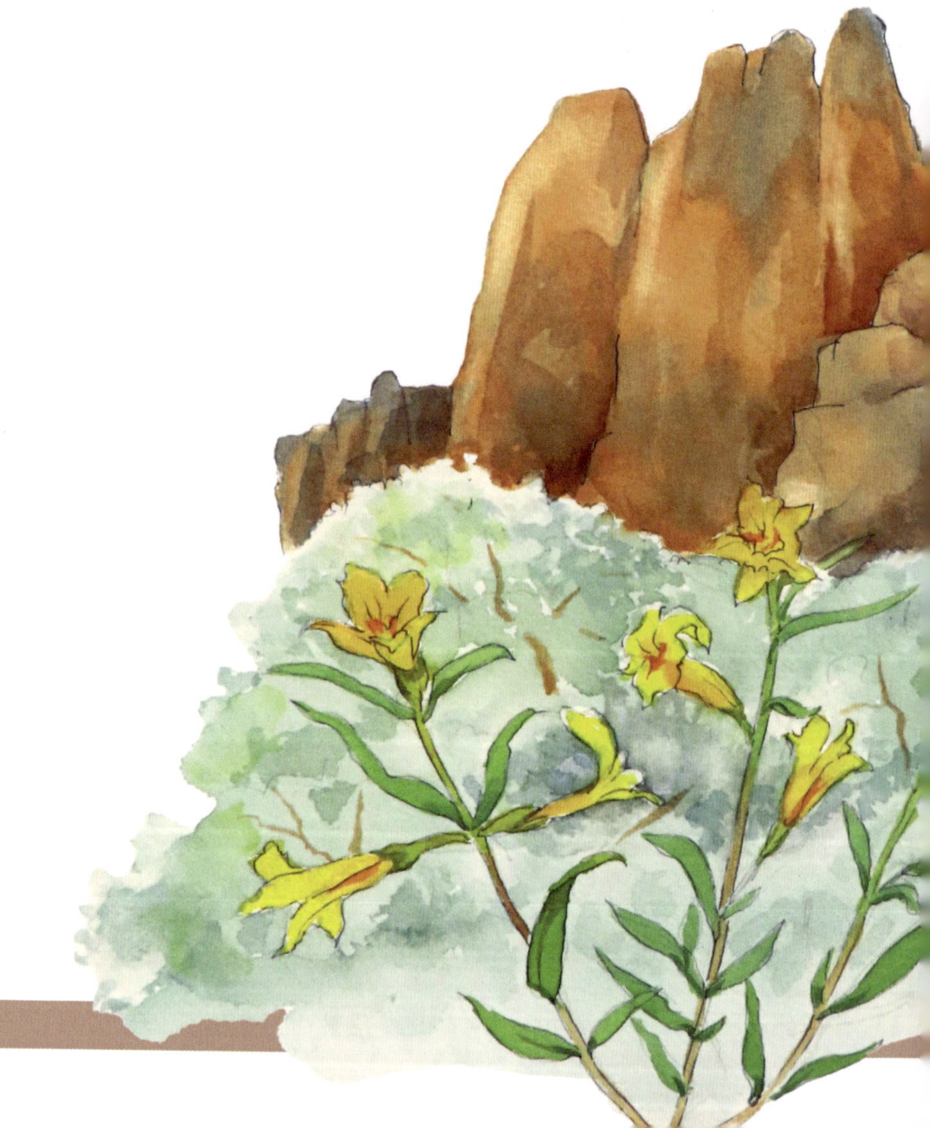

Chaparral and woodlands are found in much of California, as well as in the interior western states. Chaparral consists of brushlands, usually at an altitude of about 100 to 400 feet, featuring species adapted to extremely arid conditions, with small leaves and flowers and hard, woody stems. Characteristic shrubs are California lilac, manzanita, and mountain mahogany. Plants grow on well-drained, rocky or gravelly slopes and ridges.

Woodland habitats are generally one of two types: the oak woodlands west of the Sierra Nevada in California and the pinyon-juniper woodlands of the eastern Sierra and much of the higher elevations in the Southwest, including in Utah, Colorado, Arizona, and New Mexico.

Chaparral

Chaparral exists in much of California, as well as in Arizona between about 3,000 and 6,000 feet. In California it is most commonly found from San Diego and Los Angeles to the great Central Valley and as far north as the San Francisco Bay Area. Covering seven million acres in the state (roughly 9 percent of California's wildland vegetation), it is widespread across rocky slopes west of the deserts; this includes the interior areas of San Diego, Orange, Ventura, San Luis Obispo, and Monterey Counties. Smaller areas of chaparral also extend north from California into southern Oregon.

Chaparral is the equivalent of the Mediterranean's *macchie*, or shrubland. The word *chaparral* comes from the Spanish word *chaparro*, meaning "dwarf oak," and it describes a community of tough, fire-adapted shrubs that frequently grow in thickets, often a mix of chamise, madrone, manzanitas, and ceanothus, as well as small oak trees. Moisture in chaparral lands is very unpredictable from year to year, which leaves the chaparral prone to fire, necessary to the renewal of the plant life there. Phacelias, poppies, and lupines are common flowers that create spectacular displays after fire has burned the shrubby overstory.

Clarkia (*Clarkia speciosa*, ONAGRACEAE)

Also called godetia and farewell-to-spring, clarkia was named after Captain
William Clark of the Lewis and Clark expedition. This annual plant is widespread
in California, found in both chaparral and woodland regions. It can grow
up to 2 feet tall, with narrow leaves up to 3 inches long and four-petaled
flowers that range from light pink to rose-pink. *Clarkia gracilis* and
Clarkia purpurea are found in Washington and Oregon as well as in
California; the latter also grows in Arizona.

I came across this late-blooming specimen in August in the San
Francisco Botanical Garden's Arthur L. Menzies Garden of California
Native Plants. In the warmer temperatures of the chaparral, it is an
early spring bloomer, coloring hillsides pink from May into
June. Driving from Fresno to Yosemite in mid-May, I saw it
flowering en masse along the highway. There are numerous
species and subspecies, some delicate and others
with larger flowers. The Botanical Garden flower I
painted may have been *Clarkia speciosa*, but it could
also have been *Clarkia amoena* (the one also known
as farewell-to-spring).

I created this small painting with watercolor and
watercolor pencil, using the sharpened pencils to bring out
some of the details that are harder to achieve with watercolor
and brush alone.

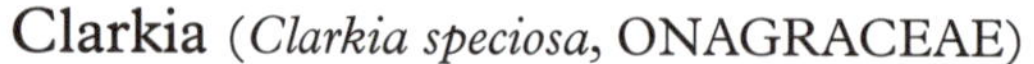

Pinnacles National Park

Pinnacles National Park lies east of the Salinas
Valley in central California, 80 miles southeast
of San Jose. It's an easy trip from Monterey,
and although several miles of Highway 146
near the park's east entrance can be a bit
nerve-racking to drive—it narrows to only one
and a half lanes (in some places only one lane),
and colossal cones from the ubiquitous gray
pine drop like bombs along the roadway—it is
completely worth the effort! The park is named
after the eroded and spectacular remains of
an extinct volcano, which "moved," starting
twenty-three million years ago, from a location
in present-day Lancaster, California, 195 miles
to the southeast. The San Andreas Fault split
the volcano, and the Pacific Plate moved north,
carrying Pinnacles' rocks and spires. The area
was declared a national monument in 1908
by President Theodore Roosevelt, and it was
redesignated a national park over a century
later, in 2013. In addition to the pinnacles,
which rock climbers frequent, there are talus

caves that house more than thirteen species of bats. California condors, hatched in captivity, are released in the park and can be seen flying above the High Peaks. Another raptor, the prairie falcon, breeds in the area—the largest breeding population anywhere in North America.

Elevations in the park range from 824 to 3,304 feet, allowing for a varied array of growing conditions. Chaparral makes up 82 percent of the park's vegetation, but Pinnacles also contains riparian, woodland, and rock and scree plant communities. Together, these diverse habitats support over one hundred species of wildflowers. In the chaparral, tiny goldfields can cover hillsides and meadows, along with Parry's larkspur, woolly blue curls, and poppies. Bush, or sticky, monkeyflowers flourish in the riparian world of Chalone Creek. High above in the rocks, spring displays include bitterroot and rock cress. Counts of bees at Pinnacles have revealed that the area has a notably dense diversity of native bee species—around 450 in the park's 42 square miles, according to a 2018 report by three researchers (including Olivia Messinger Carril, co-author of *Common Bees of Western North America*, who first inventoried the bees in the park in the late 1990s). Because of the length of the wildflower bloom, there are available plants for every species.

While the caves and peaks at Pinnacles are the main attraction for most visitors, others make the journey in springtime to enjoy the flowers. March through May are the peak times, when 80 percent of the wildflowers are in bloom. But even in January and February, you may see shooting stars and Indian warriors. By March, the bush poppy and buckbrush shrubs bloom, along with California poppies, monkeyflowers, and baby blue eyes.

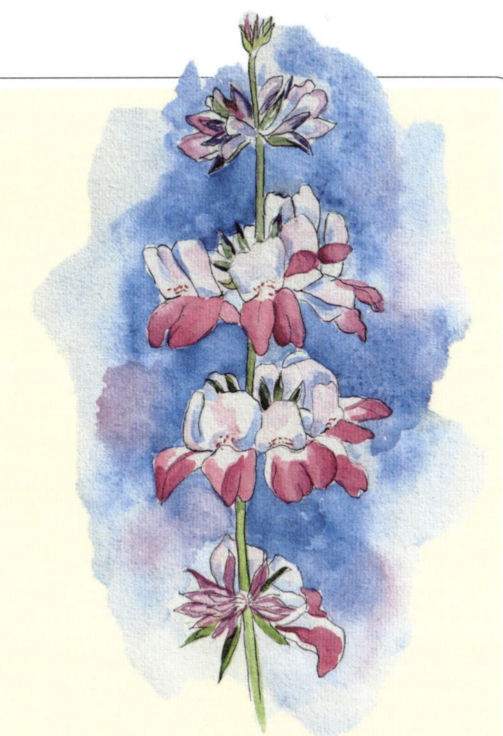

CHINESE HOUSES

In April, many of those are still flowering, but also in flower are violas, gilia, suncups, pitcher sage, larkspur, bush lupine, and Chinese houses. Then in May, plants that thrive in hot, dry weather take over—clarkias, penstemons, and wild roses. If June remains wet and cool, flowers still bloom, but normally that is the end of the spring display.

My visit toward the end of May came a bit late for the fullest floral show, but there was much to be excited about. It began with a stop at the classic 1930s-era Civilian Conservation Corps visitor center. Outside, wild turkeys disappeared into the grassy chaparral. Next, I took a hike to the towering rocks of the High Peaks area, passing through an amazing natural archway. The day ended with my discovery of Parry's larkspur and bush monkeyflower still blooming along the shade of a drying creek.

California flannelbush (*Fremontodendron californicum*, MALVACEAE)

California flannelbush, also known as fremontia, is a widespread perennial plant found between 1,000 and 6,500 feet in California's Sierra foothills—in chaparral, in oak and pine woodlands, and on rocky ridges—from Lake and Napa Counties southward, as well as in scattered sites in Southern California and central Arizona. It is a showy shrub, up to 15 feet tall and branched at the base. The flowers are composed of sepals, not petals, and are lemon yellow to golden, with a waxy coating. The leaves are broad, thick, and downy, featuring three lobes. Although California flannelbush blooms from March to June, the best time to view flowering is April and May, when the entire plant is covered in hairs, stems, leaves, and flowers. You will often see it planted alongside highways.

I encountered this specimen in early August (proof that the flowering times of plants can vary quite widely) at the San Francisco Botanical Garden, where the bees were enjoying an absolute orgy of pollen. One bee I got a close look at was flying from flower to flower, its legs so completely encased in pollen that I wondered how it managed to stay airborne.

From my journal:

> *My friend Paul and I visited the San Francisco Botanical Garden in Golden Gate Park twice while we were in the city for a family wedding. The park is an urban oasis, over 1,000 acres on the western edge of the city, stretching 3½ miles out to the Pacific Ocean, fringed with Monterey cypresses, a dramatic species endemic to a very small area of the Pacific coast near San Francisco. We visited the Botanical Garden's Arthur L. Menzies Garden of California Native Plants, where we were fortunate to observe and photograph many wildflowers, including clarkia and Matilija poppy. There were countless shrubs still blooming in the cool air of California's fog belt. Adjacent was the Redwood Grove, a*

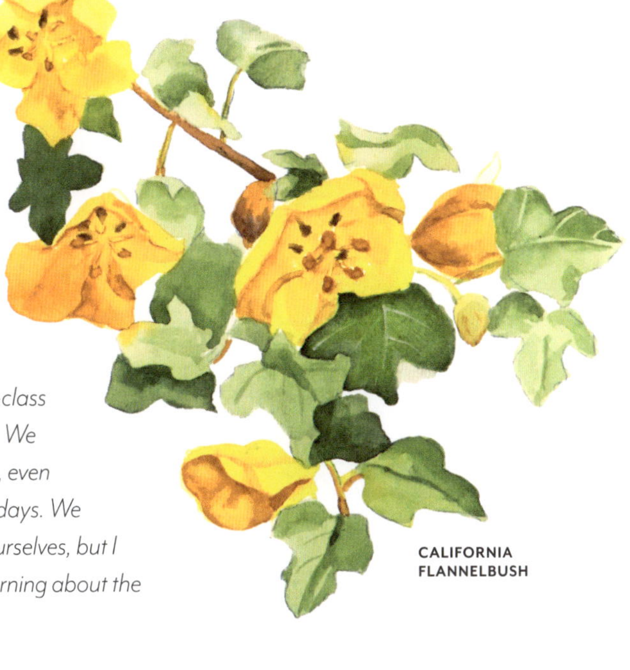

CALIFORNIA
FLANNELBUSH

Yerba santa (*Eriodictyon californicum*, HYDROPHYLLACEAE)

Yerba santa is an early-blooming perennial shrub up to 6 feet tall that is wide-spread in Northern California, growing in sunny, dry, or moist places—on roadsides, in fields, in woodlands, and in chaparral—from low elevations up to 6,000 feet. The 2-to-6-inch-long leaves are leathery and lance-shaped, and the small, delicate flowers are ⅓ to ⅔ inch long and funnel-shaped, in shades of white, lavender, and violet. Its Spanish name translates to "holy herb," and in earlier days it was used to treat asthma and colds. Bees and butterflies abound when yerba santa is in bloom.

I saw the shrub illustrated in this watercolor growing just above the Merced River in May. Its colorful flowers stood out against the foothills leading to Yosemite National Park. I sketched it in my Hahnemühle sketchbook, which is wonderful for quick treatments of panoramic landscape subjects. In contrast to Arches paper—my favorite watercolor support—Hahnemühle paper does not have much sizing, meaning you have to work faster, and mistakes aren't as easily wiped out. That can be very good for avoiding overworking a subject and maintaining a fresh and sketchy look.

YERBA SANTA ALONG THE MERCED RIVER, CALIFORNIA

Matilija poppy (*Romneya coulteri*, PAPAVERACEAE)

Also known as Coulter's poppy, the Matilija poppy, at 6 inches across, is the largest California native wildflower. Found in Pacific coast ranges and the Transverse and Peninsular Ranges, it is unfortunately no longer so common due to expanding human activities and encroaching nonnative plants. The flowers grow on a perennial shrub that can be up to 8 feet tall, and at peak season it is covered with these spectacular blooms. (Bloom time is April in dry washes and canyons up to 4,000 feet.) Each blossom has six crinkled white petals, 2 to 4 inches long, surrounding a bright yellow dome of stamens in the center. The leaves are grayish green and deeply lobed. When I saw a Matilija poppy for the first time, growing in a garden down the street from my home in Seattle, I thought it looked like a giant fried egg!

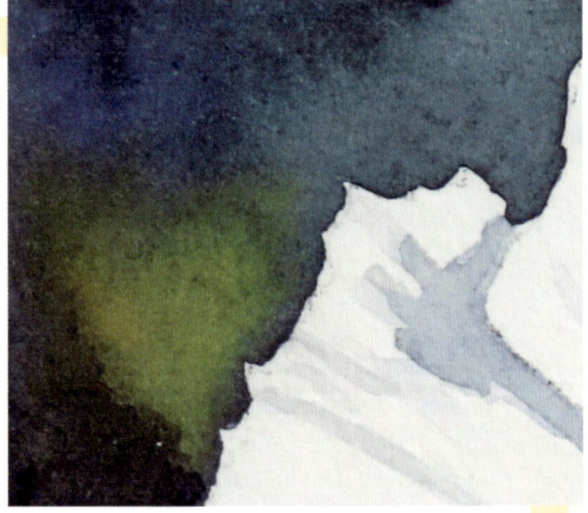

TECHNIQUE
Revealing Light Positive Space with Dark Negative Space

I illustrated several of the wildflowers in this book using the method described here. I began with the flower—bright or white flowers seem to work especially well with this approach. After I painted the center and crinkled petals of the poppy (the positive space), I taped off the outside perimeter of the painting (the negative space) and then mixed a dark wash of color, composed of perylene green, violet, and phthalo blue (red shade). I worked on dry paper; if you paint on wet paper, the mixture will be more diluted and you won't get such rich darks. Periodically, I transitioned from the base color to one with more blue, or one with more violet, and then dropped in some yellows while it was all still wet. It can create more harmony if you add drops of some of the flower color—by drops, though, I don't mean a diluted paint, because when the base color is so dark, you want to have a very saturated brighter color to "drop" in. It's also important to have enough of your dark paint mixed, as it can slow you down to try to match your initial color—mixing can take a long time. After removing the tape, I added more subtle details to the flower itself.

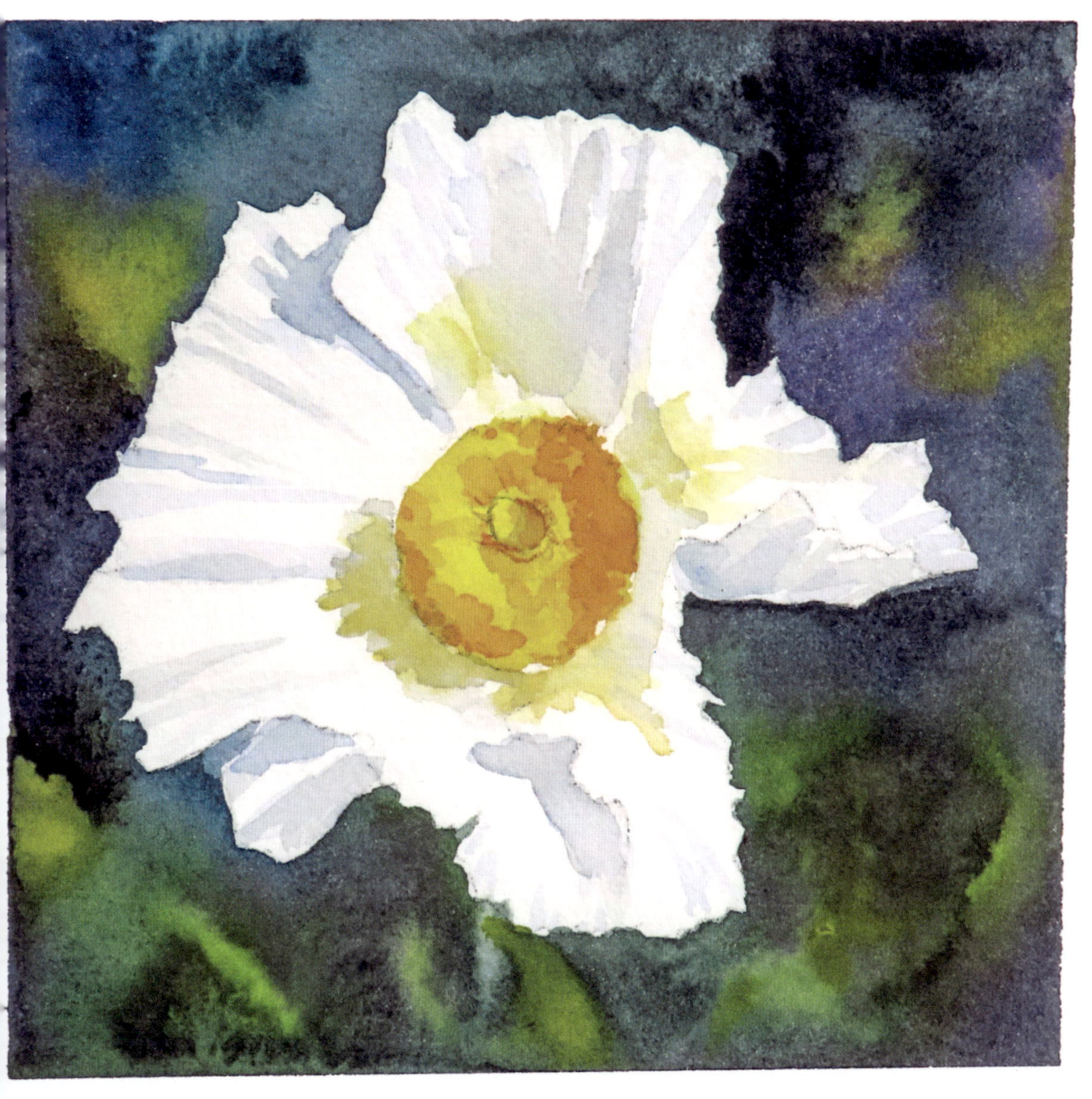

Chaparral yucca (*Hesperoyucca whipplei*, ASPARAGACEAE)

Also known as Our Lord's candle, Spanish bayonet, Quixote yucca, and foothill yucca, the perennial chaparral yucca used to be included in the genus *Yucca* but is now classified in the asparagus family. It grows in chaparral, coastal sage scrub, and oak woodland plant communities from about 1,000 to 8,000 feet, and is also found in desert and inland valleys. The sharply pointed, clustered, gray-green leaves are saw-toothed, up to 4 feet long. After five to ten years, the plant sends up a flower spike that is 10 to 15 feet tall in as little as two weeks. These spikes, which usually appear from April to June, display hundreds of bell-like white, cream, or pale violet flowers.

The chaparral yucca is pollinated exclusively by the California yucca moth. At night the female moth collects pollen grains and forms them into a huge ball; afterward, she flies to another plant and lays an egg on the ovary of a flower, rubbing her pollen mass against the stigma, ensuring pollination. Once the flowers have been pollinated, the chaparral yucca dies, although the spike will remain standing for several years. But all is not lost: before flowering, the yucca will have already sprouted smaller plants, known as pups, alongside its base—genetically identical offshoots that will grow and eventually flower. Often, hillsides are covered with yuccas blooming dramatically all at the same time, visible for miles around. Widespread blooming is common after fires.

Brush Pens

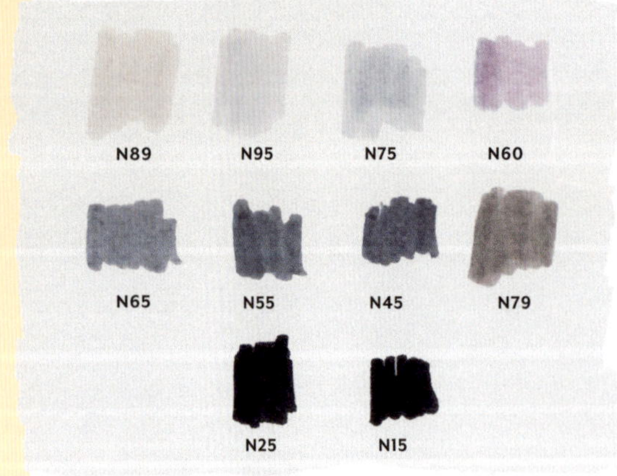

BRUSH PEN TESTS FOR CHAPARRAL YUCCA SKETCH

Because chaparral can be rather neutral in tone, I thought a monochromatic sketch might be appropriate, emphasizing the high-contrast glow of the white flowers and the dark shapes of the daggerlike leaves against the lighter tones of the chaparral landscape. I decided to use brush pens—specifically the gray to black series. These versatile pens, which have both a brush tip and a fine-point tip, come in a wide array of colors and values. The brush tip is perfect for blocking in areas of tone, while the fine point is useful for more precise details like the leaves.

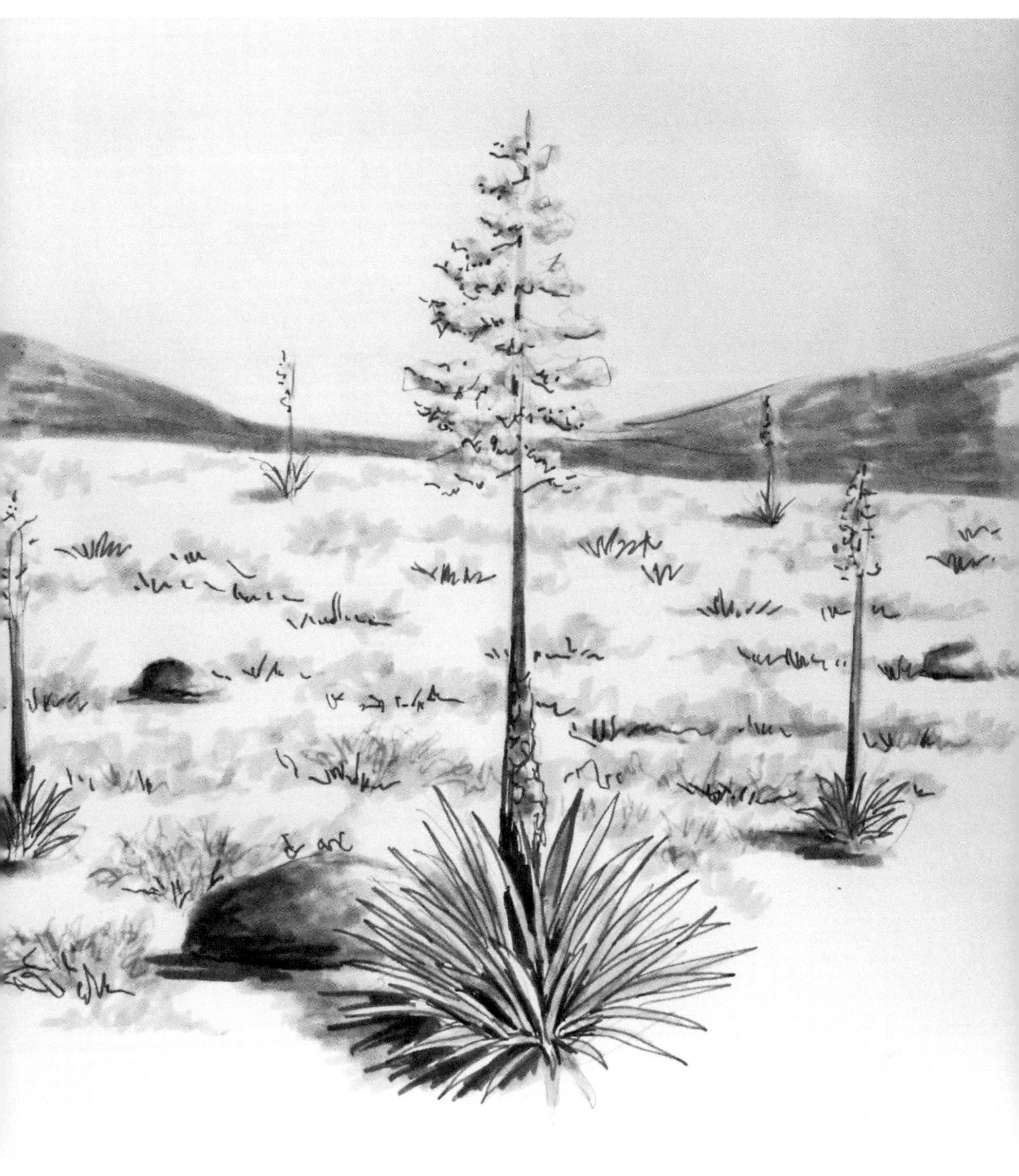

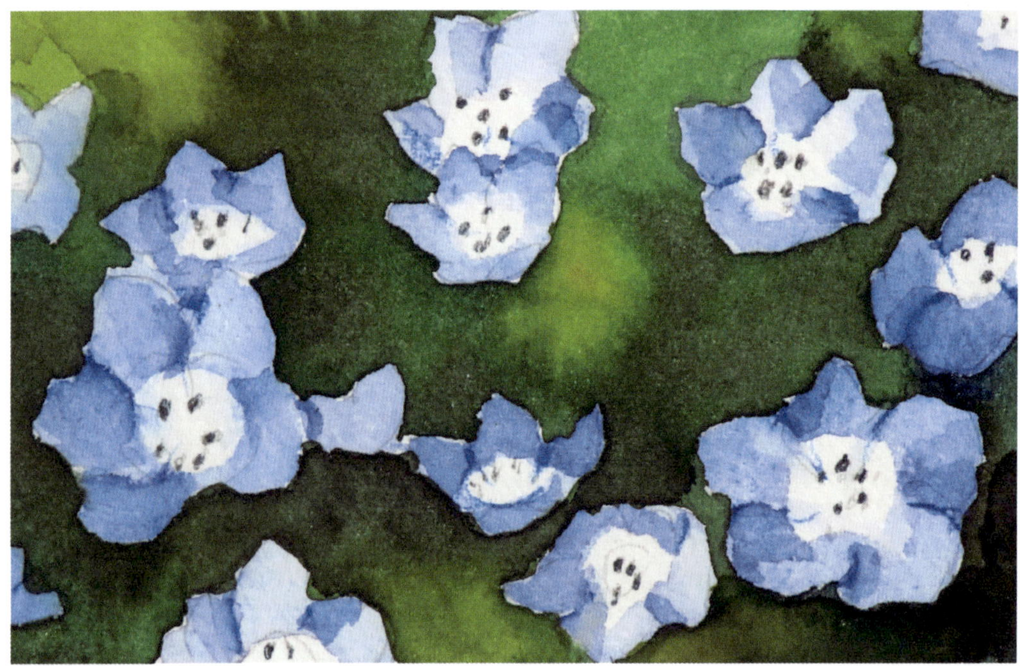

Baby blue eyes (*Nemophila menziesii*, HYDROPHYLLACEAE)

The annual baby blue eyes blooms in spring from Oregon south into California, where it is found in moist places and in grassy, brushy areas up to 6,000 feet. In California, depending on location and elevation, it is in flower from February to June. It is the loveliest shade of blue imaginable—in the watercolor here, I used cobalt blue with a very small amount of carbazole violet to try to approximate the pastel hue. Blue flowers are much prized in gardens, and you'll find *Nemophila* in almost all seed catalogs. The plant can grow from 4 to 12 inches, either sprawling or erect, and its shallow, bowl-shaped flowers are white in the centers with dramatic dark anthers atop white stamens. The opposite leaves are divided into toothed leaflets. Baby blue eyes don't appear singly, but rather grow en masse, so I painted a small group of them in this watercolor.

Woodlands

Woodland habitat is distinct from chaparral. Woodlands form a transition zone between moist conifer forests and drier grasslands and deserts. Tree species include oaks, pines, and junipers. One defining characteristic is the height of the trees—usually more than 15 feet and less than 60.

Oak woodlands are notable on mountain slopes in California. Wildflowers there include poppies, lupines, wild onion, and paintbrush. Describing the character of the California oak woodlands, botanist Willis L. Jepson writes in *The Silva of California* (vol. 2, 1910) that the blue oak in particular "plays a strong and natural part in the scenery of the yellow-brown foothills. Always scattered about singly or in open groves, the trees are well associated in memory with bleached grass, glaring sunlight and dusty trails, although for a few brief days at the end of the rainy season the white trunks rise everywhere from a many-colored cloth woven from the slender threads of innumerable millions of flowering annuals."

Woodlands are also present in Arizona and New Mexico, with oak, pine, and juniper the characteristic trees. It is not unusual to find wildflowers still in bloom there in November, members of the sunflower family in particular. By that time, the more northerly woodlands of Colorado and the Rockies foothills are experiencing the early part of winter, so flowers in those areas, including gentians, larkspur, and blanket flowers, are more limited to the summer months. In colder winter areas like the Great Basin and the Colorado Plateau, oaks are no longer part of the tree community; instead, you find single-needle pinyons and junipers. Common flowers there are lupines, paintbrush, buckwheat, cow parsnip, and irises.

Skyrocket (*Ipomopsis aggregata*, POLEMONIACEAE)

Skyrocket, also known as scarlet gilia, is unmistakable because of its brilliant orange-red flowers that grow on plants up to 4 feet tall. This biennial or perennial wildflower is very common throughout the West, growing in many different habitats, but is found most often in dry soils, including in woodlands. Bloom time is midsummer. The tubular flowers are ¼ to 1½ inches long, with pointed lobes and stamens projecting outward. I saw this individual on Patterson Mountain in the Methow Valley of north-central Washington. The precision of its pointed flowers invited me to try a combination of watercolor and pen.

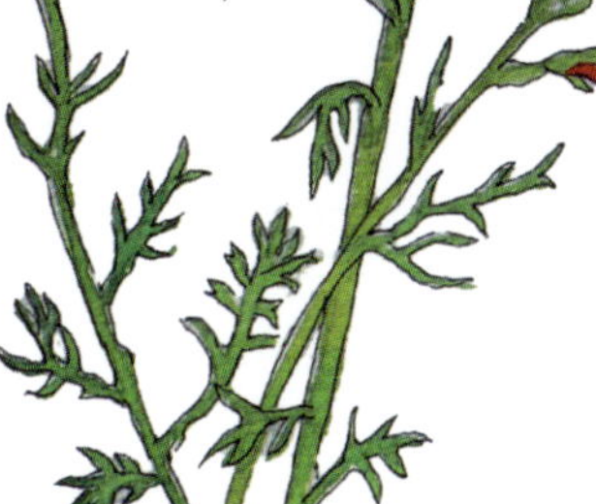

Pollinators and the Xerces Society

Conserving the diversity of invertebrates is the biggest job in the world.
—**Robert Michael Pyle,** founder of the Xerces Society

The Xerces Society for Invertebrate Conservation is a national science-based non-profit that works with land managers, educators, policymakers, farmers, and communities to conserve pollinators and their habitats. Founded by Robert Michael Pyle in 1971, with help from de facto co-founder Jo Brewer, it was named in honor of the Xerces blue butterfly (pronounced "Zer-sees")—the first butterfly known to have disappeared from North America as a result of human activities. Its habitat was destroyed by development in the sand dunes of San Francisco, and it was declared extinct by the 1940s. In the fifty-plus years since its founding, Xerces has had great success. The society has published scores of fact sheets, brochures, and conservation guides, as well as books that help gardeners choose plants that attract and feed native pollinators, including butterflies, bees, and hummingbirds. Millions of acres of habitat have been protected or improved on farms, in parks, along roadsides, and in natural areas. The society has introduced pesticide bans and created the Bee Better Certification program for fruits, vegetables, and other farm products. Hundreds of communities and colleges have committed to protecting pollinators through the society's Bee City USA and Bee Campus USA programs. And many gardeners have taken the Pollinator Protection Pledge and are welcoming pollinators to their backyards.

California milkweed (*Asclepias californica*, ASCLEPIADACEAE)

California milkweed is a gray-leaved, woolly-haired perennial that grows on grassy flats and brushy hillsides below 7,000 feet throughout much of California west of the Sierra Nevada. It can be up to 2 feet tall, with very large and fuzzy opposite leaves. The flowers are pink to maroon to violet, arranged in thick umbels several inches across. The corollas are reflexed (curved back), and the central flower parts are star-shaped, composed of five hoods with noticeable hooks. I saw a number of these plants in May in Cook's Meadow in Yosemite Valley, just ahead of the late May bloom, and they were already being visited by monarch butterflies. Milkweeds are closely monitored because they attract this vulnerable pollinator. The loss of milkweed plants in the monarch's spring and summer breeding areas appears to be a large factor in the butterfly's reduced populations, as recorded in its overwintering sites in California and Mexico. Among the reasons for milkweed habitat reduction are agricultural escalation, urban sprawl, roadside mowing, and herbicide use. The Xerces Society (see the sidebar) is actively involved in efforts to restore monarch butterfly habitat and encourage seeding with milkweed. I bought a dwarf variety at my local nursery and planted it this summer. During its peak bloom, it attracted more bees than any other flower in my pollinator garden.

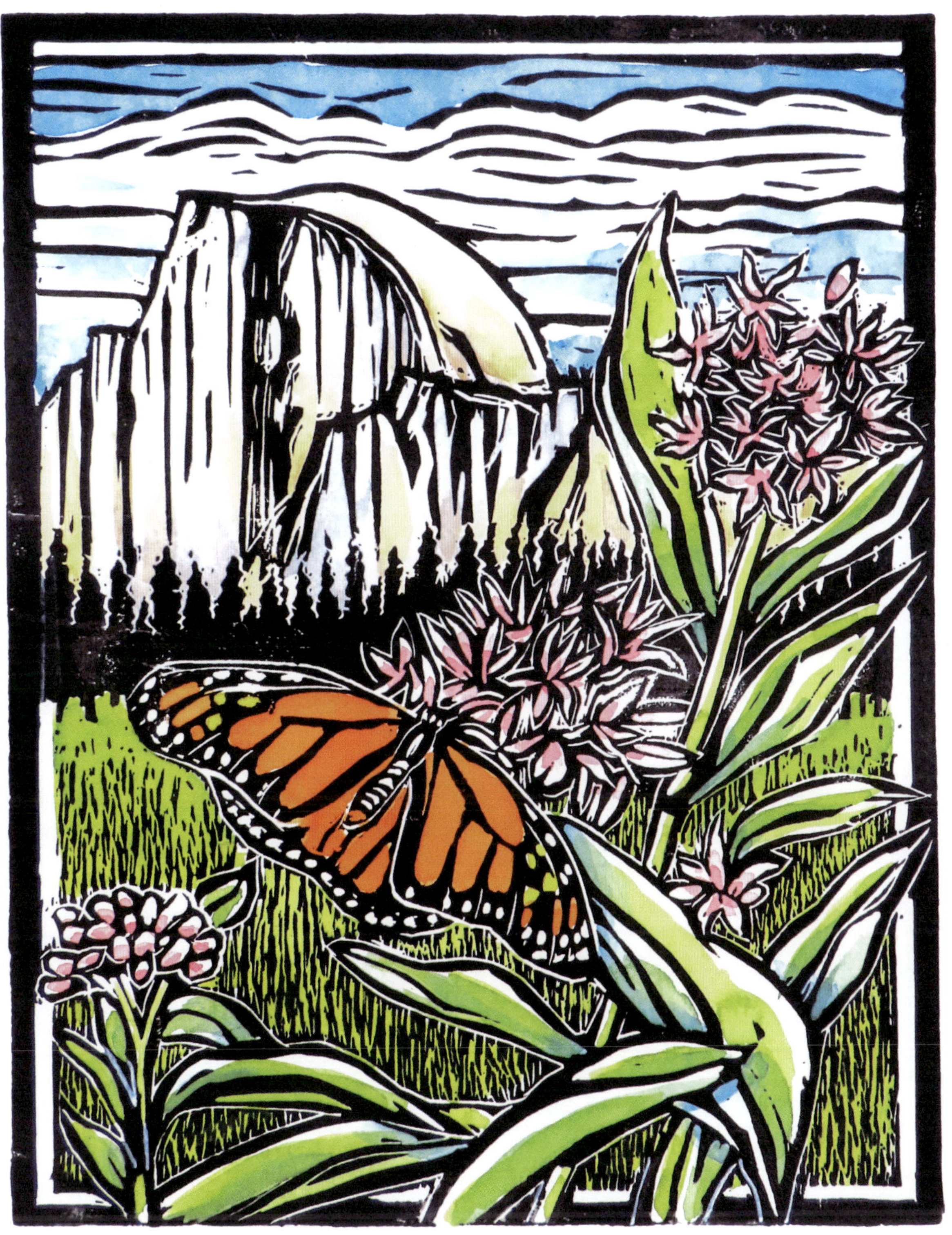

Sky lupine (*Lupinus nanus*, FABACEAE)

The annual sky lupine is found throughout much of California and extends as far north as Washington. It is a lovely bicolor blue-violet and white species. The leaves are typically palmate, with five to seven pointed lobes. Plants can grow 1 to 2 feet in height, and flowers appear on spikes in early to late spring.

It's possible the vast meadow of lupine I saw and painted might have been arroyo lupine—it's hard to distinguish among the countless varieties, and in this case both have the white patch on the upper banner. Both plants also grow in woodland settings; the sky lupine is found below 4,500 feet, the arroyo beneath 3,000 feet. It was late afternoon when I pulled off the road between Oakhurst and Yosemite to take photos of this stunning May display beneath a large oak in an area of old ranches. A breathtaking springtime panorama like this must have been commonplace before agriculture and urban sprawl overtook so many of our wildlands and roadsides.

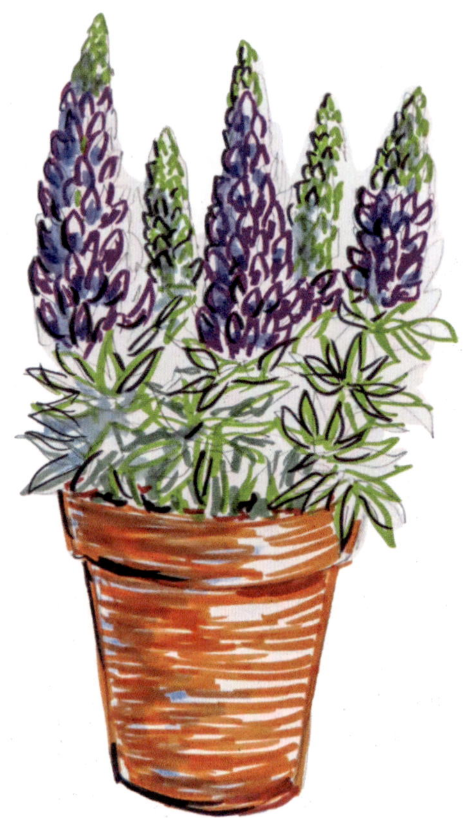

A HYBRID LUPINE BRINGS A REMINDER OF WILDFLOWERS TO MY GARDEN.

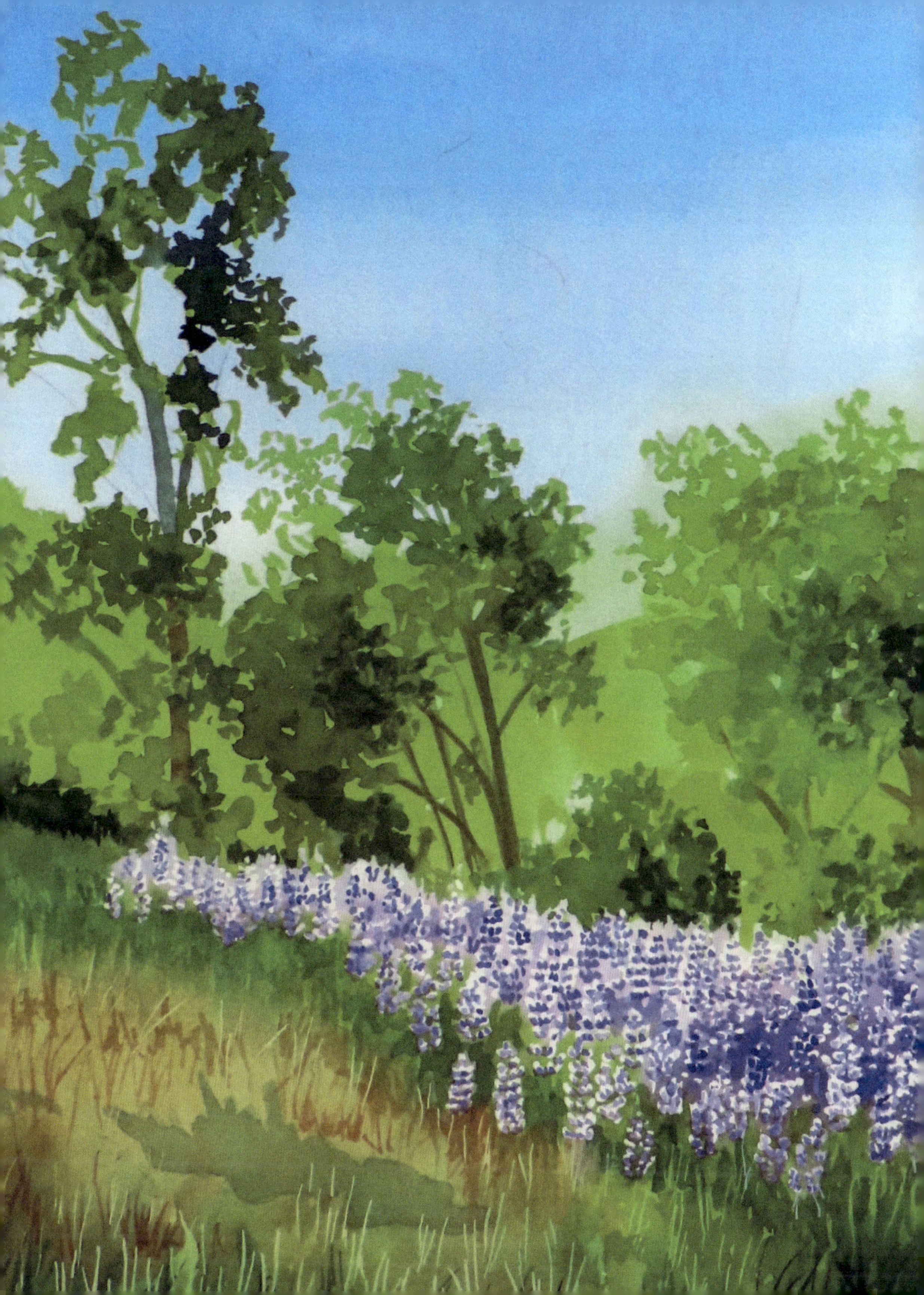

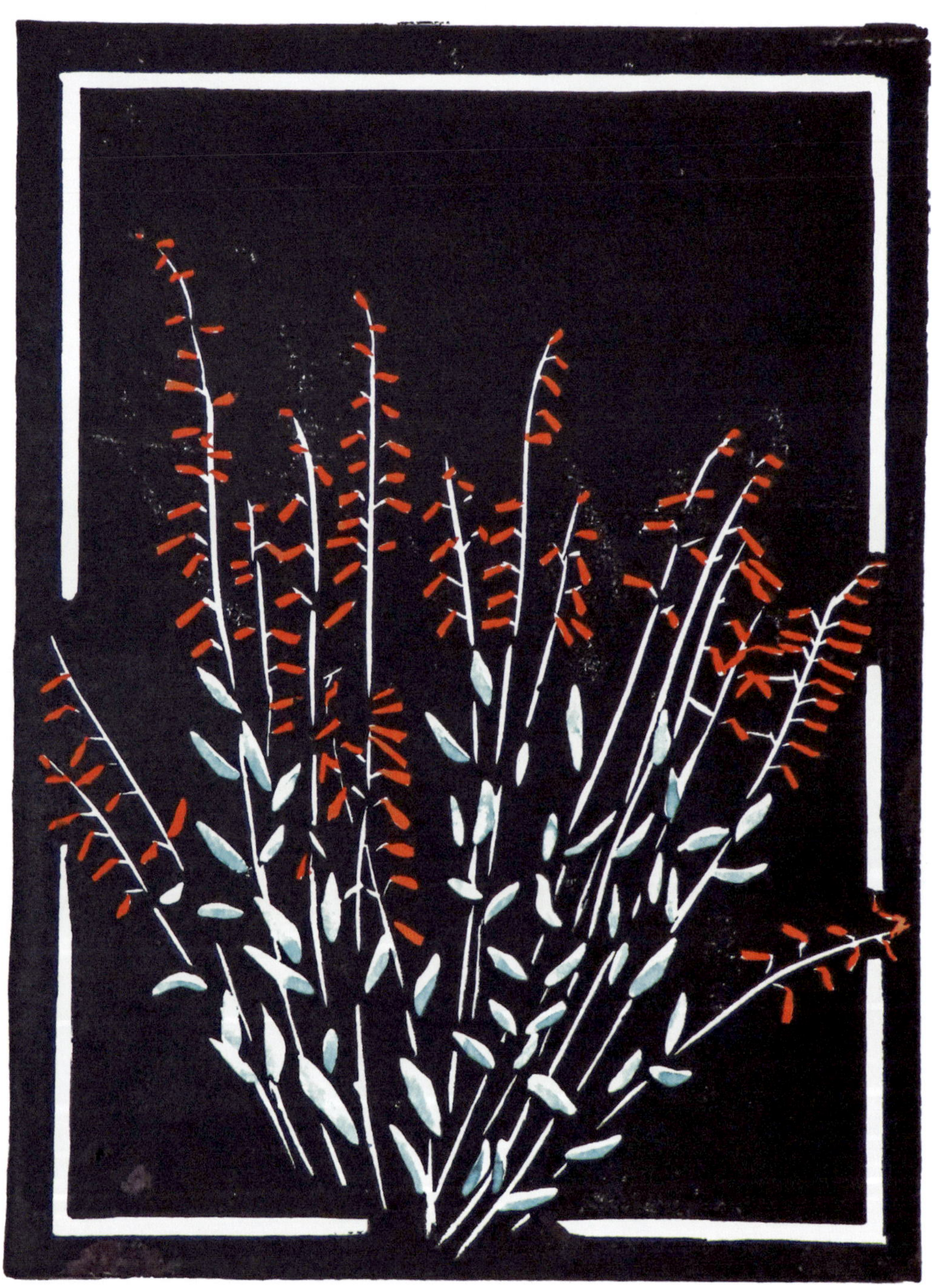

SCARLET BUGLER PENSTEMON

Scarlet bugler penstemon (*Penstemon centranthifolius*, SCROPHULARIACEAE)

The perennial scarlet bugler can grow as tall as 3 feet and has thick, heart-shaped leaves clasping several waxy stems. The tubular scarlet flowers are about an inch long, facing outward, with dozens of blooms atop the stems. It is a very common and dramatic spring wildflower of California woodland sites and other dry or disturbed areas below 6,000 feet. The simple elegance of the long stems prompted this block print, in which I did not elaborate any complex shapes or attempt to describe the surrounding landscape; instead, my intention was to imitate old woodblock herbals, in which plants were often stylized.

Woodland blue flax (*Linum lewisii*, LINACEAE)

Also known as prairie flax and Lewis's flax, this perennial grows widely in the West, although not west of the Cascades in Washington. Narrow, ¾-inch-long leaves grow on upright stems and disappear as the plant matures. Each stem produces several flowers, with petals about 1 to 1½ inches across, which last only a day before dropping. The color is a pale blue-violet, dramatic when seen en masse, which is often how they grow. Flowering time is late spring to early summer. The flower was named after Meriwether Lewis, who collected hundreds of plants on the 1804–6 Corps of Discovery expedition; unfortunately, on the outward journey, he lost all of the collection in the Missouri River near the Great Falls. On the return journey he was able to replace many of the plants, though it was a much smaller assemblage.

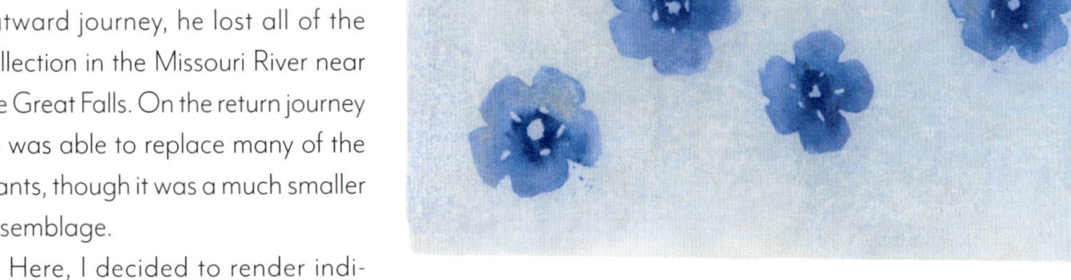

Here, I decided to render individual flowers in a *moku hanga*–style print because of the ethereal quality of the hue. I was also hoping to imitate the playful style of many contemporary Japanese prints. (For another example of *moku hanga*, see California Poppy in the Coasts & Shorelines chapter.)

Wetlands & Riparian Habitats

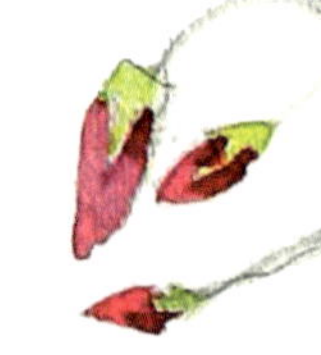

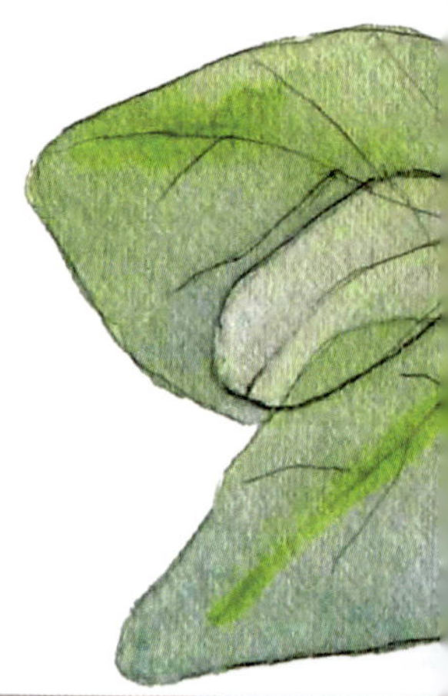

There are several different types of wetland ecosystems in the West. Marine wetlands include tidal marshes and estuaries. The other categories are freshwater systems: these include lakes, rivers, freshwater bogs, fens, marshes, vernal pools, and seasonally moist meadows. Wetlands are among the most productive ecosystems in the world because of their ability to absorb solar energy and store it as chemical energy. Year-round wetlands include bogs and fens. Bogs have very little water flow and acidic conditions with few nutrients. Here you'll find sphagnum mosses and Labrador tea, bog rosemary, and western bog laurel. Fens are a bit different in that water is continually flowing through them, and their makeup can be acid, neutral, or base. A remarkable example of a fen is the Darlingtonia State Natural Site (Darlingtonia Wayside) on the central Oregon coast, just north of Florence; this extensive fen system supports the insectivorous pitcher plant known as the cobra lily, or *Darlingtonia californica*. Also found in fens are California lady's slipper, California bog asphodel, and Vollmer's tiger lily.

Riparian habitats include the shallow edges of freshwater lakes and ponds as well as streams. These wetlands support beautiful species such as corydalis, bog orchid, saxifrages, currants, buttercups, and Lewis's monkeyflower. Even in the driest ecoregions, such as the shrub-steppe deserts of the Great Basin, where there is moisture only part of the year, colorful flowering plants can find suitable places to live.

Vernal pools are one of the more interesting wetland habitats. They exist seasonally, only after fall and winter rains on the West Coast. The pools fill with shallow water beginning as early as fall and last until late spring, but mostly become dry in summer and early fall. In drought years, they may never fill at all. Vernal pools are most often found in areas with grassy plains—in the West, only in California and southern Oregon. A habitat for many rare species, this unusual ecosystem is unfortunately threatened, with more than 90 percent of California's vernal pools now lost. In the state's Central Valley, vernal pools exist on soils that are hardpan or clay. There, the seeds of annual flowers germinate in late fall or winter, and successive blooms appear in spring as the water begins to evaporate, a phenomenon described in *Introduction to California Spring Wildflowers* as "colorful concentric bathtub rings." Typical successions are yellow goldfields, then yellow-and-white tidy tips and white meadowfoam, and finally blue downingias once the water has disappeared. Because the water does not last through the summer, these areas have resisted being over-taken by invasive species.

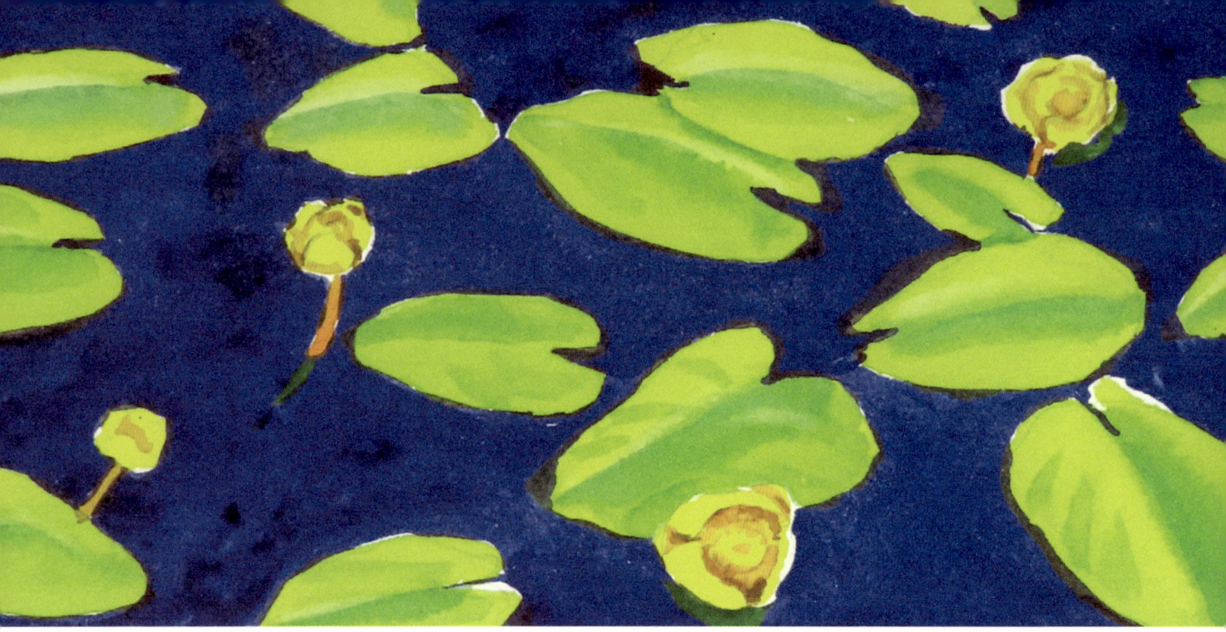

Yellow pond lily (*Nuphar lutea*, NYMPHAEACEAE)

The perennial yellow pond lily, also known as cow lily and spatterdock, is a common resident of lakes, ponds, and sluggish streams throughout the West, from Washington south as far as San Luis Obispo, California. It blooms from spring to midsummer, depending on location. The heart-shaped leaves are 4 to 18 inches long and have deeply indented bases. The flowers are cup-shaped and 2 to 3 inches wide, with two layers of large, petallike sepals—ten to twenty on each plant—enclosing a circular array of stamens. The outer sepals are mostly green, the inner ones, yellow.

I paid homage to Monet with this panoramically formatted watercolor. Monet might not have chosen such a dark color for his water, but I appreciated how the dark hue, which I created with indanthrone blue and carbazole violet, set off its complement of bright yellowy-green lily leaves.

Cobra lily (*Darlingtonia californica*, SARRACENIACEAE)

The perennial cobra lily, also known as the California pitcher plant, is the sole member of the genus *Darlingtonia* in its larger family of Sarraceniaceae. It grows in peat bogs and seeps with cold running water in Northern California and Oregon, and even as far north as Washington. Its head looks like a cobra, ready to strike, complete with "fangs" protruding from either side. The colors range from yellow to cooler green, with reddish spots. It grows 2 feet tall and flowers from April to July, before the pitchers completely develop. The flowers hang down, with five yellow-green sepals, 1 to 2½ inches long, surrounding five dark petals.

Insects are attracted to the nectar in the pitcher openings, as well as to the tonguelike protuberances. Despite this deceptive plant's intimidating appearance, insects have not learned to steer clear; the unfortunate creatures, soon to become lunch, enter the pitcher, where downward-facing hairs make it impossible for them to escape. In a short time, they fall to the bottom of the pitcher, where microbes digest them and provide nutrients to the hungry plant.

COBRA LILY PITCHERS, DARLINGTONIA STATE NATURAL SITE, WASHINGTON

One August, late in the month, I visited the Darlingtonia State Natural Site (Darlingtonia Wayside) just off Highway 101 north of Florence, Oregon. I didn't know what to expect, but my curiosity had been piqued by my botany teacher, Larry DeBuhr, who lectures about the oddball plants of California and Oregon—and then there was the description in an Oregon coast hiking guide that referred to the site as a "Little Bog of Horrors." The boardwalk that crosses the peat bog is steps away from the parking lot, and the site itself is just a minute away from the highway.

The vision that awaited me on the boardwalk was truly astounding, and yes, I was reminded of the musical *Little Shop of Horrors* and the frightening and voracious plant Audrey—only here there were hundreds of Audreys! I took a lot of photos and then drew a couple of specimens from my photos when I got back to the house I was staying in, using quick sketching methods with pen and water-color. Back home, I found a photo of the plant in bloom and decided to try working from that in gouache and pen. Finally, I wanted to remember what the sight of hundreds of cobra lilies had felt like—impossible, but I decided to try, using a set of watercolor pencils. I knew I didn't want to do an elaborate pen drawing or watercolor; instead, I hoped to capture the weird sight of dozens of these plants cheek by jowl in the bog and the immediate sensation of intense surprise.

After my trip, I visited the Biology Greenhouse at the University of Washington, home to thousands of species of plants from around the world, including a large array of carnivorous plants. I didn't see the cobra lily, but there were a number of other pitcher-type plants. Graduate students tend the plants, and some of them have mischievously placed small plastic animals in terrariums and in other somewhat inconspicuous places. I spotted a tiny plastic human skeleton emerging from a large pitcher plant.

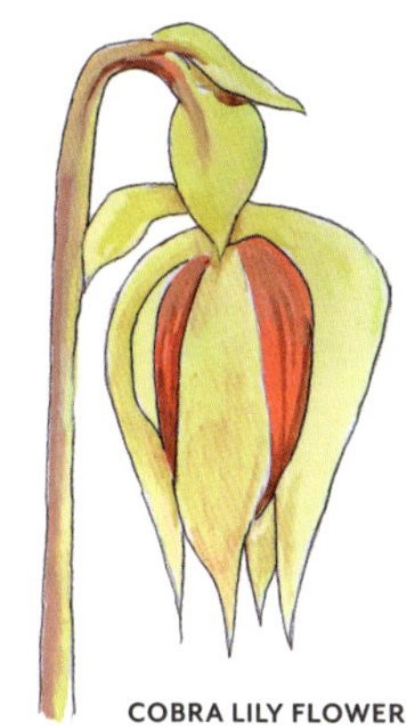

COBRA LILY FLOWER

COBRA LILY PITCHERS

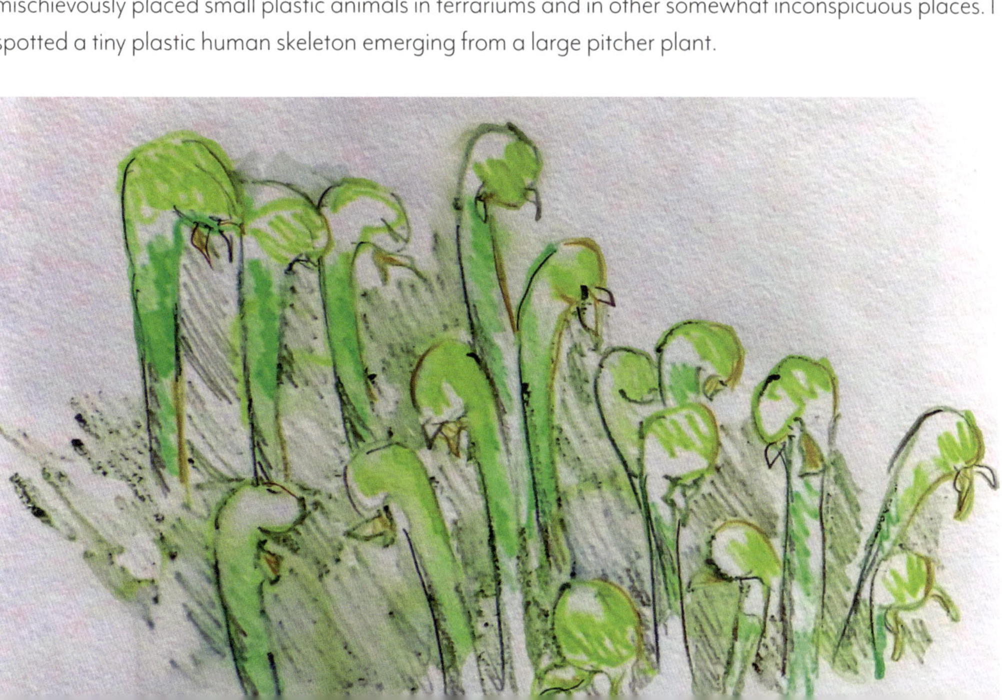

Skunk cabbage (*Lysichiton americanus*, ARACEAE)

Skunk cabbage, also known as swamp lantern, is a perennial that blooms in early spring. You can find it in wetlands, bogs, vernal pools, and, most often, tree-shaded swamps from coastal to higher elevations—from Washington in the north to as far south as the Santa Cruz Mountains in California. It has a large, petallike yellow bract known as a spathe that cups a stout spike of yellow-green flowers, called the spadix. The bright green leaves are 1 to 2 feet long and almost a foot wide. An entire bog of skunk cabbage is a beautiful sight, but many people do not care for the unpleasant musky fragrance (thus its common name); yet the scent is extremely attractive to pollinators.

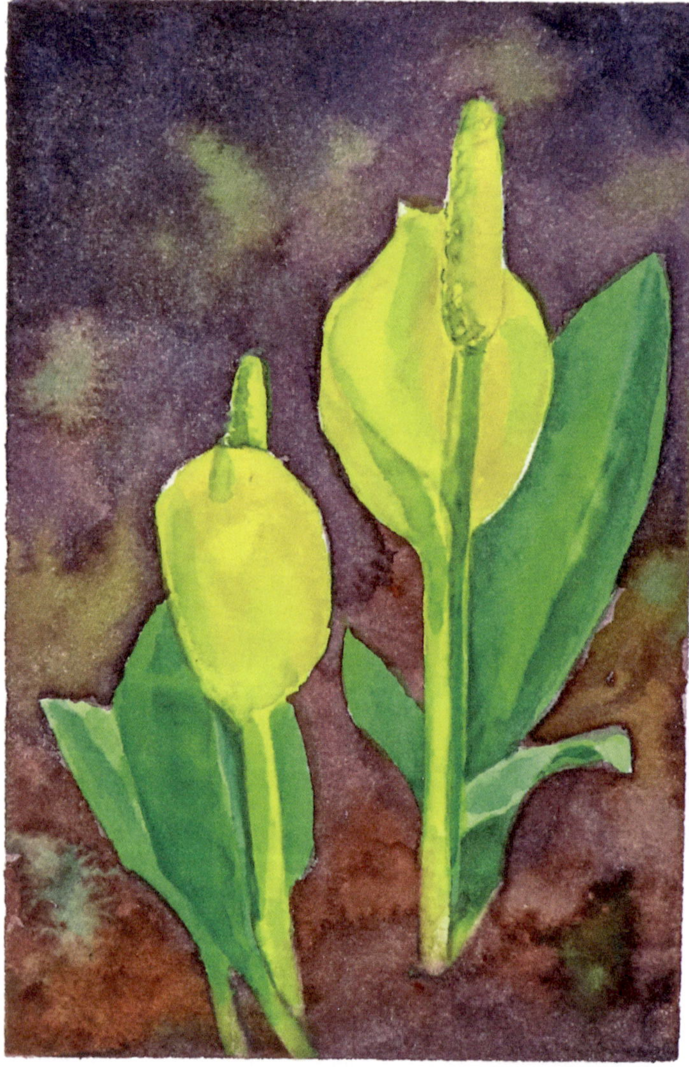

Skunk cabbage bogs are as eerie as church yards, frogs croak there, humans hurry past.

—Emily Carr,
from *Wild Flowers*

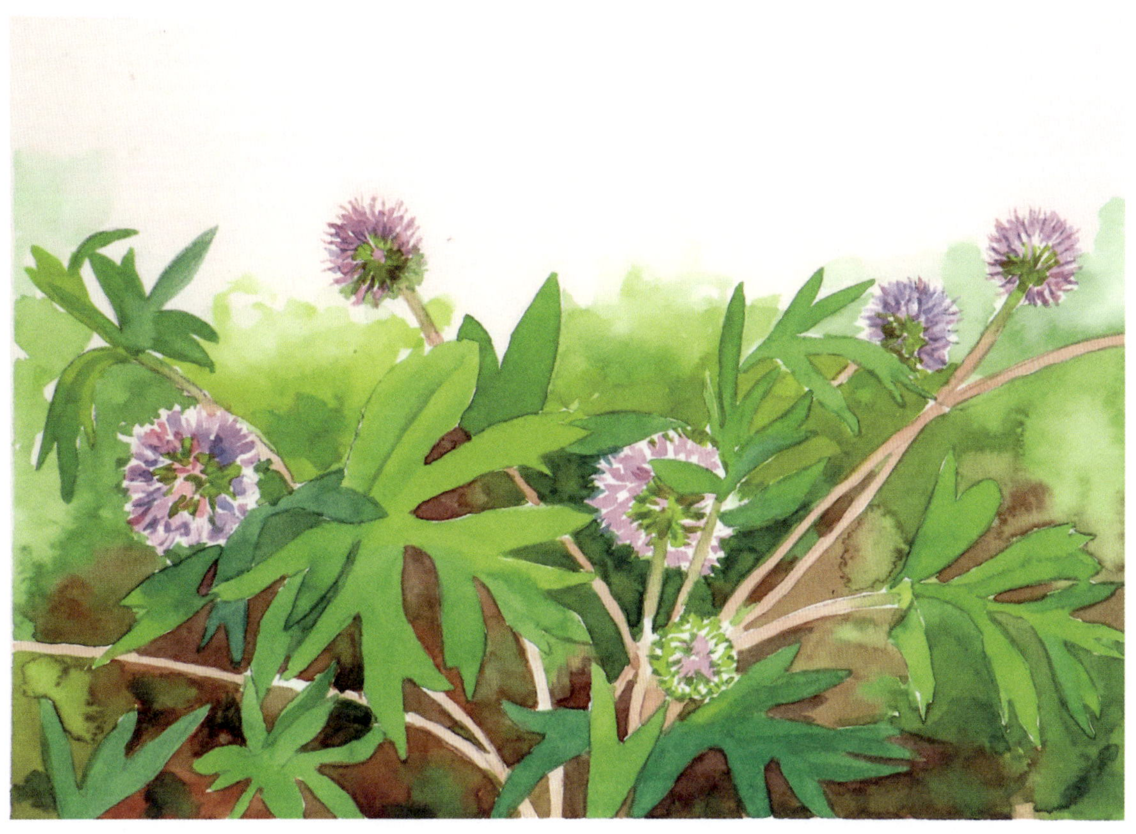

Ballhead waterleaf (*Hydrophyllum capitatum* var. *thompsonii*, HYDROPHYLLACEAE)

On an April hike in Wenatchee's Sage Hills, I spotted this low-growing perennial in a shallow ravine, where it and other water-loving plants had found a refuge from the drying sun. Somehow it looked out of place, with its luxurious bright green leaves, pinnate and irregular, and many large, ball-shaped umbels of the palest and most delicate violet-blue hue. The plant had arranged itself almost like a group of dancers, and I thought it would be very true to its essence to paint it as if it were a tableau of graceful ballerinas.

The *thompsonii* variety grows only in central Washington and the Columbia River Gorge—on slopes and in woodlands and sagebrush steppe, in areas with adequate moisture—but there are other species of *Hydrophyllum* more widespread in the West, from the coast ranges to the Cascades, and from central Oregon to California. *Thompsonii* is rather more elegant, with a long, mostly erect stem up to 16 inches. The leaves are 2 to 5 inches long, with 1-to-6-inch petioles, divided pinnately, and five to seven rounded leaflets.

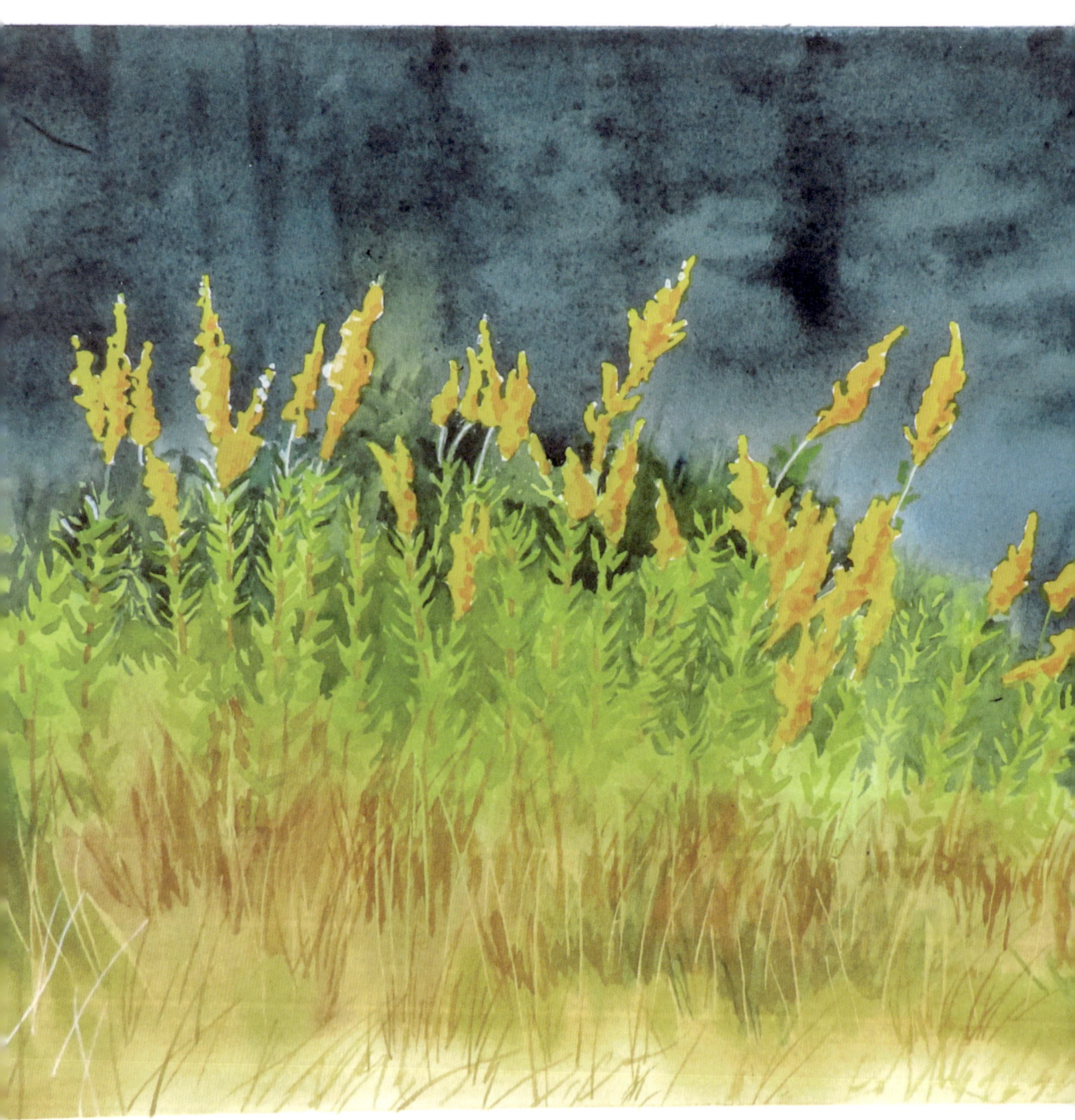

Goldenrod (*Solidago canadensis*, ASTERACEAE)

Goldenrod is also known as Canada goldenrod and meadow goldenrod. Found throughout North America, it is a very common, hard-to-miss perennial plant growing from 2 to 5 feet high. On the West Coast, it blooms from late summer into autumn in coastal areas, meadows, and forests on the west and east sides of the Cascades and into California. The leaves are lance-shaped and 2 to 5 inches in length. The golden inflorescence is long, consisting of multiple flower heads in cups with sticky bracts. Up close, you'll find ten to thirteen short ray flowers around a few central disk flowers. Goldenrod is the most important native plant for pollinators, including bees and butterflies—even the spent stalks are used by bees as nesting cavities, and the seeds are eaten by birds.

Asters commonly grow alongside goldenrod, and botanist Robin Wall Kimmerer was struck by the beauty of their complementary colors—dazzling gold against pale violet. As recounted in her book *Braiding Sweetgrass*, she set out to discover why it was so common for these late-summer species to grow together. She planted plots of asters and goldenrods alone, and then a combined plot. Bees were much more attracted to the combined plots. Even though bees have a much larger visual spectrum than our human eyes, they are just as sensitive to the heightened intensity of color when two complements appear beside each other, leading Kimmerer to conclude that bees are as drawn to beauty as we are.

From my journal:

> Before driving down to the Oregon coast in late August, I walked around my small backyard garden and looked at all the blooming plants. The dahlias and cinquefoil were in their fullest glory, and the asters were beginning early—a few days before, I'd cut bouquets of dahlias to bring into the house. I emptied the vases and threw the dahlias into the compost bin and took a photo of the backyard flowers. It surprised me how wrenching it was to leave. I thought how much more peaceful it would be if I just stayed home. I was reminded of Elizabeth Bishop's poem "Questions of Travel," specifically these lines:
>
>> Is it lack of imagination that makes us come
>> to imagined places, not just stay at home?
>> Or could Pascal have been not entirely right
>> about just sitting quietly in one's room?
>
> My friend Paul and I drove up to the house we would be staying in on the central Oregon coast, high above and inland a mile or so from the Pacific, on the flanks of Cascade Head. It was remote, on a gravel road that we could only take at 5 miles per hour. The caretaker had recently mowed the 80-acre property; the tawny late-summer meadows sloped downhill, surrounded by dark Sitka spruce giants in the forest. In the middle of one of the lower fields, he'd left three or four long swaths of goldenrod. The next morning, when we drove downhill past them on the way to

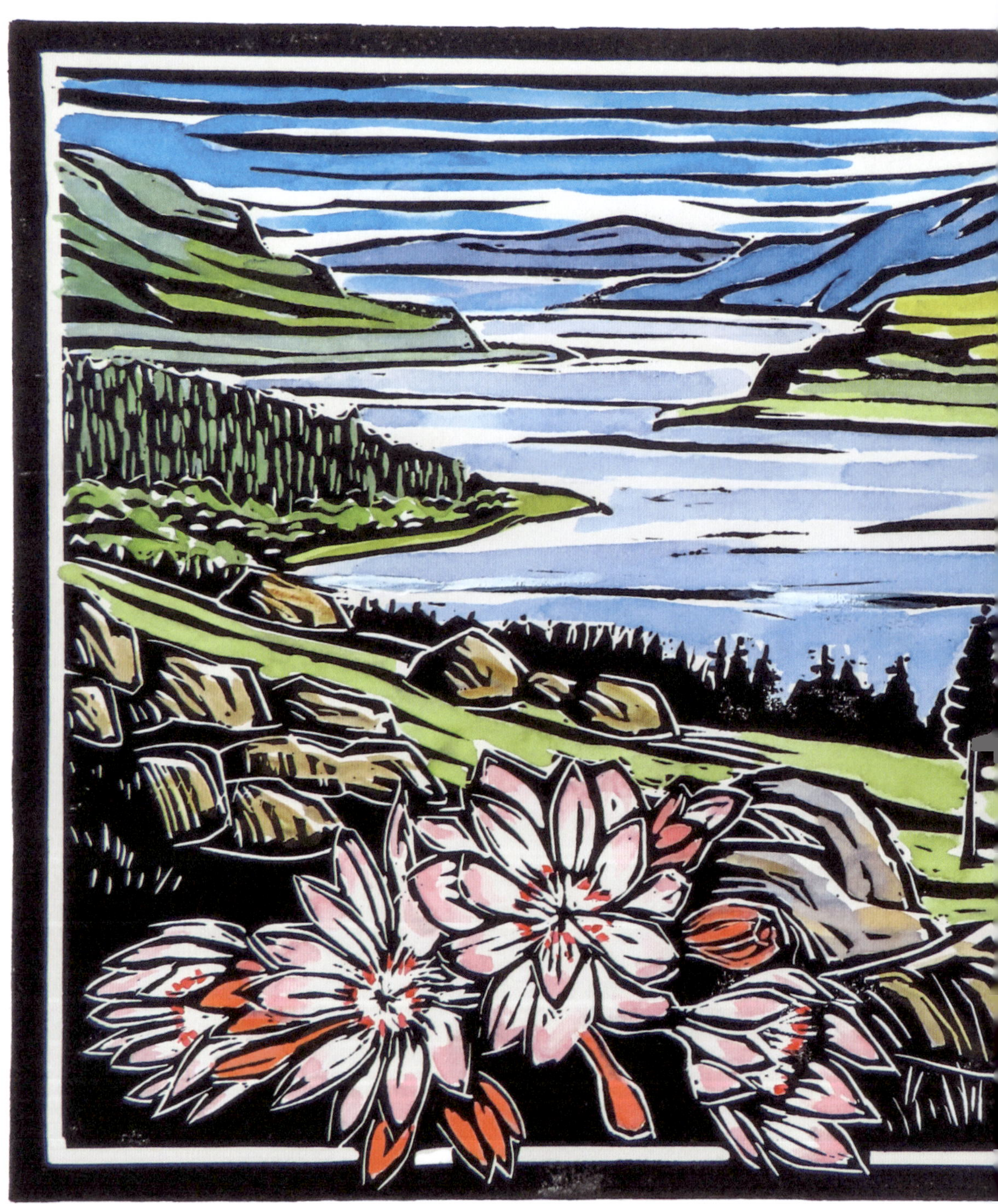

 Wildflowers of the West

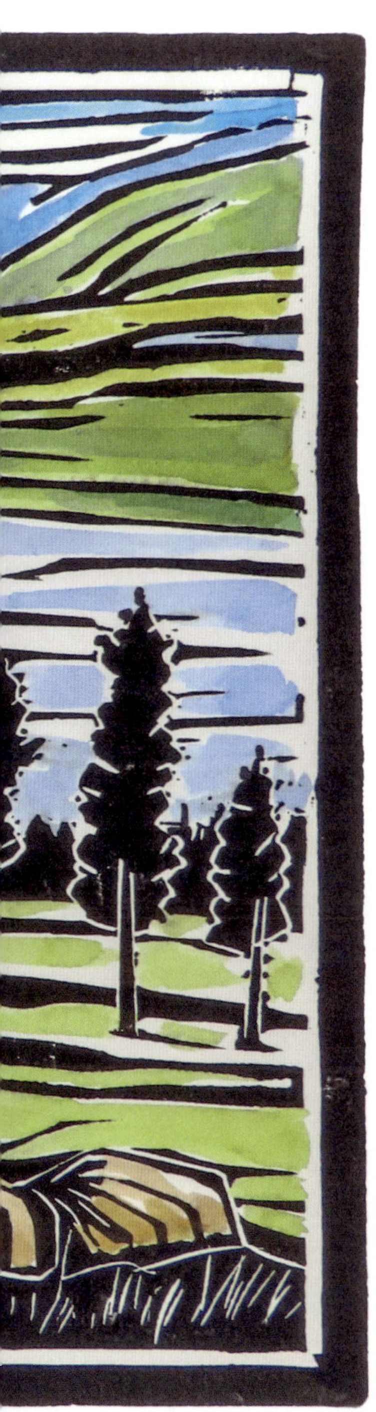

Bitterroot (*Lewisia rediviva*, PORTULACACEAE)

The perennial bitterroot grows in the shrub-steppe east of the Cascades, as well as in alpine and subalpine environments. It is found throughout the West, from Washington to as far east as Colorado and Wyoming, and south into California and Arizona, though not in New Mexico. The plant emerges in later spring as a rosette of small, reddish leaves that are fleshy and pencil-shaped, from 1 to 3 inches long. The petals are up to 1 inch long, with forty to fifty stamens and six to eight stigmas. These ground-hugging blooms are visited by many different pollinators. After flowering, the plants shrivel, and you'd never know they'd been there. The flowers are stunning—deep rose, pink, or white with a satiny sheen.

The bitterroot was prized by Northwest tribes, who collected the roots in spring and boiled them before eating. The genus is named for Meriwether Lewis, co-leader of the Corps of Discovery expedition; the species name, *rediviva*—Latin for "restored to life"—refers to the dried root's ability to revive itself, as if from the dead. Three months after Lewis collected them, the roots made it safely to the East Coast, and to Thomas Jefferson, who shipped them to Bernard McMahon in Philadelphia. McMahon had no idea how to grow an alpine plant, so the root never bloomed, though it did sprout leaves. The bitterroot is the state flower of Montana, where there is a mountain range named for them, part of the Rockies system, in the westernmost part of the state.

Even though wildflower guides say that bitterroot is common, in my decades of hiking I had never been lucky enough to be in the right place at the right time—until I made a point of visiting Catherine Creek on the Washington side of the Columbia River Gorge. The shrub-steppe landscape there is quite moist in winter and spring, and the plants were growing on basalt outcrops. The combination of the flowers and the majestic, wide-open setting made for one of the most beautiful prospects I've ever seen. I decided to pay homage to it with a block print, where I balanced the foreground flowers in their rocky home against the Columbia River panorama.

Columbia River Gorge

The Columbia River Gorge is a spectacular river canyon between Washington and Oregon. Eighty miles long and up to 4,000 feet deep, it meanders past cliffs, spires, and ridges set against the nearby peaks of the Pacific Northwest's Cascade Range. In early May one recent year, I resolved to make a trip to the Gorge in search of wildflowers. I had been there before, so I knew I'd see bright swaths of arrowleaf balsamroot blazing on the hillsides. But there were smaller gems that I was in search of: bitterroot, larkspur, lupine, Douglas' brodiaea, and camas.

About one-third of the total species of wildflowers in Oregon occur in the Columbia River Gorge, a relatively narrow geographical area in such a large state. This is due to the remarkable diversity of habitats, from low elevations (near sea level) to higher elevations (around 3,000 feet), and from moist temperate forests on the west to dry sagebrush steppe to the east. A mere two-hour drive east from Portland, Oregon, or Vancouver, Washington, can take you through many of these zones. Even if you don't get out of your car, you can't miss the dramatic shift from the dark western hemlock forests that close in on you on the west to the brighter, more open ponderosa pine woodlands as you near Hood River. Stopping at any of the many pullouts, state parks, and preserves that line the Gorge allows you to take a closer look at the unique niches that plants have found, the result of the range of elevations and climate types. Paleobotanists who study the movement of plants over eons have determined that many of these plants moved north or south over geological time. The Gorge species were able to find locations that satisfied their requirements as the West became alternately colder, drier, warmer, and wetter—here in the Gorge, there were (and still are) so many possible places to thrive.

The boundary layer, or ecotone, between the western and eastern parts of the Gorge is its own special world. One of the best places to experience it is at the Tom McCall Nature Preserve, acquired by the Nature Conservancy in the 1980s. Located about 12 miles east of Hood River, the 231-acre high-plateau

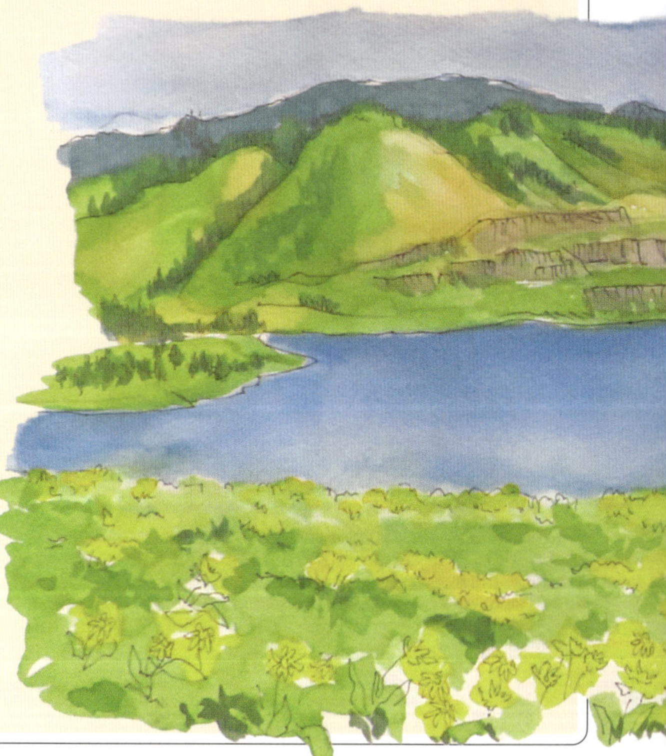

preserve contains a multitude of species in the Oregon white oak/ponderosa pine forest type. When I walked out to the preserve's Rowena Plateau around 8:45 a.m., there were no other people there. The sun was shining, meadowlarks were singing, and ravens soared in the Gorge updrafts. As I skirted a pond, several Canada geese honked and flew off. I could hear a single frog croaking. The surface of the water was placid, and pond lilies were beginning to bloom. Spring wildflowers are most abundant here in April and May.

I found the lupine not quite in full bloom, though the balsamroot was glorious. Yet later that day, over on Catherine Creek on the Washington side, about a thirty-minute drive east, the lupine was lushly flowering, making me feel as if I were time traveling.

In this remarkable landscape, where you're surrounded by the results of volcanism and erosion and the Missoula Floods (a series of massive glacial outburst floods that carved out the Gorge), you cannot escape the sense of ancient time.

Driving west toward Portland, homeward bound, it was raining heavily. Driving on the interstate behind giant semis that created their own mini-storms, I felt as if my sunny, flowery Gorge experience, like all my past adventures, was being washed away, and I was almost unwillingly being propelled into a new world. I regretted leaving the Gorge's thriving wildflowers and mighty river views, but I knew that drawing and painting what I had seen would keep those days alive in my mind.

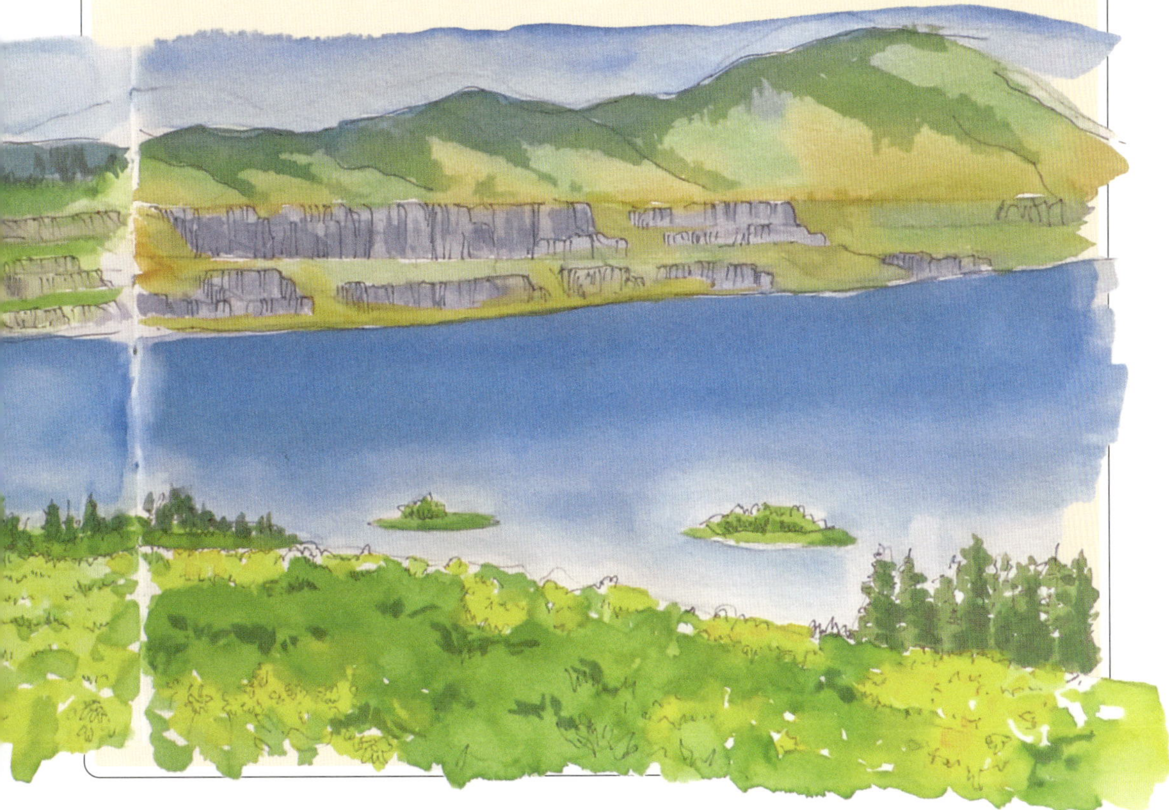

Camas (*Camassia quamash*, LILIACEAE)

Every time I've encountered the camas, I've been struck by its extreme beauty. A single flower is elegant and noticeable, but they don't just grow singly; instead, they spread, and you'll encounter entire meadows of them. An early description of camas flowers came from Meriwether Lewis, of the 1804–6 Corps of Discovery expedition. On their trip home from the Pacific, he and his party had to wait to cross the Bitterroot Mountains because the snow was still too deep. At Weippe Prairie (in what is today Idaho) on June 12, 1806, Lewis noted in his journal that the camas were in bloom: ". . . at a short distance it resembles lakes of fine clear water, so complete is this deseption [*sic*] that on first sight I could have swoarn [*sic*] it was water," he wrote. More than twenty years later, botanist and plant explorer David Douglas observed the same flower and noted its use as a staple by Indigenous peoples in both coastal and plateau cultures.

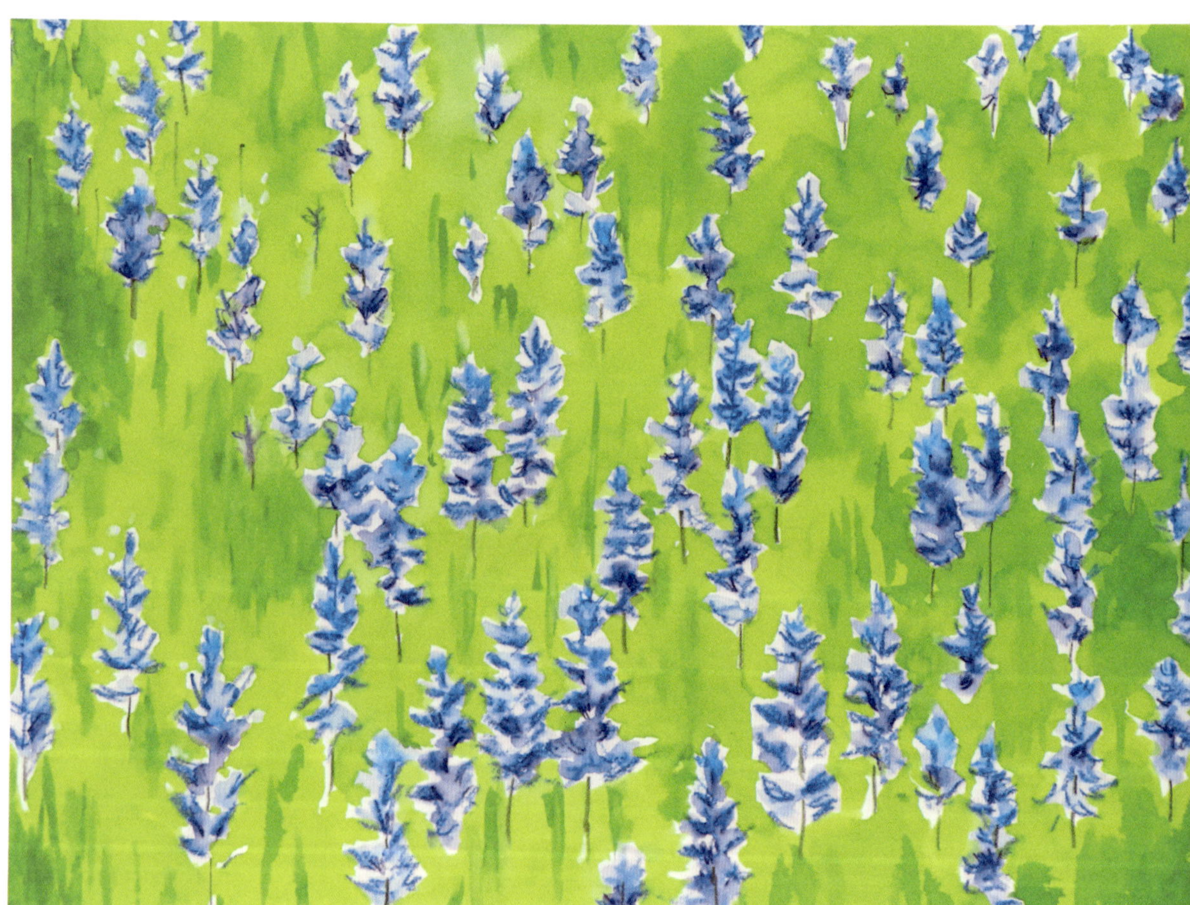

The roots are dug up after the plant has bloomed and is about to go to seed. The tubers are then roasted and dried for use in the winter.

Camas grow from 6 to 26 inches tall and have long, slender leaves. They bloom in mid-spring, sending up spikes of blue to violet, and sometimes white, flowers. The plant is common in the Northwest in Washington, Oregon, Idaho, and Montana, where it thrives in vernal pools and wet meadows that dry up by midsummer. You can also find the camas in California, from Marin and El Dorado Counties northward.

Lewis's monkeyflower (*Mimulus lewisii*, SCROPHULARIACEAE)

The perennial Lewis's monkeyflower is common in most of the West along stream banks in forests and in alpine and subalpine settings, blooming all summer. The name "monkeyflower" comes from the mouthlike shape of the blooms: some thought the flower resembled a smiling monkey. These pink to magenta flowers grow in clusters on upright stems and are 1 inch or longer, with yellow markings in the throat. The oblong leaves are 1 to 3 inches long and have pointed tips. I've seen these showy flowers on many mountain hikes, embedded in chartreuse mosses on either side of snowmelt streams— unlikely ribbons of rose in the green meadows that surround them.

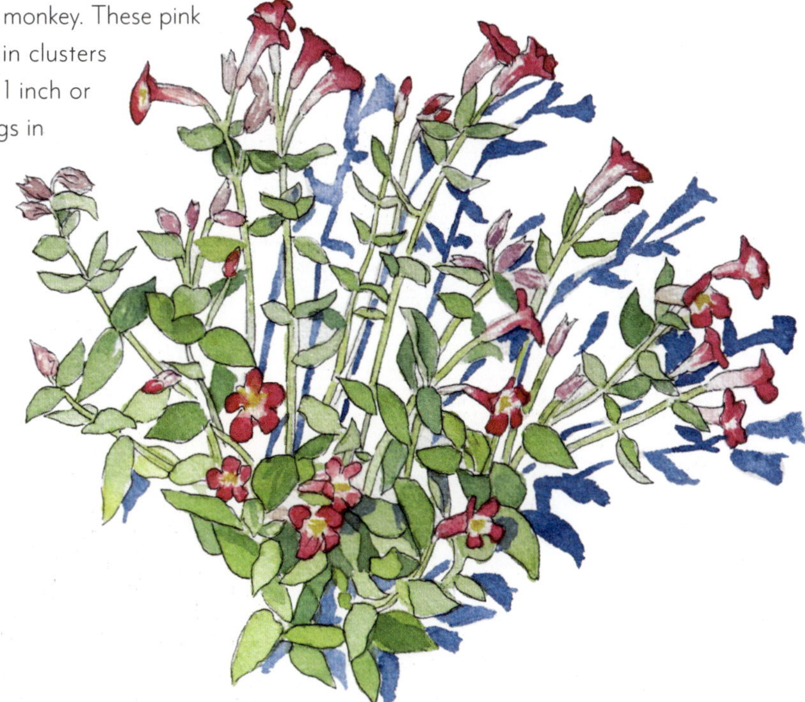

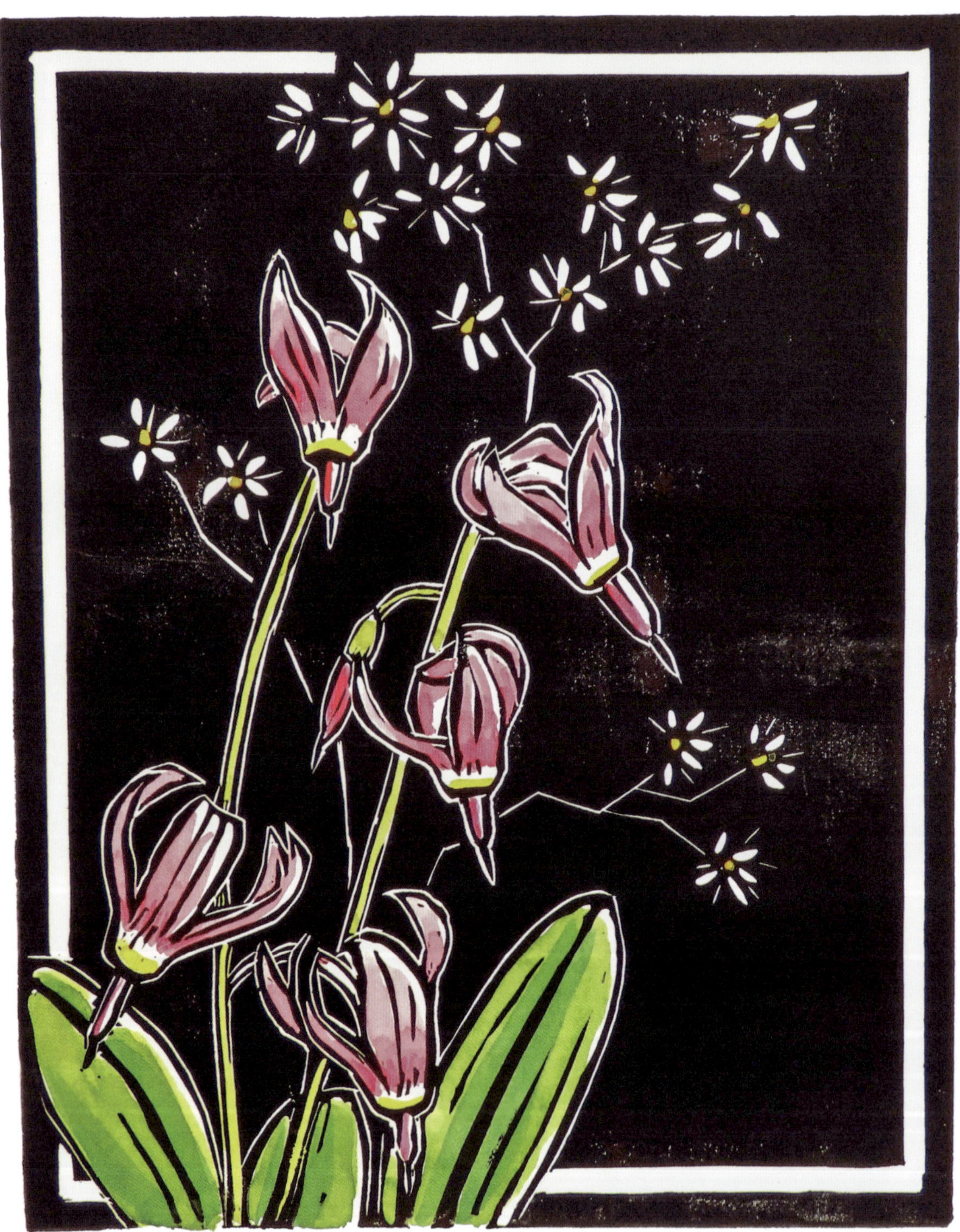

Jeffrey's shooting star (*Dodecatheon jeffreyi*, PRIMULACEAE)

Jeffrey's shooting stars thrive in very wet places that dry out in summertime, from coasts and boggy shorelines to meadows in higher elevations. I've seen them on many hikes in western Washington and on trips to the east slope of the Cascades—in Brooks Memorial State Park (near Goldendale), for one. Blooming in early springtime, with the month depending on elevation, Jeffrey's is one of the most dramatic wildflowers. The plant, a perennial, can grow from 6 to 24 inches tall and has oval or lance-shaped leaves. The flowers are pink to magenta, growing atop stems in ones, twos, threes, or more. The petals give way to cream at the base, with a red band at the bottom. Jeffrey's is found on the west and east slopes of the Cascades into Northern California; other subspecies, such as Padre's shooting star, are found in the Sierra Nevada, whereas the dark throat shooting star is widespread throughout all of the western states, even in the hanging gardens of the red rock areas of Utah and Colorado.

On a June trip to Mount Rainier National Park, I hiked to Glacier Basin, on the White River, and found an entire wet meadow dappled with these shooting stars. Back home, I created a pen and watercolor sketch of the flower. Using an approach similar to botanical illustration, I started with the watercolor painting and then outlined with pen. To keep the colors strong and vibrant, I didn't use hatching techniques, which would have shaded the darker areas but obscured the rich magenta of the petals. The shooting star is such a favorite of mine that it inspired me to try it in yet another medium, the block print also pictured here. To highlight the power of its graceful shape, I added only the small saxifrage flowers that surrounded it, rather than placing it in a larger landscape.

Coasts & Shorelines

Coastal habitats include beaches, dunes, salt marshes, and rocky shores. Because coastal weather is more consistent and cooler than that of inland areas, many coastal wildflowers, such as seaside daisies and yarrow, are found from the central California coast up through British Columbia and into Alaska. Even in summer, a thin strip of fog envelops most of the Pacific coast, resulting in up to 15 inches of additional precipitation in summer. The California coast south of Point Conception is a notable exception; there the weather changes dramatically, and fog disappears in the summer months. Remarkably, also because of the moderate temperatures, there is hardly a season in which you won't see at least a few wildflowers in bloom—at the very least, you can find them in January through October.

Salt spray influences the type of plants that can grow along shorelines, and its effects seem to be more pronounced along southern coastlines in California. Plants also have to contend with salts in the soil, as they do in desert environments. Coastal plants often develop fleshy leaves, or even replace them altogether with fleshy stems—this reduces the area of the plant's evaporating surfaces. Above the tide line on the sand, where soil has made inroads, beach peas and sand verbena thrive, along with morning glories. From Northern California to Washington, due to heavier rainfall, the forest can come right down to the bluffs and beach, so many of the flower species there overlap with forest species, like salal, Oregon grape, and ocean spray. The increased moisture reduces the saline environment, accommodating the forest species.

California poppy (*Eschscholzia californica*, PAPAVERACEAE)

California is home to countless spectacular wildflower species, but it is the California poppy that you remember once you've seen a coastal bluff, hillside, or roadside median carpeted in the gold-orange blooms. I've seen them on several visits to the California coast—at Point Lobos State Natural Reserve, Montaña de Oro State Park, and Harmony, near Morro Bay. Perhaps it's the sheer numbers of them, or the hue—a single poppy is like a sun, with its golden-orange vibrancy. The botanical name was given by the Prussian explorer Adelbert von Chamisso when he was docked in San Francisco Bay in 1816 and saw the poppies blanketing the hills around the Presidio. In 1890, when the California State Floral Society held a vote to choose a state flower, the California poppy was the hands-down favorite, beating the other two candidates, the Matilija poppy and the mariposa lily. The poppy's victory didn't make it

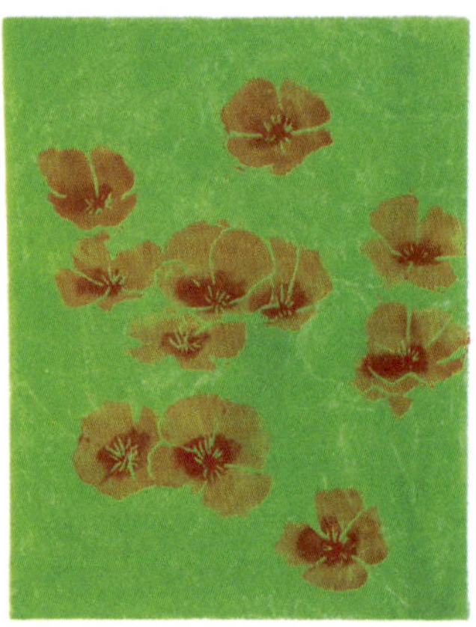

official, however. It took a decade of campaigning by Sara Plummer Lemmon (see the "Women and Early Wildflower Exploration" sidebar in the Introduction)—from 1893, when she became chairwoman of the California State Committee of the National Floral Emblem Society, to 1903, when Governor George Pardee approved the necessary legislation—for the poppy to be designated as the state's flower.

Contrary to its name, the California poppy is common throughout the western states, growing in meadows and other open, grassy areas from sea level to high elevations. It can be an annual or perennial, depending on winter temperatures, and can bloom from March to May, depending on climate and elevation. The plant ranges from 6 to 16 inches high and grows upright in a tuft from a single root. The attractive blue-green foliage is basal and delicately dissected. The flowers, 1 to 2 inches wide, are usually single on long stalks; they have four petals, in shades of orange to yellow, and many stamens. There are rare white forms as well (which Plummer Lemmon painted).

One spring I scattered some seeds in my sunny front yard and they germinated happily, thriving with little water. I was inspecting them one day and noticed a beautiful small spider, possibly a crab spider, walking inside one of the cups. It was the same gold-orange color as the bloom—an unforgettable adaptation.

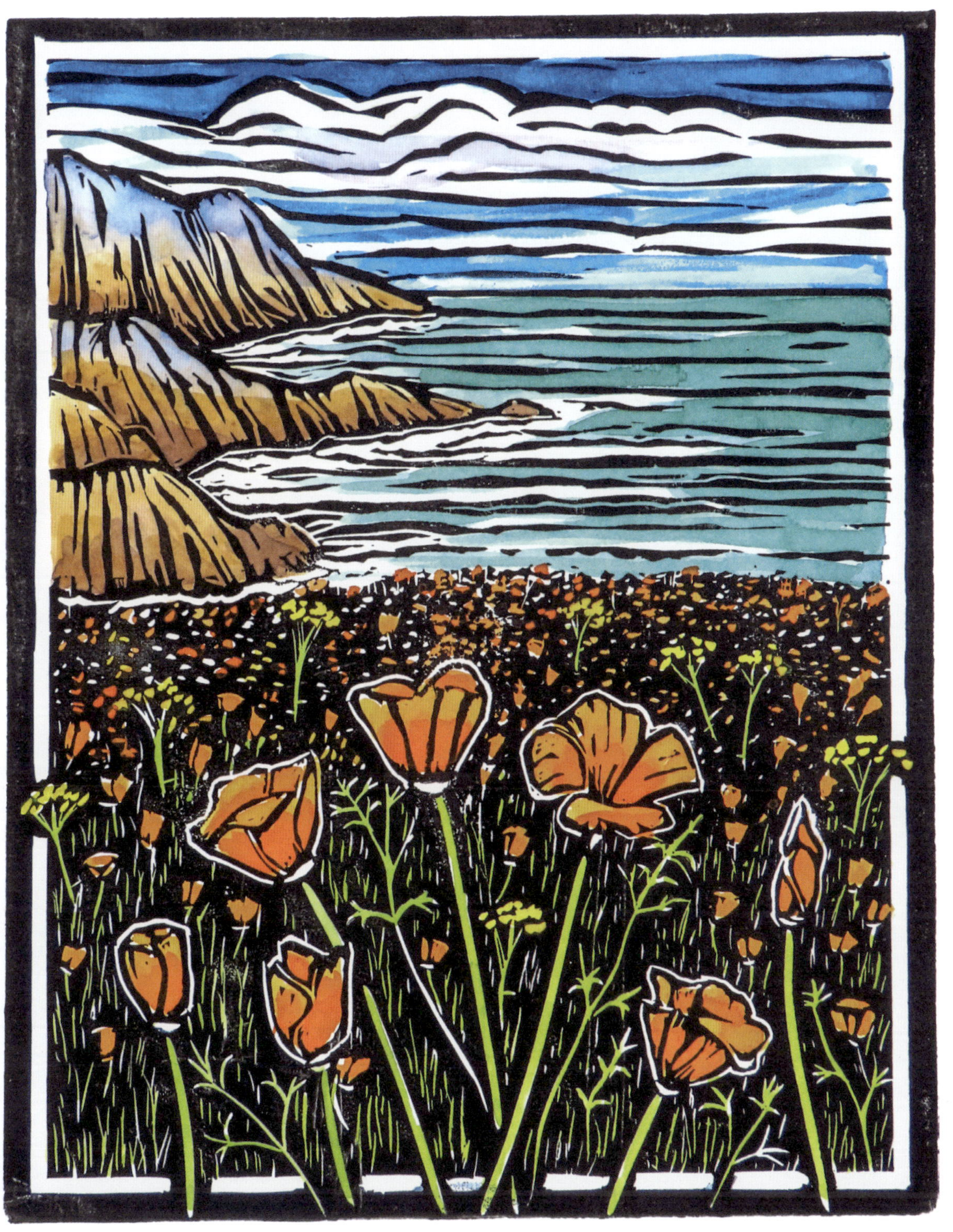

Yarrow (*Achillea millefolium*, ASTERACEAE)

The perennial yarrow, also known as achillea, is widespread throughout the West, and even across the United States. The inflorescence is composed of flat-topped disk- and ray-type white flowers—if you look closely, you'll see that this plant is related to others in the aster family. The gray-green leaves are aromatic and deeply lobed on erect stems; the plant height is 1 to 2 feet. Yarrow grows in both wet and dry places and is one of the most common flowers on the Pacific coast, blooming throughout the summer. Northwest coast tribes used it to treat colds and stomach ailments, and as an aid in childbirth.

Yarrow

Some words you just like to say: yarrow,
sparrow, arrow, marrow tomorrow, sorrow.
Even when it hurts, the tongue can taste savor.

Feather leaves of yarrow staunch blood
in wounds. Eat some, they say, not much.
Make weak tea for fever, ache, and sleep.

You may flavor beer. You may plant it for bees.
From peeled stems, you make pick-up sticks, or
a bundle to throw the I-Ching.

But mostly, in joy or sorrow, wandering
the prairie, you may crush yarrow leaves
in hand and find your pleasure.

—**Kim Stafford,** from *Earth Elements*

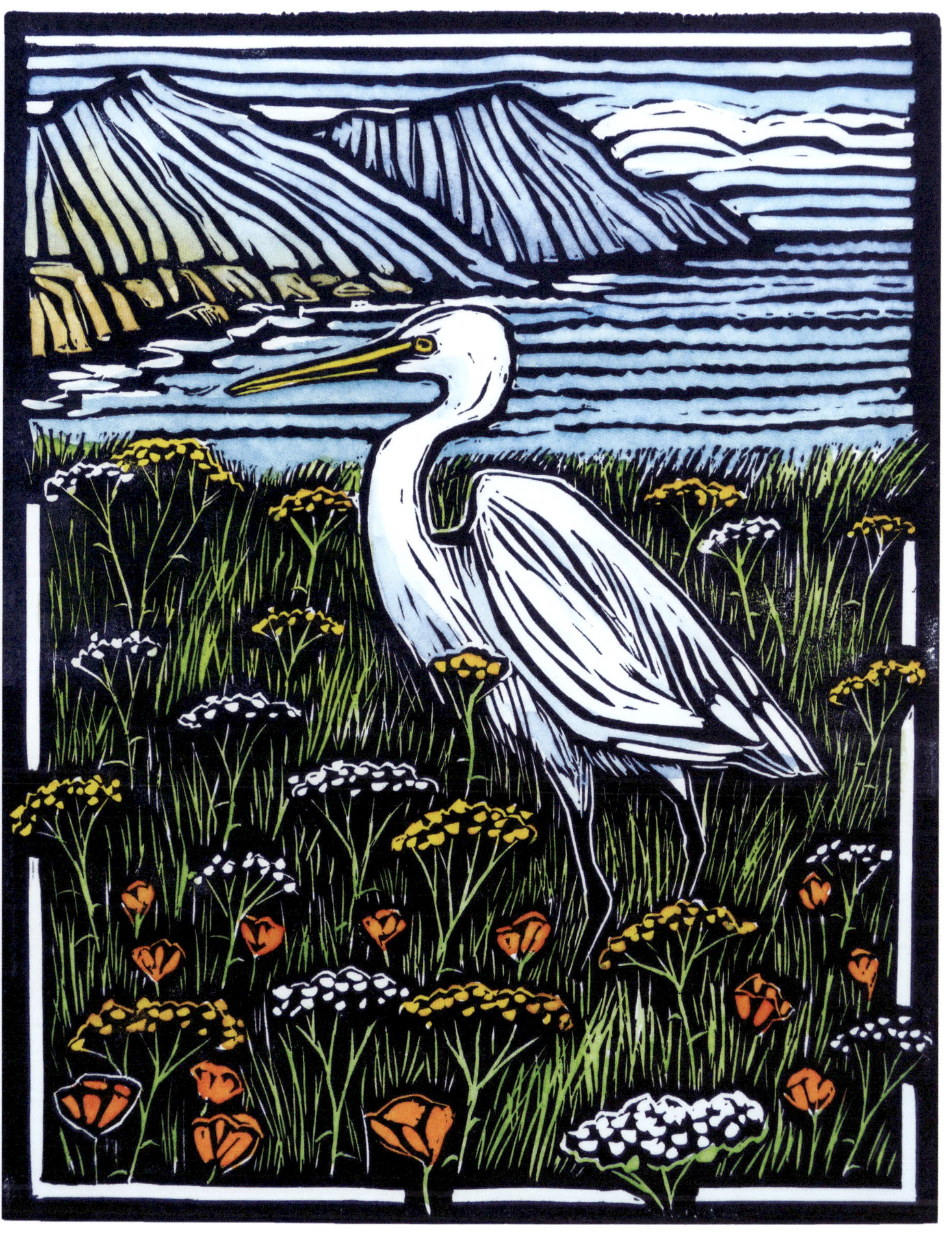

Seaside daisy (*Erigeron glaucus*, ASTERACEAE)

This compact perennial daisy grows from 2 to 12 inches high, forming dense mats with its slightly succulent oval to spoon-shaped leaves, which are up to 4 inches long, attached to a thick stem. The leaves can be shiny, hairy, or covered with a white, waxy powder. The flower heads are single, up to 1½ inches across, with petals on the ray portion. The tiny flowers in the central disk can number up to 160! The rays are pink, white, or reddish violet; the disks are bright yellow. The seaside daisy is common on the Pacific coast from southern Washington southward down the entire length of California. It is limited to seaside locations and can bloom from spring through summer.

I encountered a meadow of seaside daisies on the California coast near Harmony, north of Morro Bay, a picturesque display with the backdrop of mountains and coastal rocks (see the sidebar). The daisy's flowers and foliage are colorful and lovely enough to belong in any garden, and in fact, I found the plants for sale recently at my local Seattle nursery. I'm trying them out in my backyard native perennials garden to see what kinds of pollinators are drawn to them. My reference book says they attract bees and butterflies.

TECHNIQUE
Using Markers to Define Shapes

Painting a field of flowers can be difficult if you rely on watercolor alone. The details often call for the use of a darker medium that can provide more definition, such as colored pencils or fine-point markers. Here, I used brush-tip and fine-point markers to create darker areas around both the individual flowers and the groups of flowers.

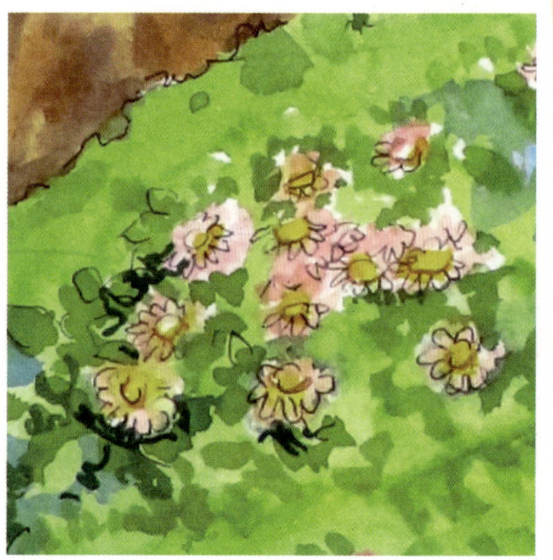

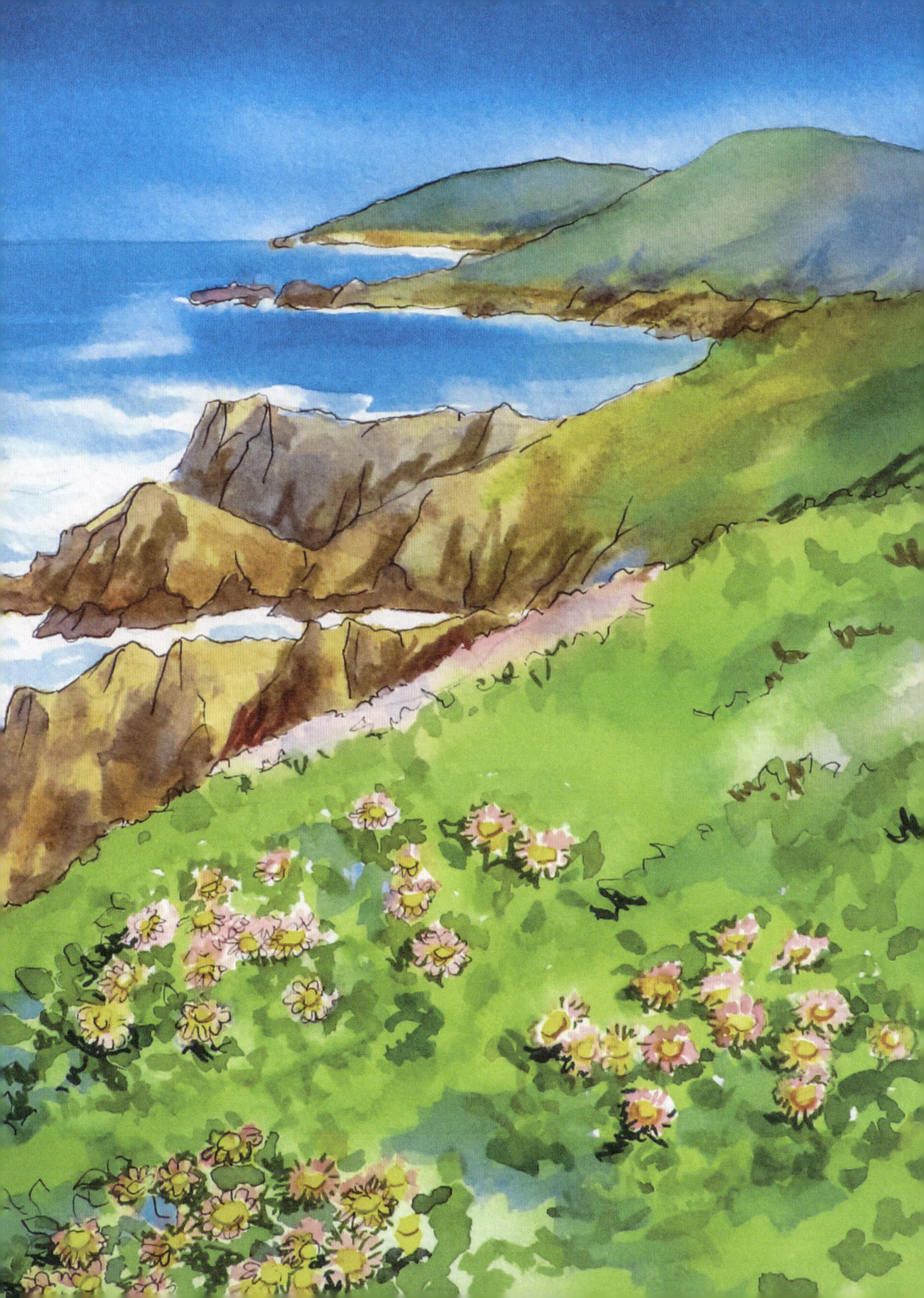

Sand verbena (*Abronia latifolia*, NYCTAGINACEAE)

I saw this verbena, a member of the four o'clock family, growing on the sand just north of Monterey, California. It is a perennial that forms mats several feet across with fleshy, shiny leaves, which I represented using a little bit of white gouache to create the gloss, after painting the base watercolor. The cheerful bright yellow flowers form tight clusters, with seventeen to thirty-four flowers per cluster. Below the five spreading petal lobes, each small flower has a narrow ½-inch tube, which holds four or five stamens and a pistil with a linear stigma atop it. The plant grows all along the West Coast as far south as Santa Barbara and can hybridize with the two pink varieties that grow in the same preferred coastal sand and scrub. Flowering time is from May to October.

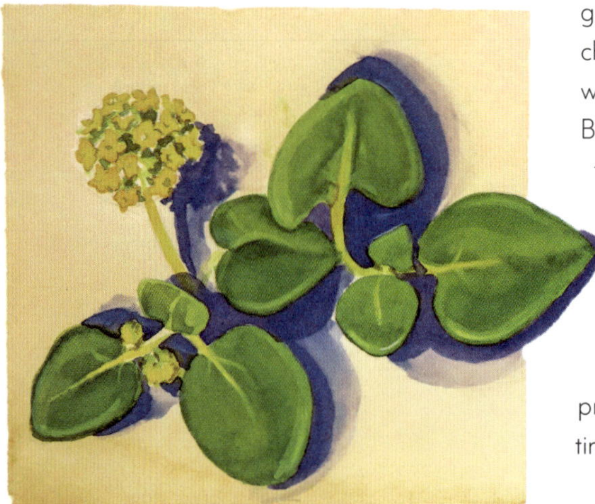

SAND VERBENA

Woolly sunflower (*Eriophyllum lanatum*, ASTERACEAE)

Also known as the woolly yellow daisy, the woolly sunflower is a common plant of many western locales, ranging from Washington and Oregon to Montana, Wyoming, Utah, and California. It sometimes grows as a perennial but more often as an annual. I saw this one at Point Lobos State Natural Reserve, near Monterey, California, with a white-crowned sparrow perched on one of the stems, presiding over the stunning view. I love to create block prints where a bird is situated in an unforgettable landscape appropriate to the bird.

The woolly sunflower is shrubby, reaching up to 1 foot high. Single flower heads sit atop long stems, with eight to thirteen yellow ray flowers and many yellow disk flowers. The individual flowers are small, up to an inch in diameter, and the yellow flowers can be two-toned, with yellow on the ends and orange toward the disks. The plant is found mostly on dry lands with sandy or rocky soils and frequently along coastal bluffs. The white woolly hairs on the plant help it survive the drying effects of the sun in places as diverse as the coast, the foothills, and even above timberline, although it is not found in the desert. Bloom times are from May to August.

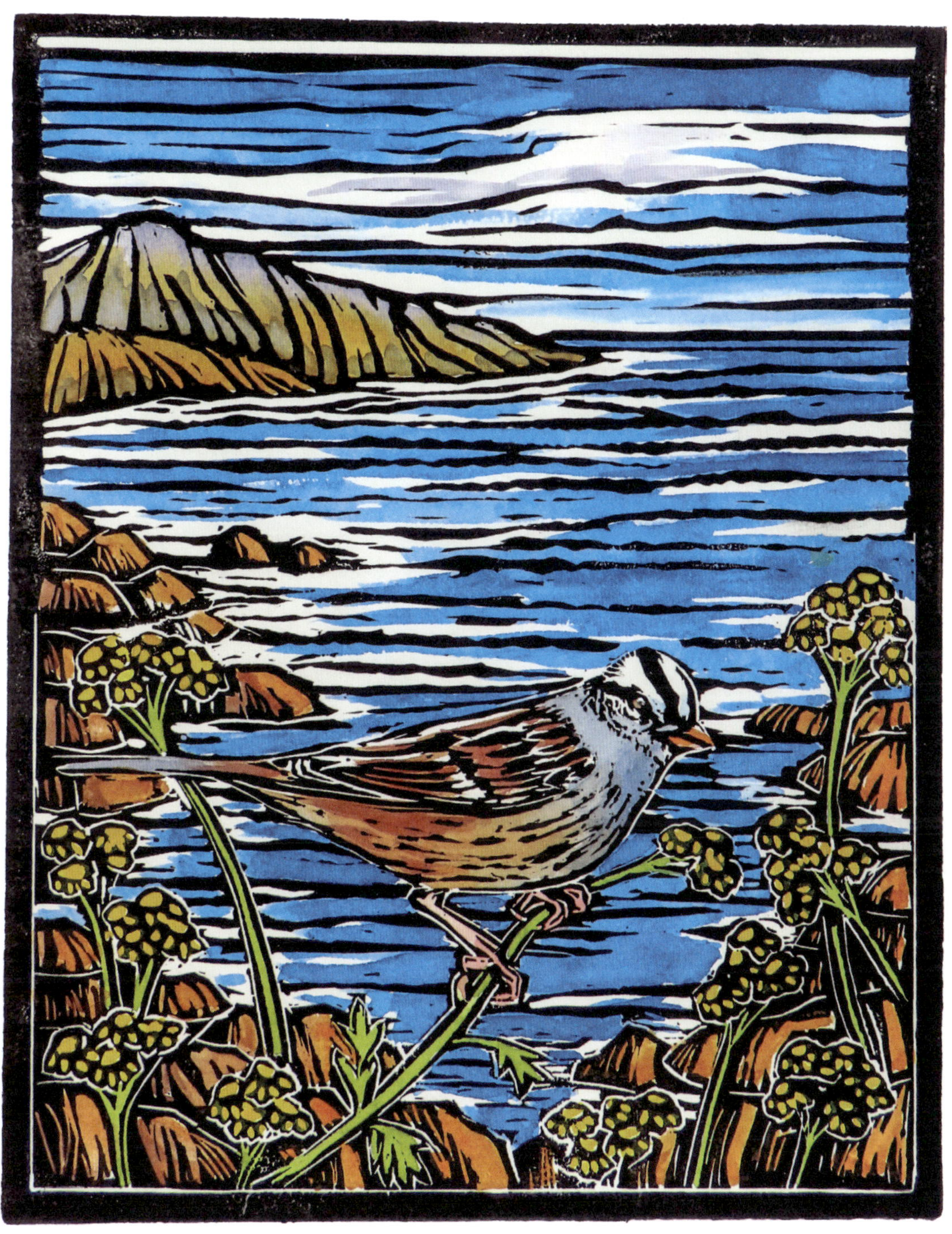

WOOLLY SUNFLOWER AND WHITE-CROWNED SPARROW, POINT LOBOS STATE NATURAL RESERVE

Beach evening primrose

(Camissonia cheiranthifolia,
ONAGRACEAE)

The beach evening primrose is a common flower on sandy beaches and coastal dunes. This perennial blooms from spring through summer from Coos Bay, Oregon, all the way down the California coast. South of Point Conception, it becomes a larger, woodier plant with larger flowers. The plant height is less than 2 feet, with occasional

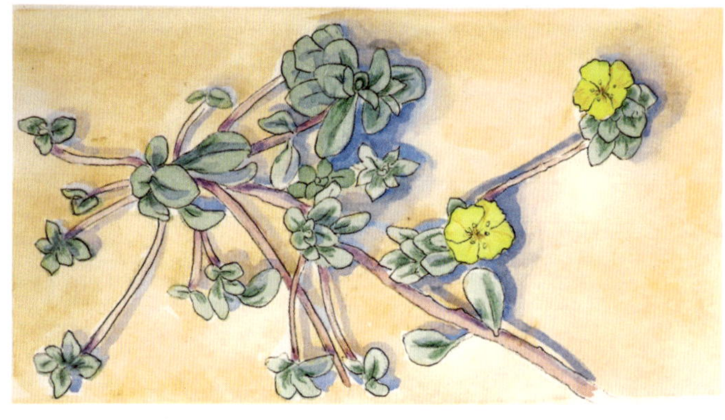

upright stems, though it is mostly prostrate, generally forming flat mats. The leaves are a lovely grayish blue-green and are oval to egg-shaped. The plant sends out long stems, with leaves and one yellow flower on each stem.

I have found that yellow flowers work very well with pen line, so for this illustration I began with watercolor, simply coloring in the larger shapes, like the flowers, leaves, and stems. Then I added pen line, using a size 03 felt-tip pen, and I heightened some of the colors and deepened the shading with watercolor pencils.

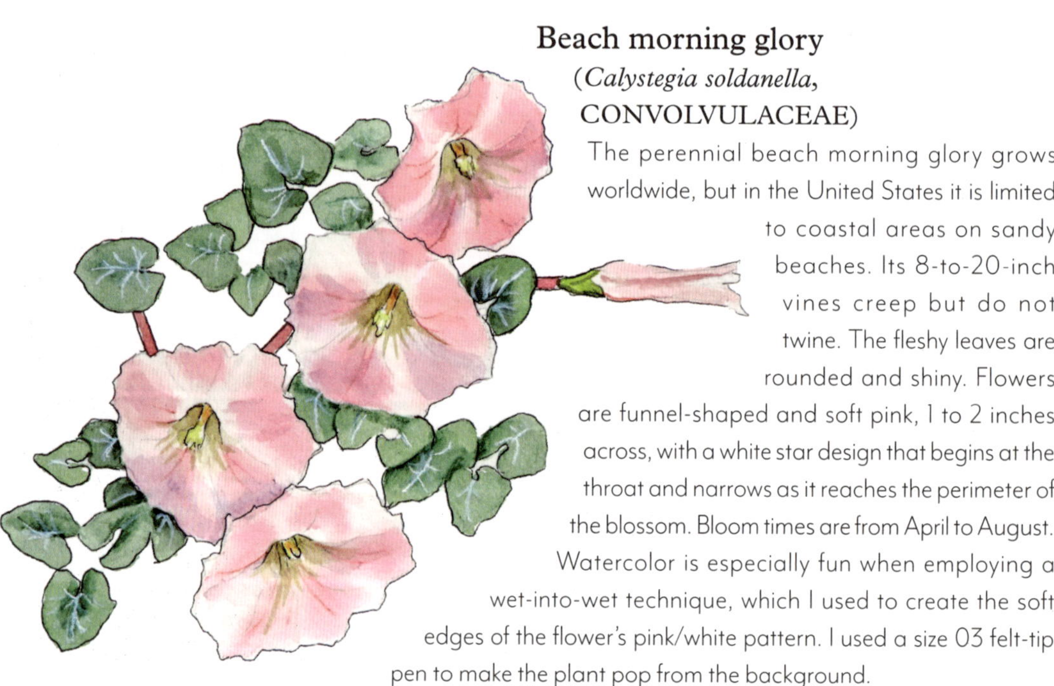

Beach morning glory

(Calystegia soldanella,
CONVOLVULACEAE)

The perennial beach morning glory grows worldwide, but in the United States it is limited to coastal areas on sandy beaches. Its 8-to-20-inch vines creep but do not twine. The fleshy leaves are rounded and shiny. Flowers are funnel-shaped and soft pink, 1 to 2 inches across, with a white star design that begins at the throat and narrows as it reaches the perimeter of the blossom. Bloom times are from April to August. Watercolor is especially fun when employing a wet-into-wet technique, which I used to create the soft edges of the flower's pink/white pattern. I used a size 03 felt-tip pen to make the plant pop from the background.

Douglas iris (*Iris douglasiana*, IRIDACEAE)

Growing on coastal cliffs and grassy slopes in southern Oregon and Northern California, the perennial Douglas iris is never found more than 2 miles away from the coast or higher than 300 feet above sea level. It blooms in late spring. The 1-inch-wide leaves are evergreen, as with so many other coastal plants. Each branched stem has clusters of one to nine flowers. The petals range in color from deep violet to lavender, blue, or cream with purple, and they can have violet, blue, or gold veins. I grow tall bearded irises in my garden, and their shape is quite similar to the wild species; both remind me of my childhood in St. Paul and our kind neighbor on Laurel Avenue, Mr. Ritt. The elegant shape along with the delicate veining led me to add pen to the initial watercolor.

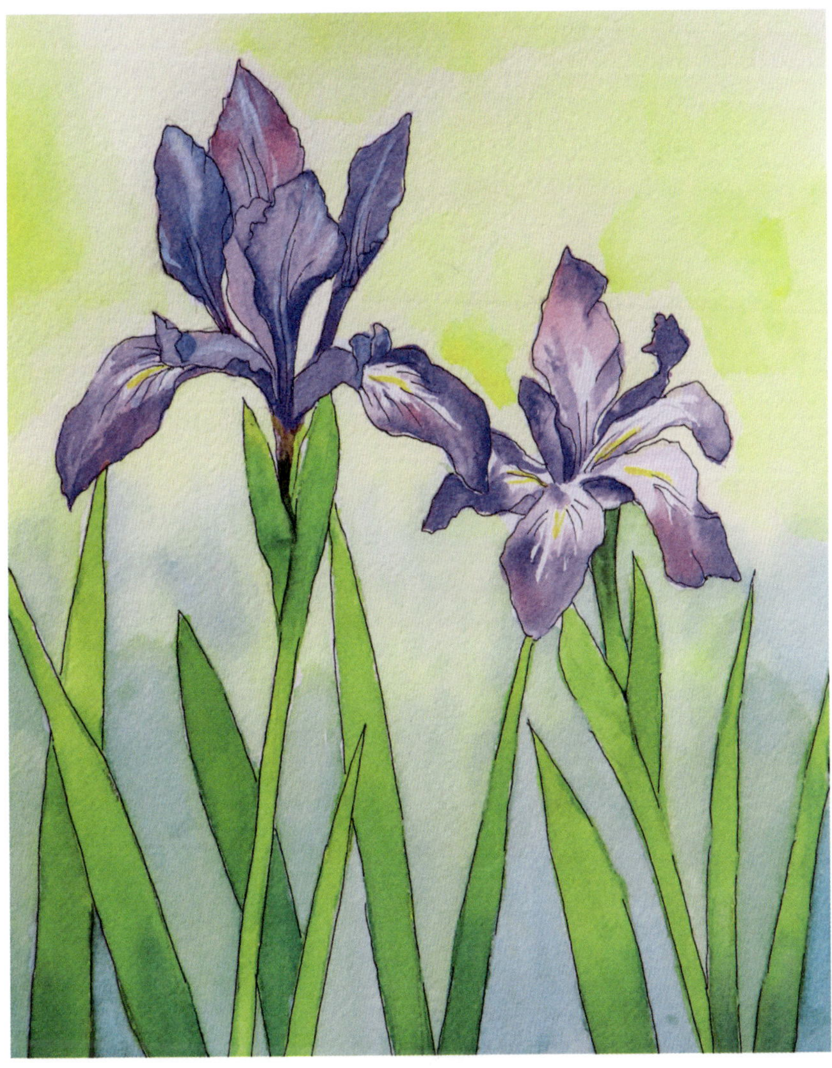

Fireweed (*Chamerion angustifolium*, ONAGRACEAE)

Fireweed is a beautiful perennial plant, ranging from 2 to 5 feet tall, that is ubiquitous in disturbed sites and recently burned or logged areas, where it is among the first plants to come back. After the eruption of Mount St. Helens in 1980, fireweed was quick to colonize the devastated slopes. One June day several years ago, on a trail just east of Winthrop, Washington, I hiked through a forest of burnt ponderosa pines, a shocking sight, yet it was brilliantly illuminated by flowering fireweed. To my unthinking eyes, it seemed a tragic beauty. Of course that was only from my human perspective. Fires are beneficial and necessary to the health of a forest, killing pests and refreshing the soil to encourage new growth. Fireweed is perhaps the most obvious proof of that.

Fireweed is such an adaptable plant that it finds suitable habitat all over the West, from coastal areas to moist meadows and forests, and is unmistakable on roadsides through the summer months. Its green leaves are numerous and lance-shaped, 2 to 8 inches long. The flowers can be pink to magenta, forming a dense spike at the top of the stem, with the spacing between the blooms increasing as the plant matures. Flowers bloom all summer, and when the petals drop, the stamens remain, eventually turning into seed fluff. This fluff was prized by Northwest Indigenous peoples for weaving—it was mixed with dog hair and goat hair to make blankets. In fall, the leaves turn scarlet and magenta so that, through the seasons, the plant never goes unnoticed.

When I first visited Yaquina Head Outstanding Natural Area, on the Oregon coast north of Newport, I saw the stunning meadow of pink flowers illustrated here and struggled to identify them. They were quite a bit shorter than the taller fireweed I'd seen in the Cascade foothills and mountains. It may have been the subspecies *circumvagum*. When I returned the following August, just a month later in the season than the first time I'd seen the plant, it still transformed the meadow into a pink haze, even though most of the petals had dropped. The long pink stamens remained.

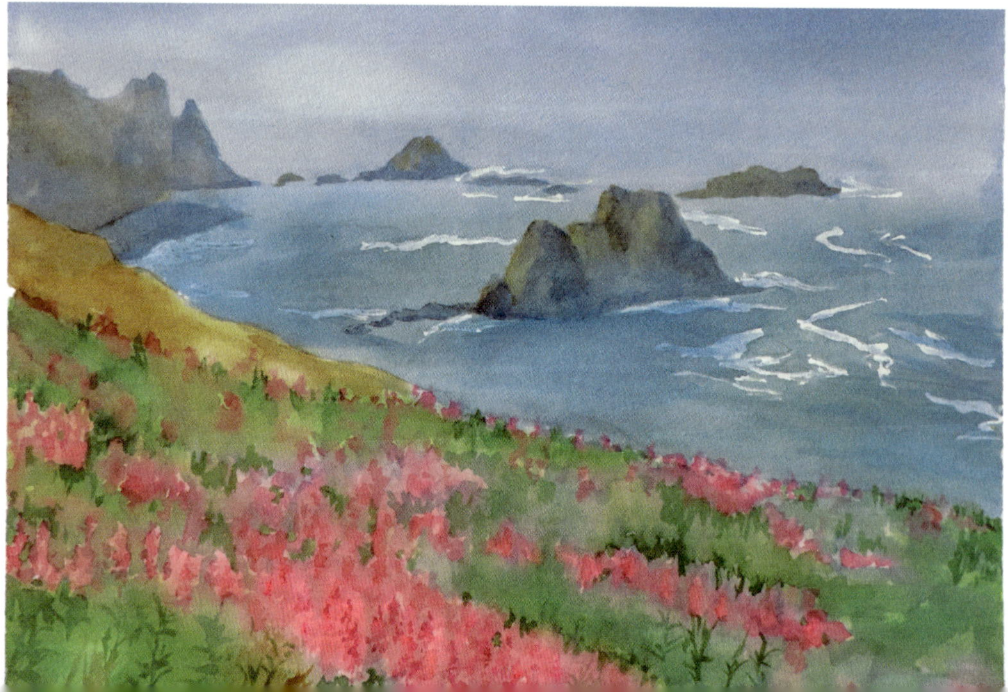

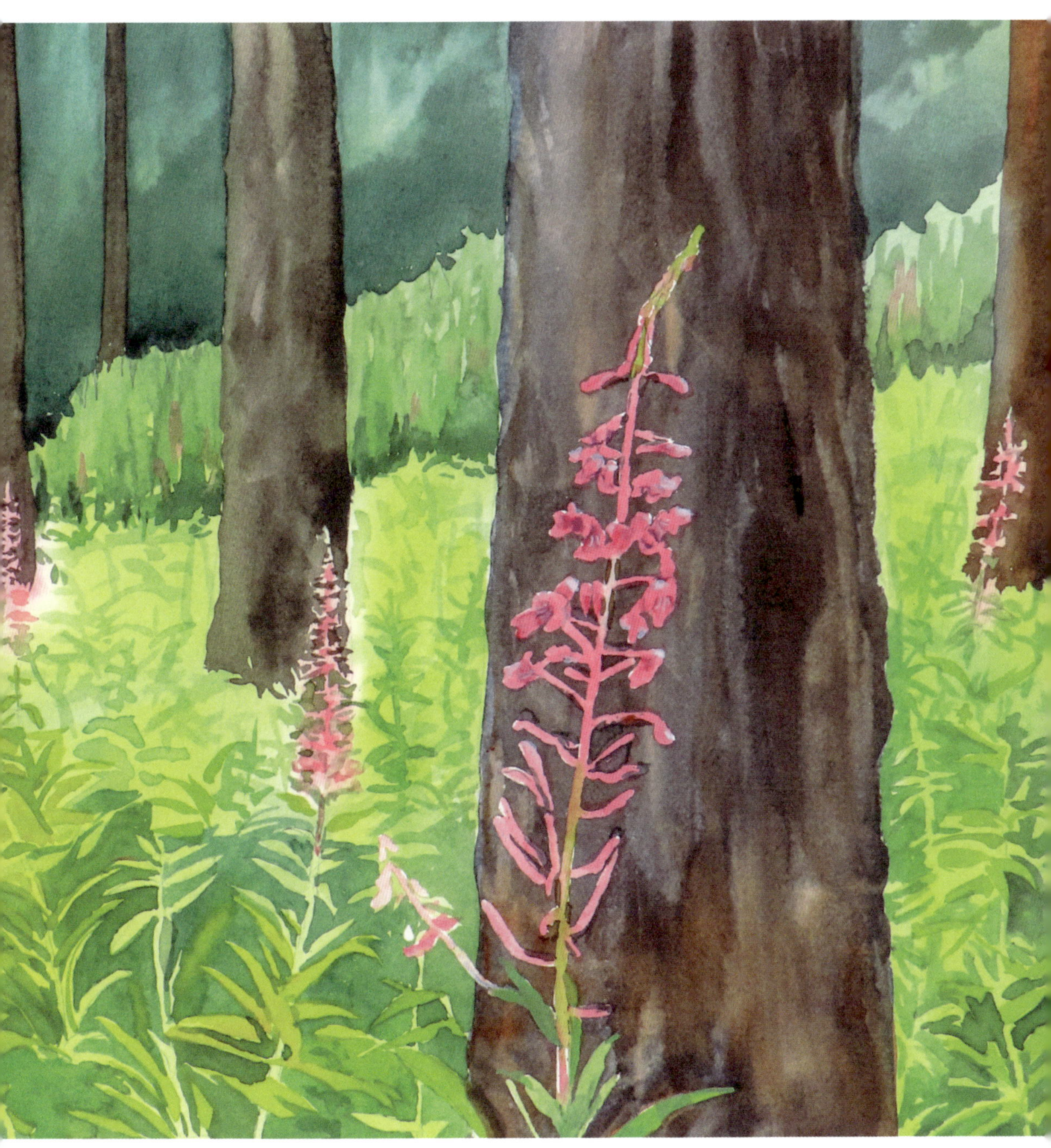

Shrub-Steppe & Grasslands & Prairie

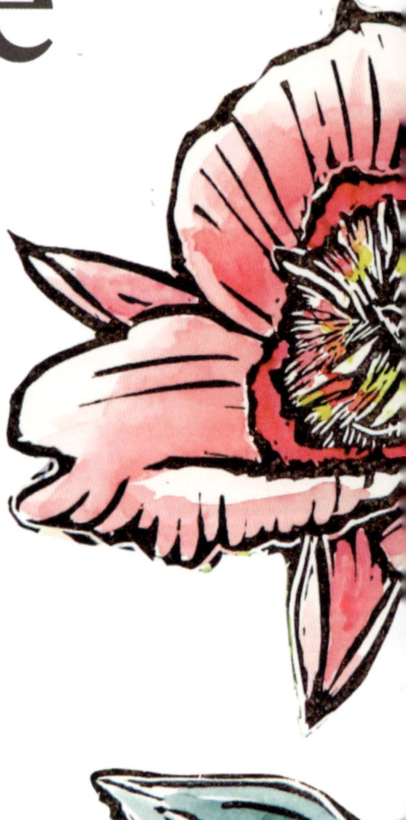

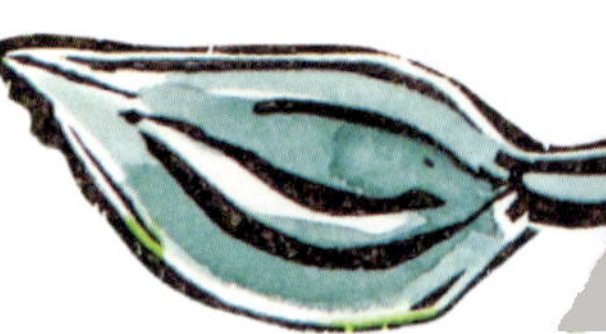

Shrub-steppe, also known as sagebrush steppe, is widespread in the West. It can be found in eastern Washington and Oregon, northeastern California, northwestern Nevada, southern Idaho, and western Wyoming. Just as climate varies depending on latitude, there are also unique vegetative zones based on the chemical properties of the soil. The standard sagebrush steppe zone is characterized by a lack of extremes, with deeper soil and slightly alkaline and somewhat moist conditions. Lupines, balsamroots, buckwheat, paintbrush, phlox, larkspur, and several daisies, plus onions and death camas, thrive here. The lithosol ("rock-soil") zone—characterized by shallow, rocky soils—is found in shrub-steppe areas where there is a lot of basalt, a volcanic rock widespread throughout the western states. Even though this zone is not as rich as other shrub-steppe habitats, it supports dazzling displays of wildflowers similar to the cushion plants of the Arctic and alpine zones, hardy flowers such as cushion phlox, rock penstemon, daisies, and some members of the sunflower family.

Grasslands and prairie include terrain as diverse as open valleys, foothills, and even deserts. In the West, *prairie* might be defined as wide-open landscapes from low elevations to near timberline. Although much of the open land in the West has been converted to crop cultivation and grazing, many of the flower species continue to live along roadsides. South-facing slopes, in contrast to the timbered north-facing slopes in the West, are often treeless, thus supporting prairie-type vegetation.

Colorado Plateau semidesert grasslands and shrub-steppe occur in northern Arizona and northern New Mexico, as well as in southern Utah and southwestern Colorado. These habitats are found on nearly level landforms of sedimentary and igneous origin. Grass species include blue grama and western wheatgrass, with sagebrush and saltbush as the predominant shrubs; springtime wildflowers are often sheltered by these shrubs.

Desert grasslands and shrub-steppe include low-elevation grass and shrub communities adjacent to the Chihuahuan, Mojave, and Sonoran Deserts. Common grass species include black grama; prevalent shrub species include spring bloomers like creosote bush, mesquite, ceanothus, and soaptree yucca.

The flora of the California Floristic Province, as the plant communities in the state are sometimes referred to, is quite notable: almost 50 percent of the native species grow nowhere else in the world. Because of its many specialized environments, such as the Central Valley prairies and the high mountains and deserts to the east, the province—which extends into southern Oregon and northern Baja California—is much like an island "in space and in time," according to Laird Blackwell in *Wildflowers of the Sierra Nevada and the Central Valley*. Living in California gives one the opportunity to travel through the seasons with the wildflower bloom—first to the plains of the Central Valley, ablaze in huge fields of flowers, then to the foothills and eastern desert, and finally to the Sierra Nevada, with its subalpine and alpine species.

California's Central Valley is not a true grassland; originally, it supported vegetation that included mainly annuals and not the bunchgrasses commonly associated with prairie. This is obvious in a superbloom year, when the valley becomes a kind of giant vernal pool due to the heavy winter rains that precede the bloom. Yet, for the purposes of the book, I've considered it a plain, illustrating some of the grassland species.

As California's Central Valley and other western valleys were transformed into pasture and agricultural lands, many of the once-abundant wildflower species became rare, endangered, or extinct, and grassland species invaded. There are still places, though, where one can see glorious spring wildflower shows in California, including the Carrizo Plain National Monument in San Luis Obispo County, Bear Valley in Colusa County, the Antelope Valley California Poppy Reserve in Los Angeles County, and Table Mountain in Butte County.

This apron is Goodlow Rim
slowly weathering,
crumbling toward the valley floor.

Junipers and sagebrush
are my neighbors, amply spaced,
agreeably quiet.

Yellow balsamroots,
bright lanterns of sun,
splotch the upper apron.

On the rimrock crest
stand ancient junipers, roots
clenched in cracked basalt.

Way down on Smith's pond,
sober white pelicans drift, mute
their entire lives.

Black angus dot green pastures.
Far across Langell,
one moving car flashes sun.

Clouds trail their shadows
along mountain and valley
like slow-passing thoughts.

—John Daniel

Arrowleaf balsamroot (*Balsamorhiza sagittata*, ASTERACEAE)

This common member of the sunflower tribe, along with many similar species and subspecies, grows in the cold, dry areas of the West, from the Dakotas and Colorado westward to the Cascades and the Sierra Nevada, and from Canada south to Arizona and Utah. My first sighting of it was in Augusta, Montana, in the north-central part of the state. I was amazed at its size and brilliance as it covered large aprons of

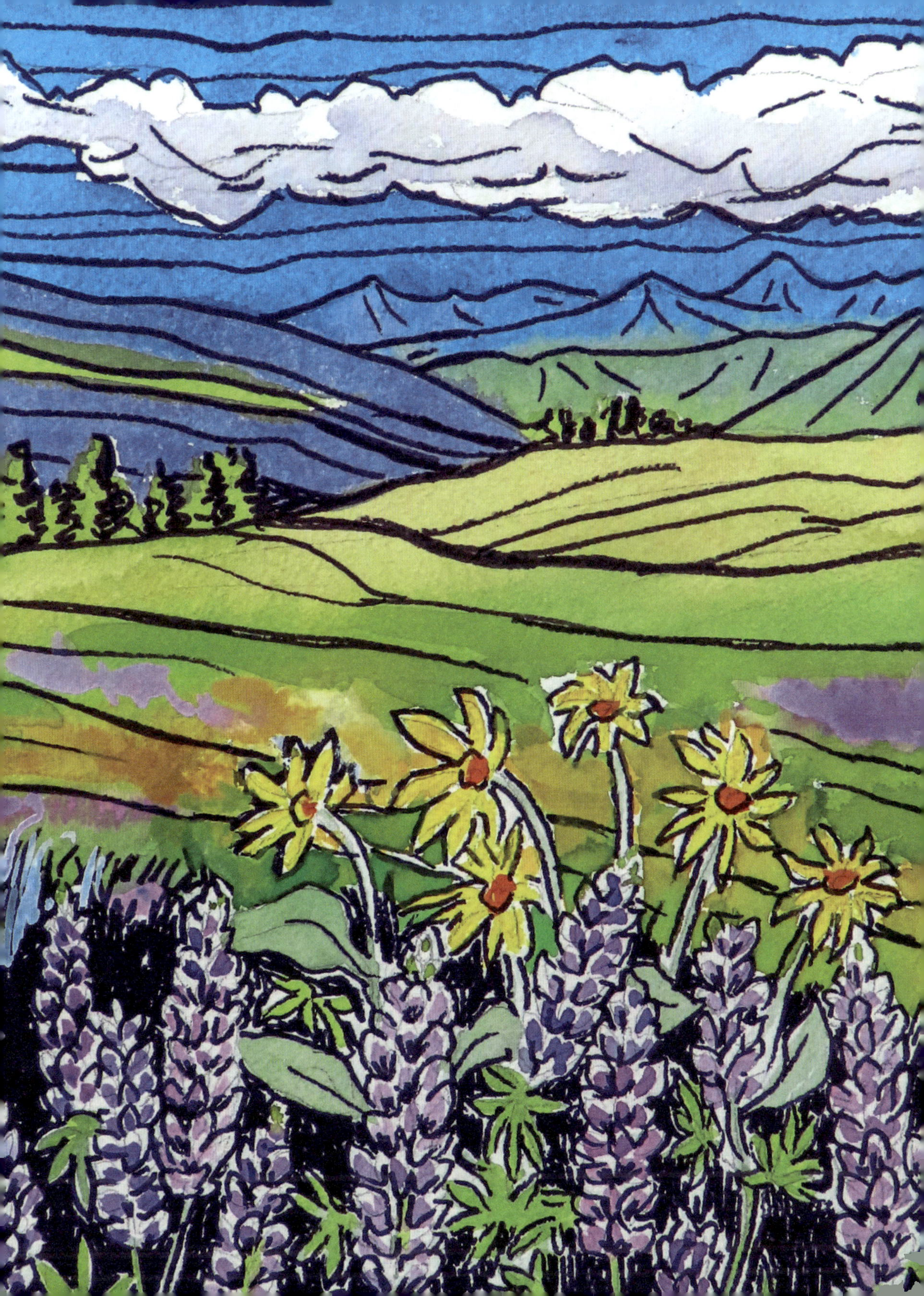

the highway roadside. The plant, a perennial, grows to 36 inches with clumps of upright leaves and erect stems. Its namesake arrow-shaped leaves resemble wide triangles with heart-shaped bases, each one up to 24 inches and colored an attractive olive-green, fuzzy or hairy on both sides. The leaves shrivel soon after the flowers bloom, becoming hairless and twisted. The flower stem is 1 to 3 feet tall, and the golden flowers are up to 4 inches across, above woolly bracts, with rays 1 to 2 inches long.

In north-central Washington's Methow Valley in spring, the balsamroot displays are spectacular. But when I arrived in early June, in most places there and on the east slope of the Cascades they had already peaked and were shriveling up. From a hiker on the Cedar Creek Trail, I learned there was still a marvelous display in one location, so I set out one morning quite early and arrived at the Rex Derr Trail at Pearrygin Lake State Park around 8:30. The light was perfect, angling in from the southeast, and the tall sunflowers exhibited heliotropic orientation in a most dramatic way—there were thousands of them, all facing the sun at once. Lupine bloomed in large areas beside the balsamroot, both species fairly isolated in their own areas, almost as if they'd been neatly stroked onto the landscape with a broad, flat paintbrush. I wondered why these flowers were still blooming and speculated that perhaps this area north of and a bit higher than the main valley had a slightly cooler microclimate.

Sagebrush violet (*Viola trinervata*, VIOLACEAE)

The perennial sagebrush violet is an outlier in the Violaceae family, growing in poor soils around rock formations in the lithosol zone—one expects to see violets in moist forest settings. This wildflower benefits from spring moisture and appears quite early in the season. I encountered the illustrated specimen on the ridge above Cowiche Canyon, near Yakima, Washington, on a sunny day in early April. It was among the most beautiful of the flowers I saw. Surprisingly, it looks very much like a pansy cultivar that you might find in a nursery, with two darker, deep magenta-violet petals above and three paler lilac ones below. The fleshy leaves are also remarkable, growing on short stems, slightly blue green in color. The plant is 2 to 3 inches tall and grows in a mat-like manner.

NAPHTHAMIDE MAROON

GUINACRIDONE MAGENTA

PHTHALO BLUE RED SHADE

MIXTURE - MORE MAGENTA

MIXTURE - MORE BLUE

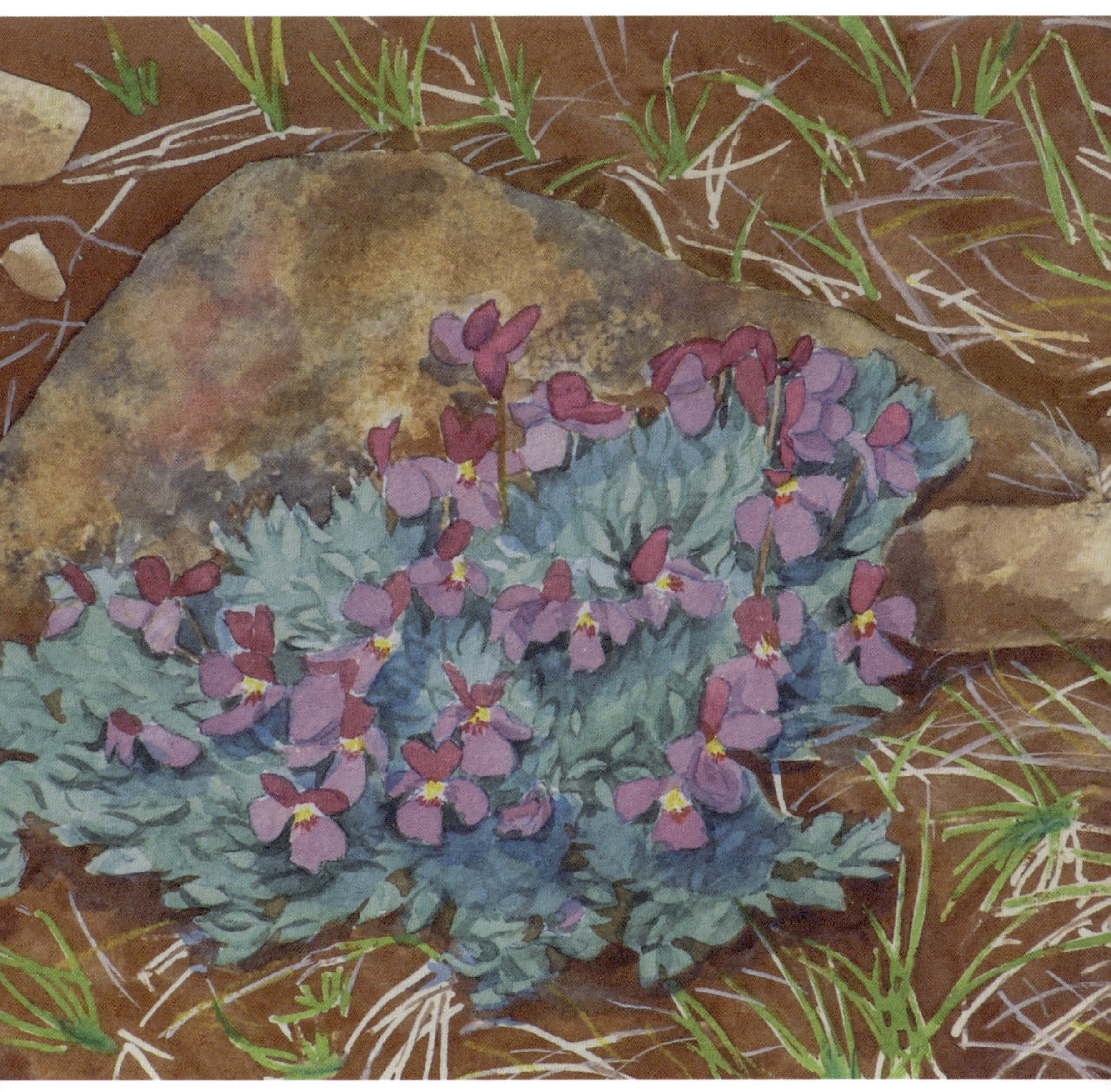

Painting the violets growing beside the lichen-encrusted rocks required a careful approach; each petal had to be well crafted to reveal the violet's surprising resemblance to a cultivated pansy. I tried out most of my reds, violets, and blues to achieve the right hues. I found that it didn't take very many colors to get it right: I used phthalo blue (red shade) and quinacridone magenta for the lower, lighter-colored petals, and naphthamide maroon and quinacridone magenta for the upper petals.

From my journal:

> *I started out on Interstate 90 in Seattle on a cold and rainy morning. The drive itself was a mete-*
> *orologist's dream: The eastern suburbs of Bellevue and Issaquah brought much heavier rain, and*
> *then as I continued east into the foothills, a beautiful mist draped the summits. At Snoqualmie*
> *Pass, huge snowflakes hit the windshield and there were no visible mountains, only a pure white*
> *blanket of fresh snow along the interstate. By Cle Elum on the east side, blue sky began to appear,*
> *and at Ellensburg the sun was fully shining. All of this weather drama took place traveling east*
> *for only two hours—a very immediate example of the climatic effects of Pacific storms along the*
> *West Coast, as they drain themselves of moisture over the foothills and Cascades. I had checked*
> *the forecast ahead of time and fully expected it, but a forecast is nothing like experiencing the real*
> *thing. Cowiche Canyon was not in bloom, but the rocky sagebrush uplands above the canyon,*
> *still part of the Cowiche Canyon Conservancy lands, were glowing with small wonders: sage-*
> *brush violets, grass widows, and yellow bells.*

Green-banded mariposa lily (*Calochortus macrocarpus*, LILIACEAE)

The perennial mariposa lily grows in sagebrush and pine forests from mid- to high elevations on the east side of the Cascades, from Washington to Northern California. The *Calochortus* genus is full of lovely variations throughout the West. Alexis Madrigal, who writes the *Oakland Garden Club* newsletter on Substack, offers a playful description of the genus in a July 2023 post: "Perched on thin and unadorned stalks, they are like a grass that decided to be fabulous." He notes that each individual within a species is unique in coloration and form.

I saw the green-banded variety on Patterson Mountain in early June outside Winthrop, Washington. It was impossible to miss, with its lovely rose-violet petals and pointed sepals, completely unlike any other wildflower I've seen. The plant can grow from 8 to 23 inches in height; the single leaf dries up before the flower blooms. Each flower, like most lilies, has three petals, three sepals, and six stamens. Flowers can be dainty or large, with petals 1 to 3 inches wide. The inside of each flower is strongly marked with a purple band and a small fringe of hairs. "Green-banded" refers to the green stripe that appears in the center of each petal, more noticeable on the outside of the petal.

Leafy bluebells (*Mertensia longiflora*, BORAGINACEAE)

On a visit to the Beezley Hills Preserve, north of Ephrata, Washington, early in wildflower season, I was drawn to a beautiful outdoor still life: bicolor bluebells, pale blue and magenta, growing beside a twisted sagebrush trunk. Of the many flowers growing in the shade of both living and dead sage shrubs—with the sage bushes forming a kind of dwarf canopy—the bluebells were by far the most appealing. I consulted the guidebook I had with me, *Wildflowers of the Pacific Northwest*, and discovered that this perennial species, also called trumpet lungwort, is fairly common in the high plains of the sagebrush steppe, where there is a lot of spring moisture (flowering in early spring, it favors wet springs and dry summers). The plants have erect stems up to 8 inches high and leaves with indistinct wide veins. The tubular flowers, which grow

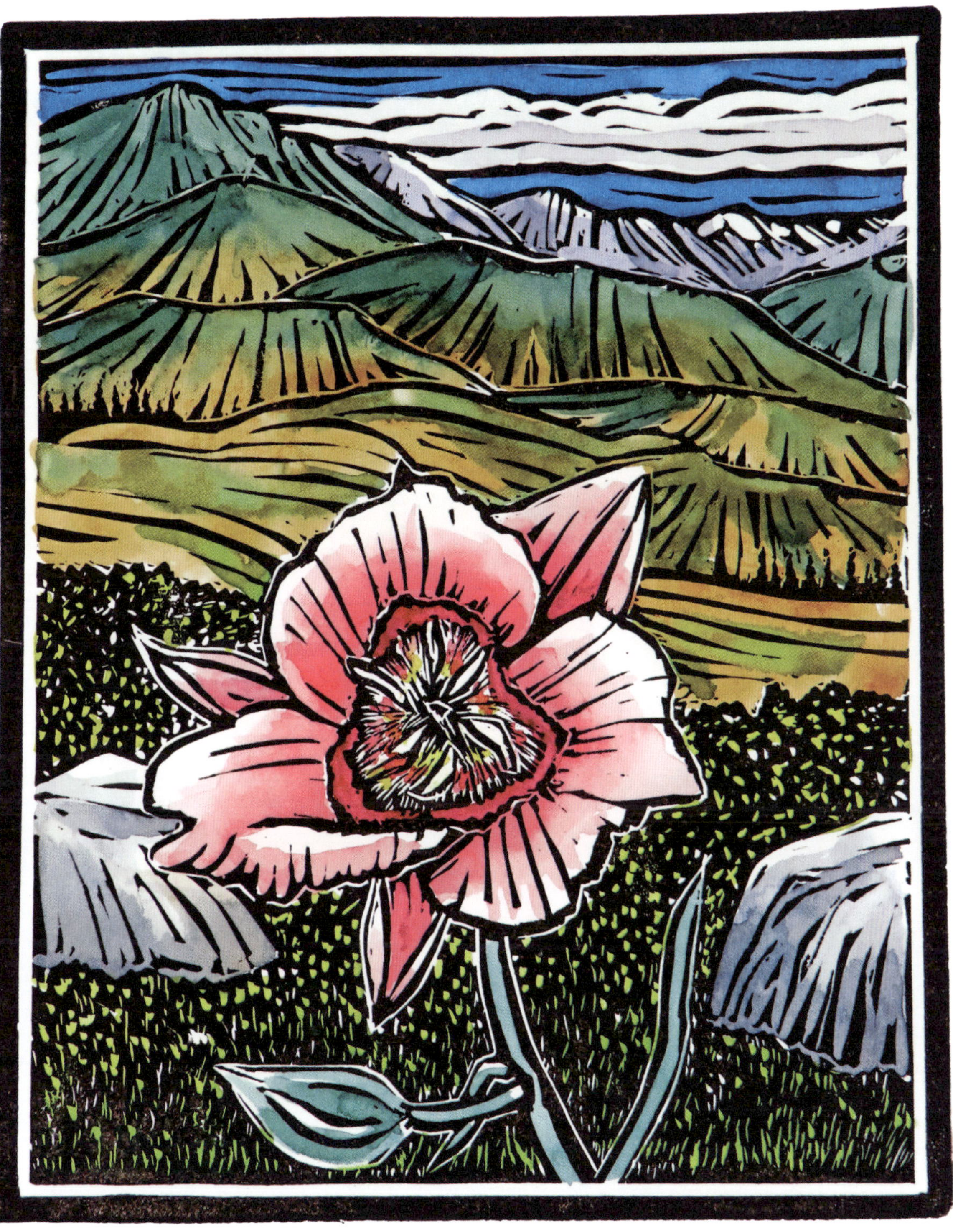

GREEN-BANDED MARIPOSA LILY, PATTERSON MOUNTAIN, WASHINGTON

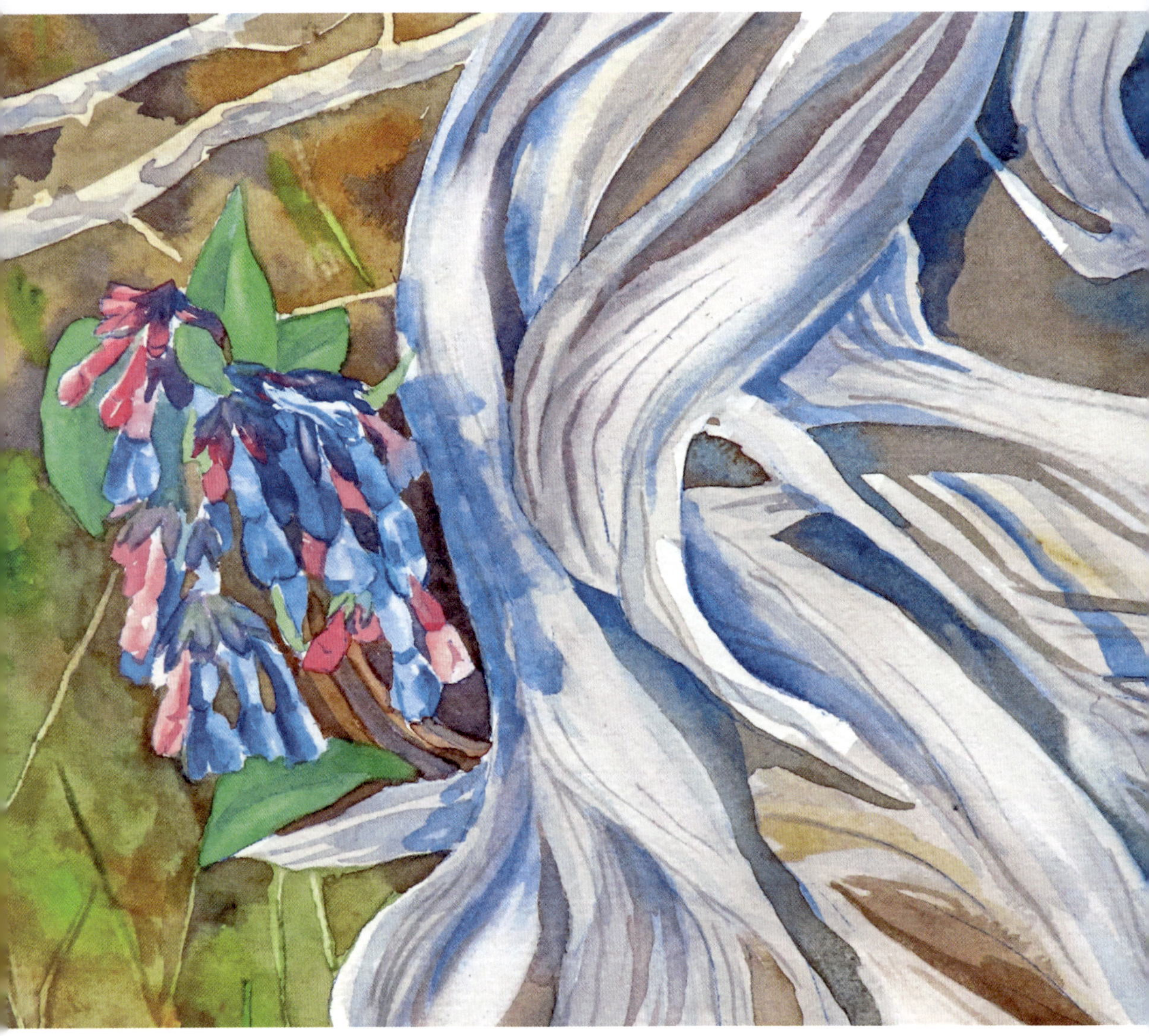

LEAFY BLUEBELLS, BEEZLEY HILLS PRESERVE

in dramatic clusters, are up to 1 inch long and are the loveliest shade of blue with hints of magenta—a rather opaque and chalky hue.

Once I'd painted the base gray of the sagebrush trunk, I used a rigger brush (so called because it was invented to paint the delicate lines of a ship's rigging) to paint the darker swirling grooves. Had there been pounding surf nearby, the trunk might have been a piece of ocean driftwood, a beautiful reminder that nature's patterns repeat themselves endlessly in every corner of the earth.

Grass widow (*Olsynium douglasii*, IRIDACEAE)

Also known as the satin flower, as well as blue-eyed grass and purple-eyed grass, this perennial blooms in earliest spring. It can grow in a variety of habitats, but since I saw it on the shrub-steppe of eastern Washington, I included it in this chapter. Found from Washington east into Idaho and as far south as Northern California, it is most common in seasonally wet locations that become dry in summer, notably vernal pool areas.

Grass widow is one of the most beautiful wildflowers. The grasslike leaves, up to 12 inches tall, emerge from the base. The flowers disappear after the spring bloom, leaving behind their grassy leaves. The flower parts come in sets of three: three sepals, three petals, three stamens, and three compartments in the ovary. Even though *Olsynium* are widespread in other locations, the most beautiful species is the *douglasii*, because of its comparatively large rose-violet flowers. Other *douglasii* colors are magenta, white, and pink. I used watercolor to paint this group that I saw in the Cowiche Canyon Preserve near Yakima, Washington. I added watercolor pencil to heighten some of the details.

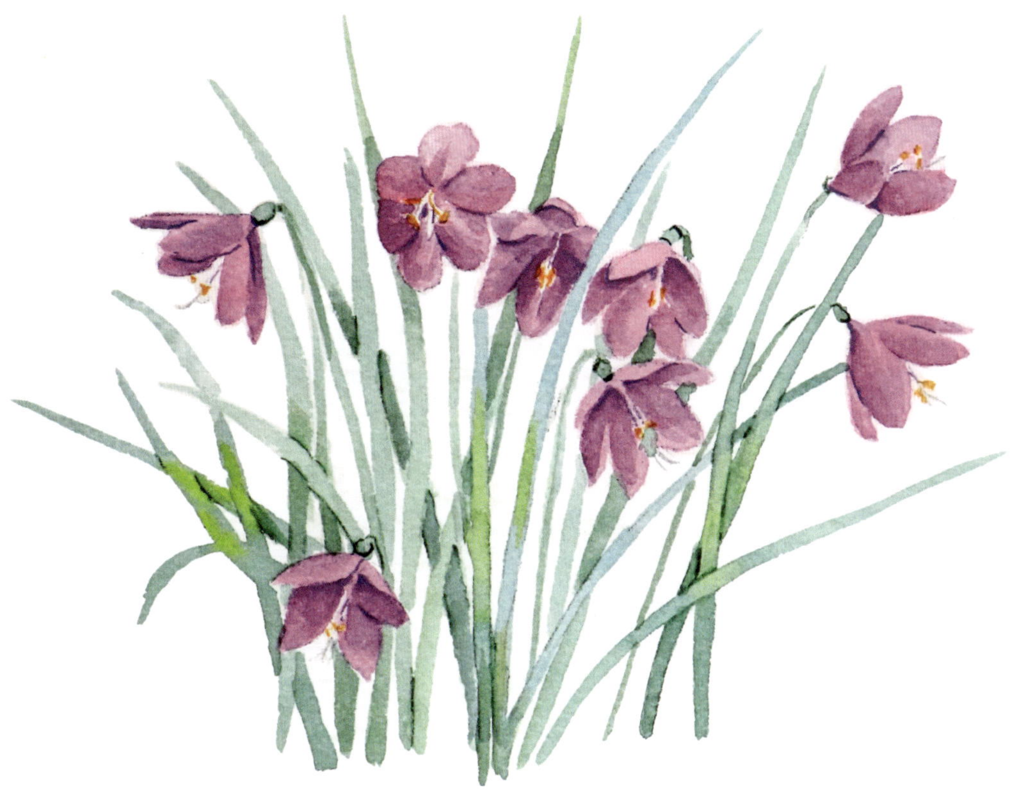

Yellow bells (*Fritillaria pudica*, LILIACEAE)

Yellow bells, or yellow fritillary, is an early spring perennial that is very common in eastern Washington, eastern Oregon, and northeastern California. It prefers heavy soils that dry out in summer and is found in both low and higher elevations. The plant is 3 to 12 inches tall, with strappy leaves along the erect stem. Nodding, bell-shaped flowers hang atop the stems, in rich yellow to gold colors, aging to orange. In *Sagebrush Country*, botanist Ronald Taylor describes yellow bells as "one of the most unforgettable characters" of the sagebrush steppe. "Undoubtedly, its popularity relates in part to the fact that it flowers in very early spring when the desolate recesses of winter linger over the drab countryside," he writes. Walking along the ridgetop at the Cowiche Canyon Preserve in April, I saw yellow bells blooming simultaneously with grass widows and sagebrush violets, all of them opulently hued, their colors standing out bravely from the landscape surrounding them.

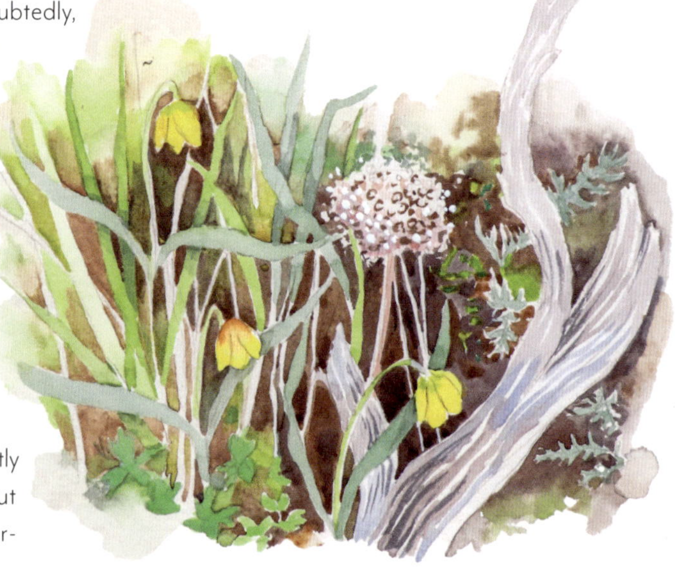

Blanket flower (*Gaillardia aristata*, ASTERACEAE)

The perennial blanket flower blooms in spring and summer and is quite common in eastern Washington and in the northern part of eastern Oregon. It can be found at elevations up to 6,500 feet—along roadsides, in ditches, and in grasslands.

Gardeners are probably familiar with the blanket flower since it is offered in many nurseries and seed catalogs, where it is often called gaillardia. (The plant was named after Gaillard de Charentonneau, a French magistrate who encouraged botanical studies in the eighteenth century.) Single flower heads of ray- and disk-type florescence top stems that are 1 to 3 feet tall. Six to sixteen bright yellow rays, often orange or purple at the base, surround the reddish, brown, or purplish central disk. The leaves are 2 to 6 inches long, becoming smaller the higher they appear on the stem. Another species, *Gaillardia pinnatifida*, grows in Arizona and has narrower leaves than blanket flowers found in other states.

On a June visit to the Methow Valley in Washington State, I observed a field of blanket flowers, as well as a lazuli bunting singing in a tree in roughly the same area. I decided to illustrate them together in this block print.

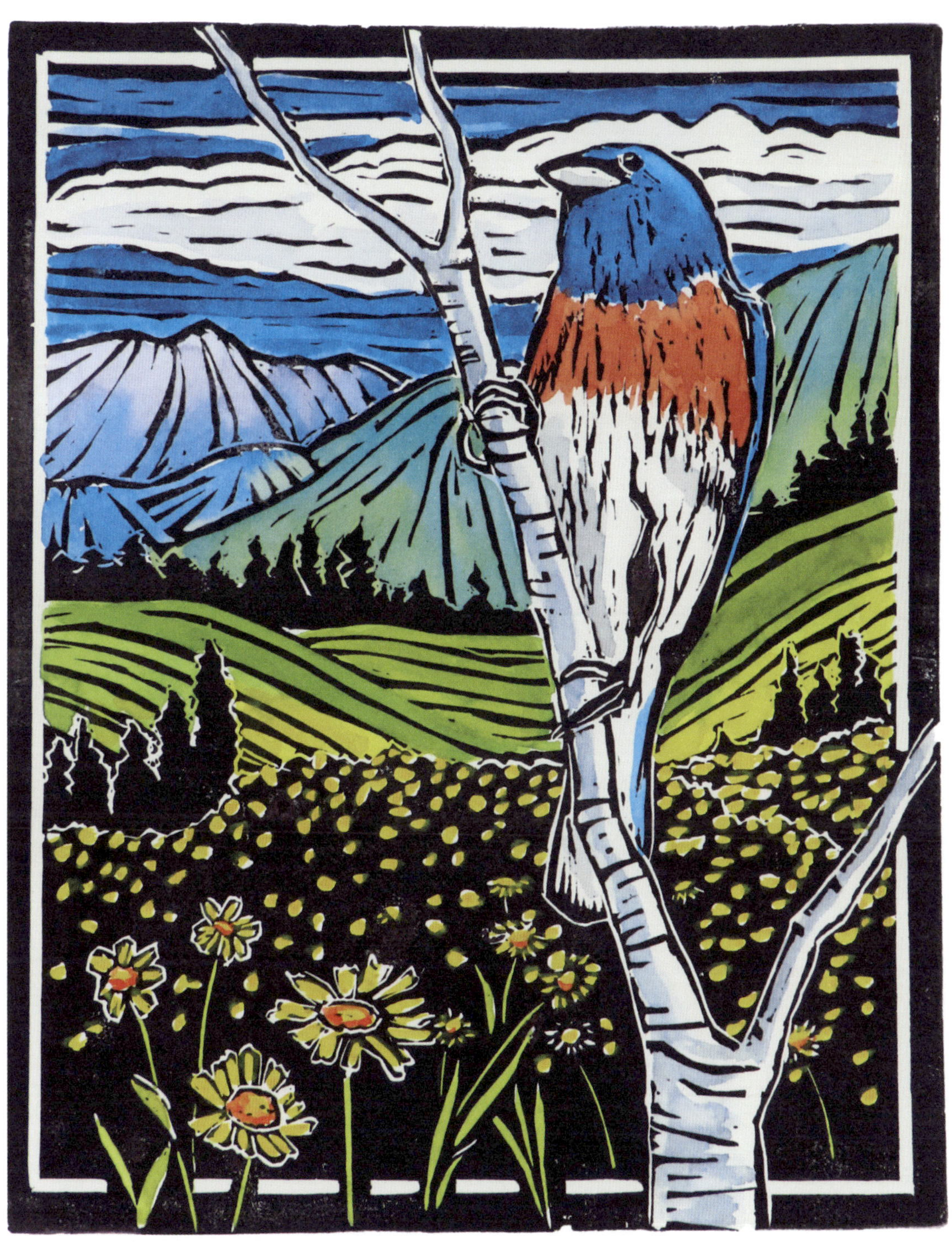

BLANKET FLOWERS AND LAZULI BUNTING METHOW VALLEY, WASHINGTON

Hedgehog cactus (*Pediocactus nigrispinus*, CACTACEAE)

The hedgehog cactus grows in drier areas throughout the West, but I found it in its northwesternmost reach, near the Columbia River and the town of Ephrata in Washington State. In Washington, it grows at a lower altitude than anywhere else in the West. The spines of the cactus can be black, gray, or even golden; dazzling pink flowers, 1 to 1½ inches across, bloom in early May. Anywhere from four to eight buds can form at the top of the cactus, and flowering groups are large enough to make for an impressive display, even at a distance. The hedgehog can grow as a solitary cactus, but some develop as many as thirty offshoots and can form mounds up to 1 foot tall and 2 feet across. The individual cacti are 2 to 8 inches tall and 3 to 6 inches across.

From my journal:

I had several locations in mind to scout for wildflowers. The Beezley Hills Preserve in eastern Washington wasn't a first choice because it was a long drive from Leavenworth, where Paul and I were staying. But spring was so delayed in the state that flowers were late, and I thought that by driving east toward the Columbia Plateau we might find warmer temperatures and more flowers.

I'd forgotten Craig Romano's guidebook, so we were forced to rely on an app that led us astray and we ended up at an organic farm. As bundled-up farmworkers swung hoes in the field, we walked along a dirt track on a berm, looking for any sign indicating a nature preserve, but there was only the track and farm fields stretching into the distance. Among the sagebrush plants on the berm was a white-and-magenta wildflower with dozens of snapdragon-like flowers growing out from a central mat. I thought it might be a weed, but Paul used his PictureThis plant identification app and we determined that it was a woolly milkvetch. How jewellike and lonely it seemed in that place.

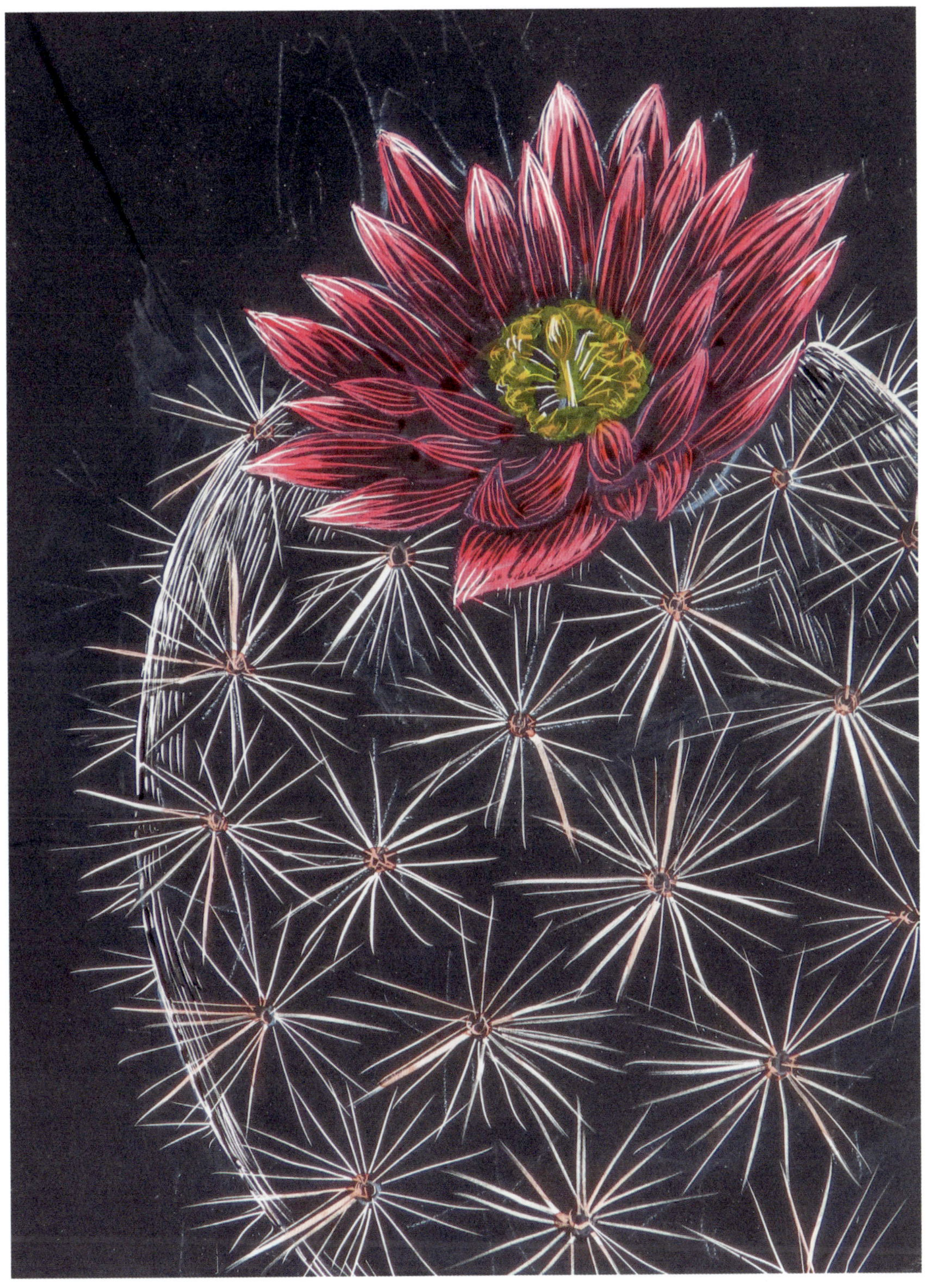

Back in the car, we tried another navigational app, which sent us in the right direction. From Ephrata we drove up a gravel road to Monument Hill, where a radio tower presides over the Nature Conservancy's Moses Coulee and Beezley Hills Preserves. A turnstile and small sign barely visible from the road identified the site. Several beer cans and broken bottles littered the ground beneath the sign, its metal face pocked with bullet holes. The panoramic view below us reached east and south to the agricultural lands and then west to the Columbia River. A cold wind blew, the distant ground alternately alight in sun and shaded in great circles cast by the towering clouds. Rain fell to the west, slanting gray strokes against the dark blue of the Columbia's vast canyon walls.

We saw several wildflowers in bloom—yellow bells, bluebells, woolly milkvetch, and Hooker's balsamroot. Sagebrush was everywhere, and some of the flowers grew cautiously beneath it. I was surprised in the midst of flower-spotting by a tiny round cactus, about 6 inches in diameter, rust colored and with silvery spikes, not yet in bloom. I later identified it as a hedgehog cactus. It seemed out of place, yet we encountered a half dozen or more. It is one of only two cacti that

Penstemon's Many Forms

Penstemon is the largest genus of flowering plants native to North America, consisting of about 280 species. It belongs to the larger figwort, or snapdragon, family. You can find penstemons at garden nurseries, and I've successfully grown them as perennials in my dry front yard, a xeriscape, which I never water in summer. Hummingbirds love their tubular flowers.

Penstemons are happiest in the drier habitats of the West, especially Utah, where there are about seventy species. They grow on roadsides, in gravel, in sand, and even on cliffs, like the rare Barrett's penstemon, which is found in the Columbia River Gorge on basalt escarpments. People who love them are called "penstemaniacs," and if you're one of them, you probably already have a copy of Dee Strickler's *Northwest Penstemons*.

Penstemons are perennials, generally sending up one or several stems from a base clump that emerges from a branching woody root crown. Some penstemons are evergreen, but most die back during the winter. I've found that the most beautiful penstemons form low mats. I remember one in particular—a cliff penstemon growing on the roadside between Paradise and Stevens Canyon Road at Mount Rainier National Park in Washington. I had to pull over to take a photo of it, marveling at how it had spread for yards across the roadside gravel. I thought it was more exciting than the black bear I'd seen on the same trip! And then there was the dazzling mountain pride penstemon (see the Alpine & Subalpine Zones chapter) growing out of cracks in the granite rock off the Tioga Road in Yosemite—yet another surprising appearance of this remarkably adaptable plant.

grow in the Great Basin and sagebrush steppe, the other being the prickly pear. Before land reclamation, it was much more common and widespread in northern locales.

Oddity was the defining feature of this adventure. Two city folks on a cold spring day, dressed in outdoor gear, prowling with cameras and smartphones along the edge of an organic farm field; I had no doubt we were a comical spectacle for those hardworking men and women, completely out of place. A beautiful and dainty wildflower growing among weeds and dirt near an irrigation canal. Sagebrush steppe on a high hill, pristine, preserved, yet still used by local teenagers for beer parties and target practice. And a diminutive cactus that you'd expect to see in the desert Southwest, thriving in this high northern climate.

But maybe most of this wasn't odd at all. I'd never thought about what a large-scale organic farm looked like and how the work was done. Nor did I know about the small beauties and species that lived only a few short hours from my home in Seattle, though I'd lived here for decades and could easily have visited. A reminder to myself to keep the view wide and long.

Lowly penstemon
(*Penstemon humilis*, SCROPHULARIACEAE)

I had a lot of trouble identifying this penstemon, probably because there are so many penstemon species (see the sidebar), and a large number of them are blue. But this perennial individual is uniquely multicolored, bright blue to rose-violet with the insides of the tubes white or lavender; you really have to see the flowers in person to appreciate that particular blue. I encountered the plant in May at Lava Beds National Monument in northeastern California, where it was thriving in sandy, rocky soil. I decided to paint it on a creamy beige paper to show how striking the flowers appeared against that backdrop of pale brown. I used a Twinrocker handmade paper with a deckle edge; the completed illustration is reminiscent of an old-fashioned needlepoint sampler. The "lowly" name is appropriate only because this penstemon is a low-growing variety, from 4 to 10 inches tall, with small, narrow, spoon-shaped leaves up to 3 inches long and 1-inch flowers atop the stems. It is one of my favorite penstemons, not lowly at all!

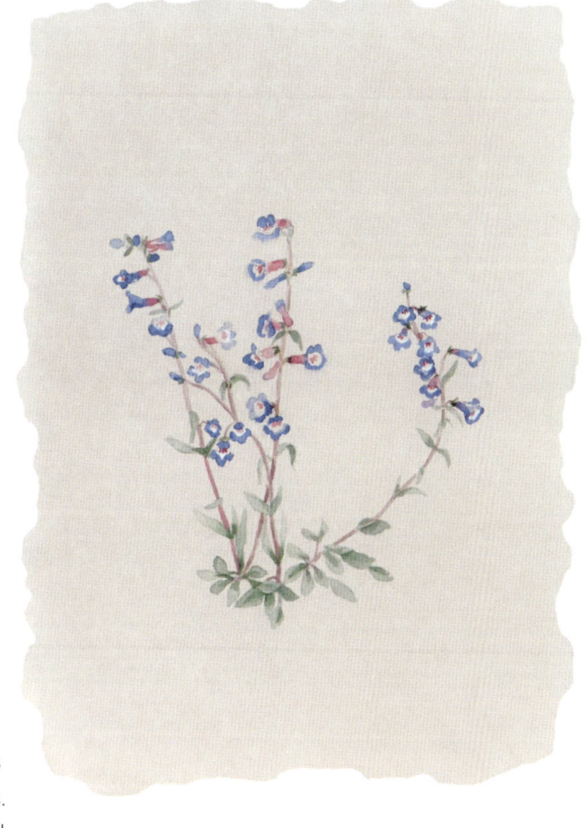

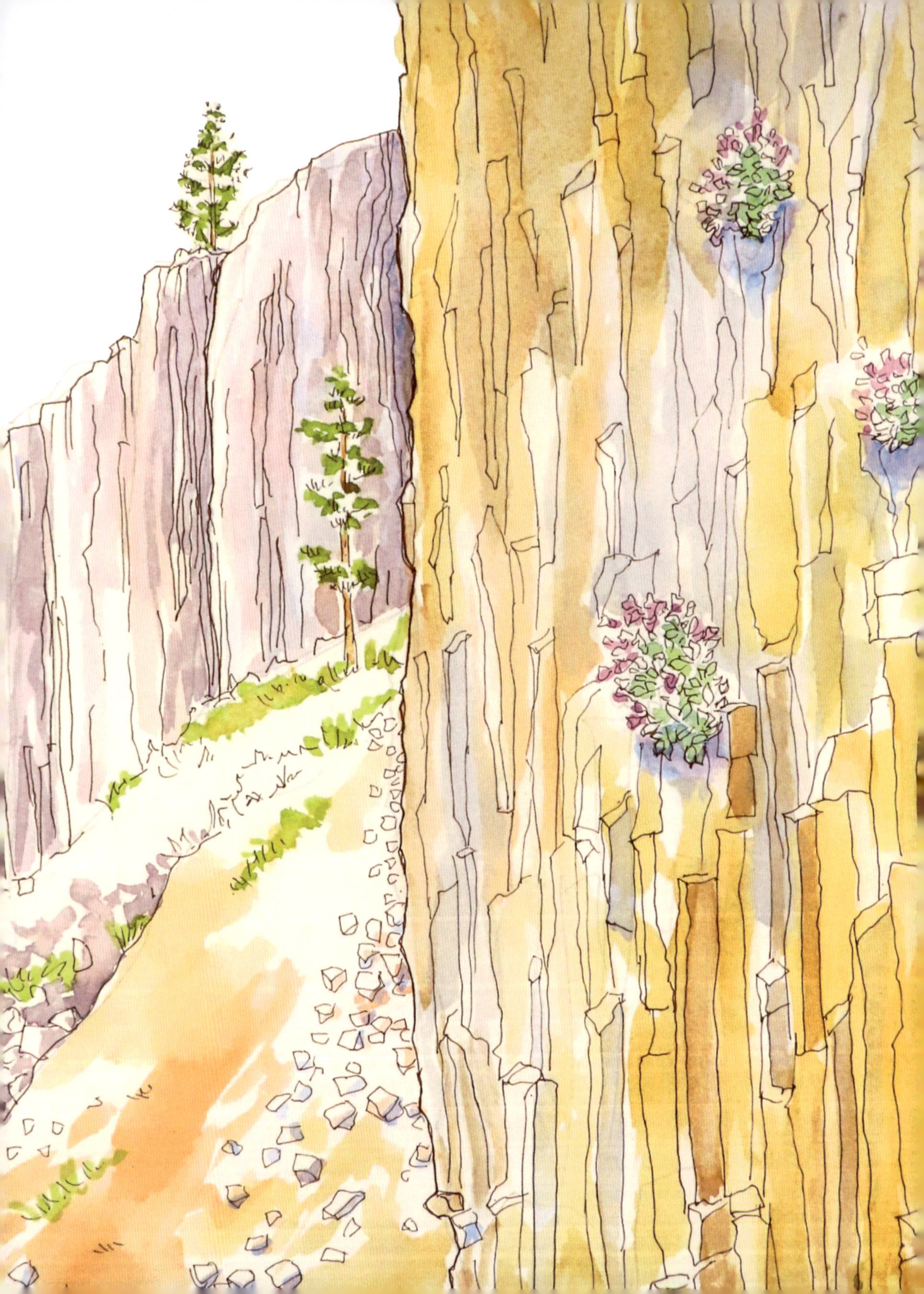

Barrett's penstemon (*Penstemon barrettiae*, SCROPHULARIACEAE)

Barrett's penstemon is a perennial that grows from 9 to 15 inches tall, often forming clumps, with multiple showy blooms per stem, in colors from pink to lilac. The succulent-like leaves are up to 3 inches long, with a tapered tip, and are covered with a waxy powder, which gives the leaves a blue-green hue. Barrett's is a very rare plant, growing only in the Columbia River Gorge in the transition zone between the dry lands of the Columbia Basin, the eastern slope of the Cascades, and the wetter western slope. It grows in very specialized locations along cliffs or in talus, preferring drier sites at lower elevations. Bloom time is early to mid-May. (For more on penstemons, see the "Penstemon's Many Forms" sidebar, page 120.)

I visited Catherine Creek, in that transition zone, to see wildflowers in early May. On the drive back along Washington State Route 14 on the north side of the Columbia River, where basalt cliffs loom above the road, I was startled by the appearance of these lush blooms hanging from almost invisible ledges. I'm always full of admiration for any plant or tree that manages to find a foothold in inhospitable surroundings, but this fulsome penstemon was among the most stunning of all the plants I've seen in unwelcoming sites. Of course that begs the question: Unwelcoming to whom? Seeing something from only a human point of view makes many locations seem unappealing. But it's clear this plant has found the perfect spot for itself. Barrett's penstemon doesn't exist anywhere else but in this very small geographic area, like so many endemics in the Gorge (see the "Columbia River Gorge" sidebar in the Wetlands & Riparian Habitats chapter).

I wasn't sure how to do justice to the flower and its cliffside residence of complex, blocky basalt columns, but I thought it might be best represented with the crisp lines of a pen. I made the pen drawing first and then added the color.

Alpine & Subalpine Zones

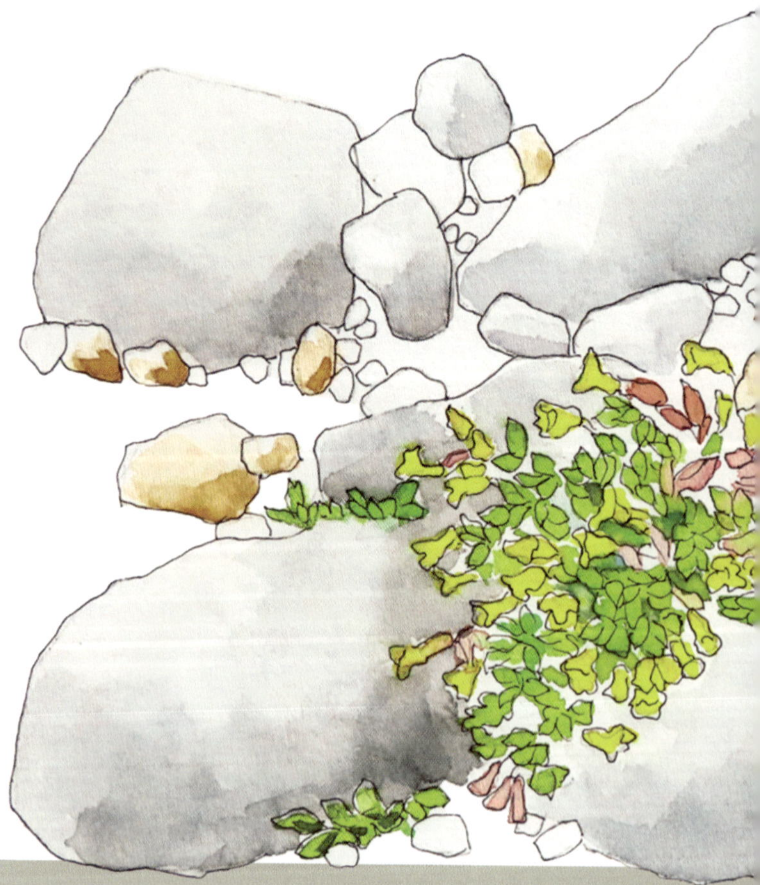

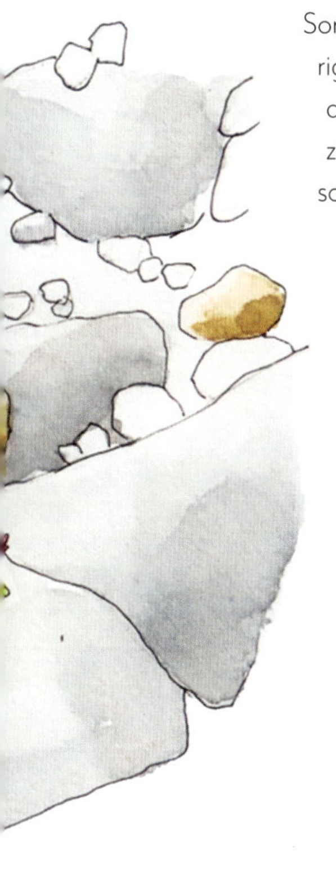

uch of the alpine and subalpine West lies on federal lands—in national parks, wilderness areas, and national forests. The alpine zone is defined as the elevation above which no trees will grow. The subalpine is an intermediate zone between montane forests and the treeless alpine zone. Common trees of the subalpine include firs and Engelmann spruce, whitebark pine, and mountain hemlock. Floral wonderlands interrupt these forests of spare-looking and picturesque trees. In the Rockies of northern Idaho and northwestern Montana, the subalpine flora begins at about 6,000 to 6,500 feet, but in Colorado and northern Utah, at 9,000 to 10,500 feet. The subalpine zone is characterized by a very short growing season, nourished by a lot of precipitation that falls mostly as snow in winter, although rain is common in fall and spring. In the Pacific Northwest, wildflowers in this habitat are found in the Olympic Mountains and to both the east and the west along the Cascade crest. They are notably abundant on Hurricane Ridge in Olympic National Park, at Heather Meadows near Mount Baker, at Paradise and Sunrise at Mount Rainier National Park, and at Crater Lake in Oregon.

Some of the more spectacular species are glacier and avalanche lilies, blooming right beside melting snowbanks, plus Sitka valerian, paintbrush, bistort, lupines, and western pasqueflowers. Interestingly, spring comes later to the subalpine zone than the alpine zone: because the alpine zone is exposed to more wind and solar radiation, snow melts faster there than in the forested areas of the subalpine.

In all the western mountain ranges at alpine elevations, the soils are very thin and rocky. Grasses and sedges grow there, but the soils are not rich, due to erosion from wind, water, and glaciation. Plants are forced to grow deep roots for nutrients and moisture and usually grow as small, cushion-like forms to protect themselves from the harsh winds; these tough survivors are often found in the lee of large rocks. On a hike from forest to subalpine to alpine, you will see marvelous adaptations of species—a lush lupine in the subalpine forest may give way to a tiny dwarf version in the harsh, tundra-like conditions of the alpine zone. Other common flowers are sedum, phlox, heather, and moss campion. I have not painted many of these because the flowers are very dainty, not well suited to block prints or watercolor.

In much of the Rockies, the elevation of the subalpine zone is much higher than in the Cascades: from 10,000 to 11,500 feet. This zone is heavily forested in the Rockies, so understory plants are sparse except for at forest edges and in clearings. Many flowers are found in the meadows and rivulets of this zone. Above where the forests give out at timberline, plant growth is very spare and tundra-like. On protected southern exposures, the tree line can go higher, and on cooler north-facing slopes, it can be less than 11,500 feet. Many of the plants are quite similar to those found in the subalpine and alpine zones of the Cascades and the Sierra Nevada, although there are some very striking endemics, such as the subalpine Colorado columbine, the state flower of Colorado.

In the Sierra Nevada, the altitude is similar to the Rockies, yet the climate is closer to that of the Cascades; a few of the most notable subalpine flowers are Lemmon's paintbrush (named after Sarah Plummer Lemmon—see her paintbrush watercolor in the "Women and Early Wildflower Exploration" sidebar in the Introduction), mountain pride, and Sierra gentian. The Sierra subalpine zone may have almost six hundred species, two hundred of which are endemic. As in the other ranges, much of the flora includes plants that survived the glaciation of the last ice age. These so-called relict plants continued to thrive because they were on mountain peaks that stood above the ice, like islands.

As an artist, I've long been thrilled by one of the most wonderful aspects of subalpine flowers: their intensely saturated hues. The flowers are often also quite large, even on a small, or dwarf, plant, and many are fragrant. All of this is to ensure they're a seductive presence for pollinating insects, as the plants are in a huge hurry to complete their seasons of growth and regeneration. Most of these flower displays occur in June, July, and August, when daylight hours are at their peak.

Avalanche lily (*Erythronium montanum*, LILIACEAE)

The perennial avalanche lily is the first wild-flower to bloom in high-elevation meadows in the Washington and Oregon Cascades, often in June or July, depending on altitude. The flowers appear in the melted-out areas of large snow patches, their delicate white petals in perfect harmony with the snow that surrounds them. The plant grows from 6 to 8 inches high and has shiny leaves, 4 to 8 inches long and half as wide. As the snowmelt accelerates, the lilies spangle entire meadows with their starry shapes, a scene I painted after a visit to Nisqually Vista at Mount Rainier National Park (see page 129).

Glacier lily (*Erythronium grandiflorum*, LILIACEAE)

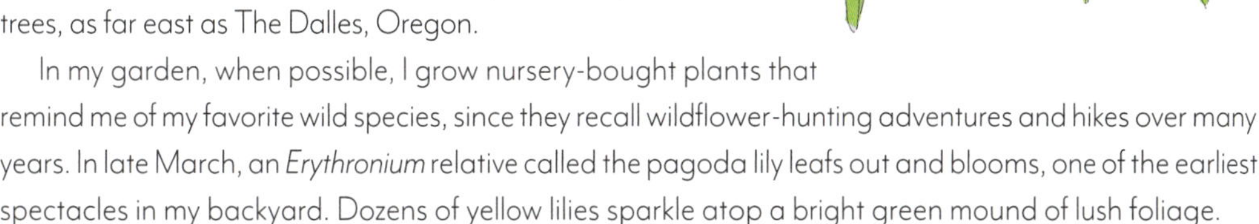

The perennial glacier lily blooms very early as the snow melts, in June or July, depending on elevation. Look for it in high-altitude meadows throughout the West, from the Cascades into Montana, including in Yellowstone National Park and the Rockies. Similar in appearance to the avalanche lily, it can be distinguished by the bright yellow color of its starry petals. It grows from 6 to 12 inches tall, with shiny leaves 4 to 8 inches long and half as wide. Surprisingly, glacier lilies grow in the Columbia River Gorge at much lower elevations, where you can find them on wooded slopes, usually near oak trees, as far east as The Dalles, Oregon.

In my garden, when possible, I grow nursery-bought plants that remind me of my favorite wild species, since they recall wildflower-hunting adventures and hikes over many years. In late March, an *Erythronium* relative called the pagoda lily leafs out and blooms, one of the earliest spectacles in my backyard. Dozens of yellow lilies sparkle atop a bright green mound of lush foliage.

Small-flowered penstemon

(*Penstemon procerus*, SCROPHULARIACEAE)

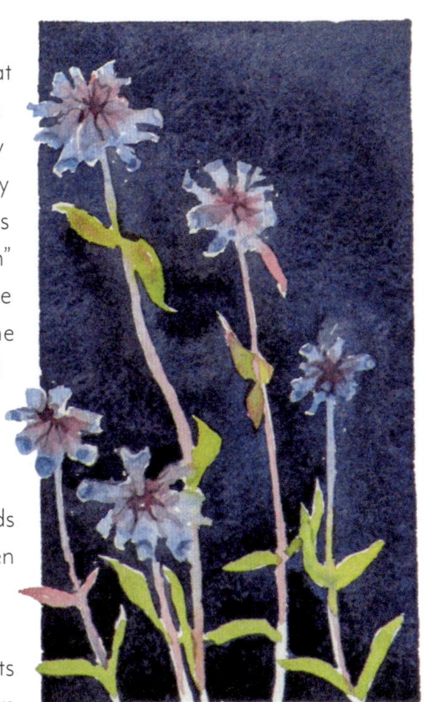

The small-flowered penstemon is a widespread perennial that grows from mid- to high elevations. It can be found as far north as Alaska, south into the Sierra Nevada, and east to the Rocky Mountains in Colorado. Like many penstemons, it prefers rocky slopes, so it is readily found in subalpine habitats. Its species name, *procerus*, is a bit of a misnomer because it means "high" or "tall," whereas this plant is short, only 2 to 12 inches tall. Dee Strickler, penstemon expert, has speculated that the name references its high-altitude habitat. The leaves are thin and lance-shaped and point upward. The tubular flowers grow in tight clusters around the stem, almost forming a ball shape. They are deep blue in color, tinted rose along the outside of the tube, and with a white throat. The flowering time depends on altitude but can occur anytime from May to August. I've seen it on Mount Rainier in August.

I painted this penstemon with watercolor, creating a dramatic dark background to set off the delicate blues and violets of the flowers, a technique I used often in illustrating the flowers in this book.

Mount Rainier National Park

Mount Rainier National Park has been called the most flowery place in the world. The high-elevation meadows there have no equal anywhere, as they are positioned perfectly to receive the onshore flow of Pacific storms. This is especially true at Paradise, the most luxuriant of the park's alpine natural gardens. Located at 5,400 feet on Rainier's south slope, Paradise lies directly in the path of most storms (which usually come from the south and southwest). Its elevation is ideal for maximum snowfall and high moisture levels throughout the year, with most of the snow and rain falling at 5,000 feet. Paradise is typified by a Sitka valerian and showy sedge meadow, alternating with heather woodlands. These higher-altitude flowering communities occur all around the mountain, perched between rocky ridges above the deep glacial valleys.

There are flowers in bloom at all times during the summer at Rainier, beginning with avalanche lilies, followed by glacier lilies and western pasqueflowers, then lupines, monkeyflowers, and asters, and concluding with gentians. Many of these are more intensely hued than in other western locations. In *Wildflowers of Mount Rainier*, Laird Blackwell compares the colors of Lewis's monkeyflower at Rainier to the same plant in the Sierra Nevada, writing that the Rainier flower is "brighter and more vibrant, a touch more intense." This is

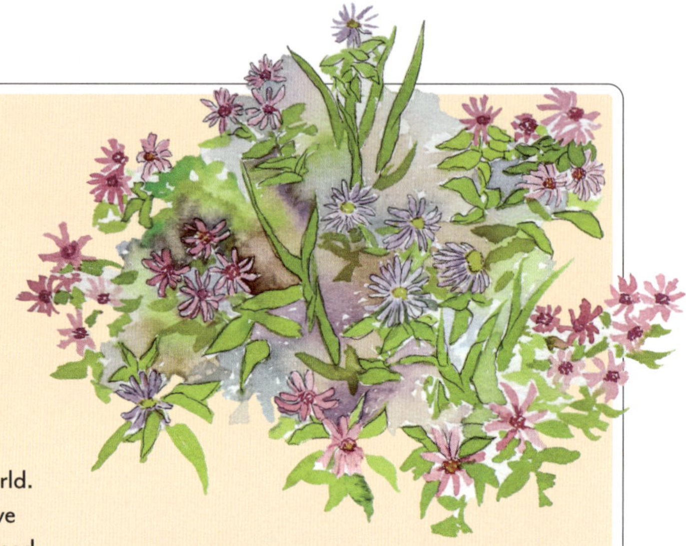

MOUNTAIN ASTERS

because plants adapt to seasonal temperatures by displaying deeper pigmentation; in their cooler and shorter bloom periods, they must try even harder to attract pollinators. Another common high-elevation strategy is dwarfing, as are features like dish-shaped flowers and hairiness (for warmth).

Climate change is shifting the landscape at Rainier. As studies of current and historical trends have shown, Rainier's subalpine forests of firs and hemlocks advance into the meadows in periods of warming. This gradual encroachment threatens not only the wildflowers but also their pollinators. Without sufficient nectar, adult butterflies won't have the necessary energy to reproduce. The warmer, drier conditions created by climate change mean plants shrivel sooner. Pollinators lay eggs on leaves, but if there is nothing left for the larvae and caterpillars to eat, they won't mature into the beautiful fritillaries, blues, and swallowtails that are part of the meadow experience at Mount Rainier. Park and citizen scientists are monitoring the health of the meadows and the butterflies, documenting changes that will then influence public policy.

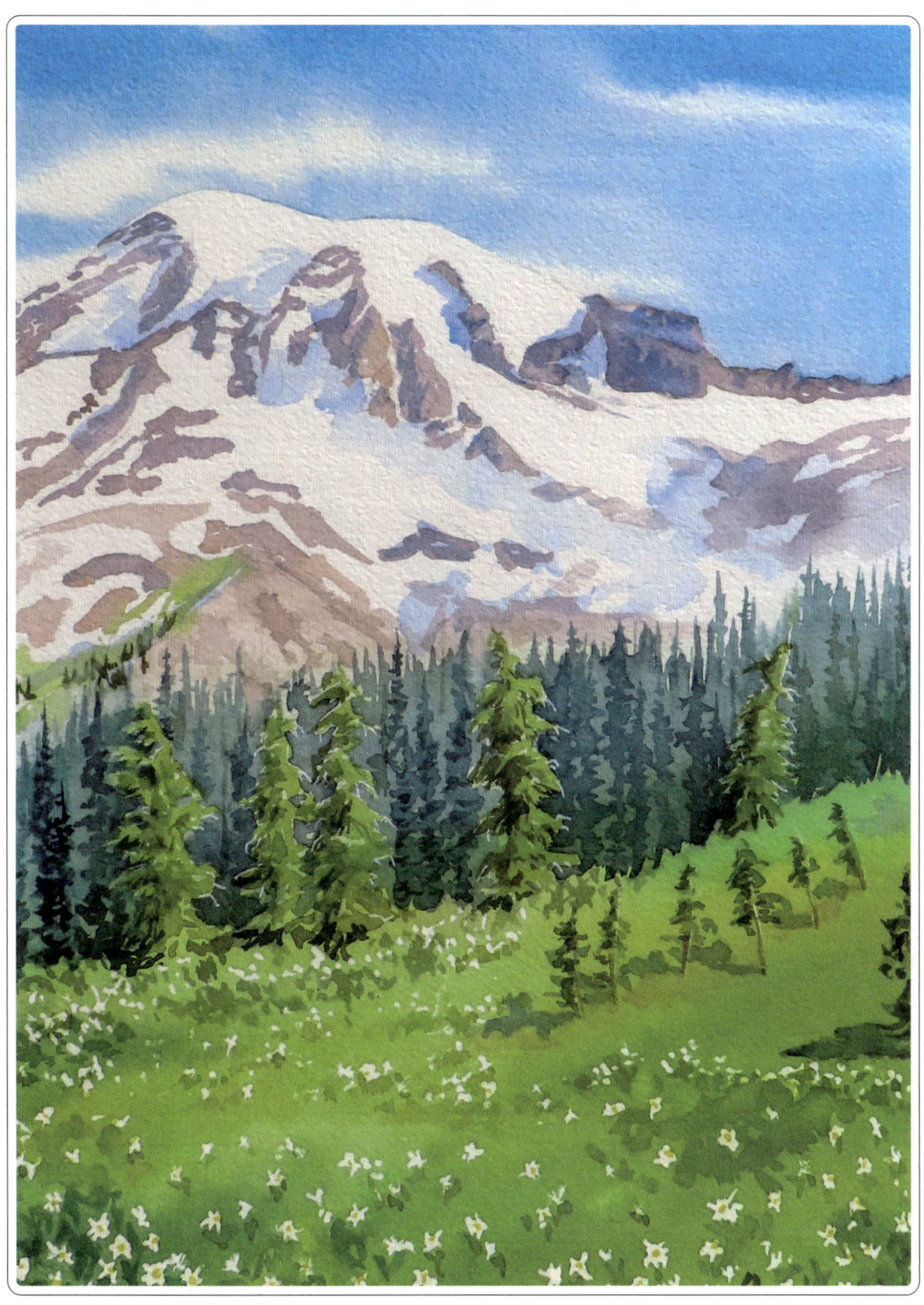

AVALANCHE LILIES, NISQUALLY VISTA, MOUNT RAINIER NATIONAL PARK

Cascade aster (*Aster ledophyllus*, ASTERACEAE)

Asters are very common late-summer ray-and-disk-type perennials that grow at elevations from 4,000 to 6,500 feet, in meadows and on rocky slopes in the Cascades of Washington, Oregon, and Northern California. The stems are up to 3 feet tall, and elliptical leaves with shiny upper surfaces and hairy undersides emerge from the hairy stems, all growing from a woody base. The lower leaves are smaller, with the middle and upper leaves equal in length. The daisy-like flowers consist of up to twenty-one rays emanating from a central yellow-orange disk. Colors range from pink to pinkish-violet to blue. The flowers attract many pollinators, including the fritillary and the alpine blue butterfly, as I've observed along the trail at Sunrise in Mount Rainier National Park. On a September visit, the only flowers remaining were gentians and asters. I loved the visual drama and strong values contrast of the aster, the butterfly, and the white snow of Rainier. Fritillaries and bees were desperately seeking pollen, and they reminded me of the human visitors on this sunny fall day, all of us grasping at our last chance for sunshine before the rains came.

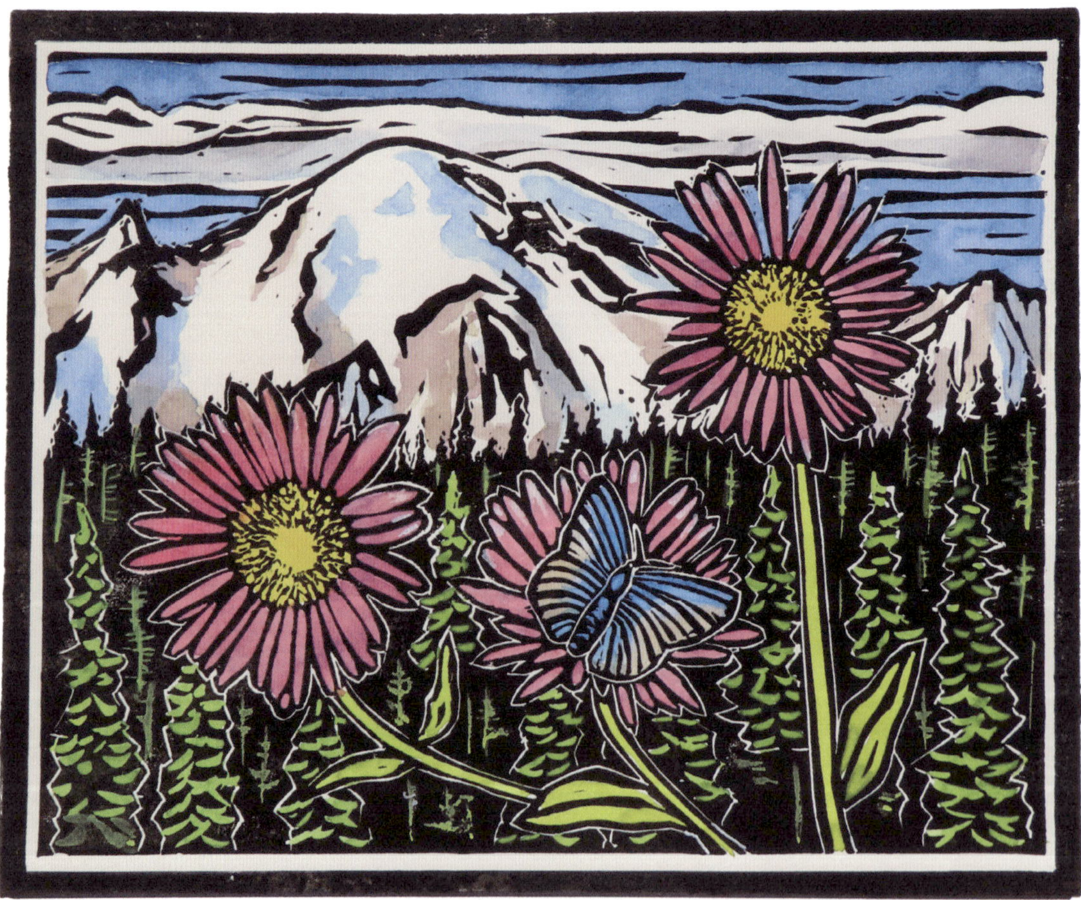

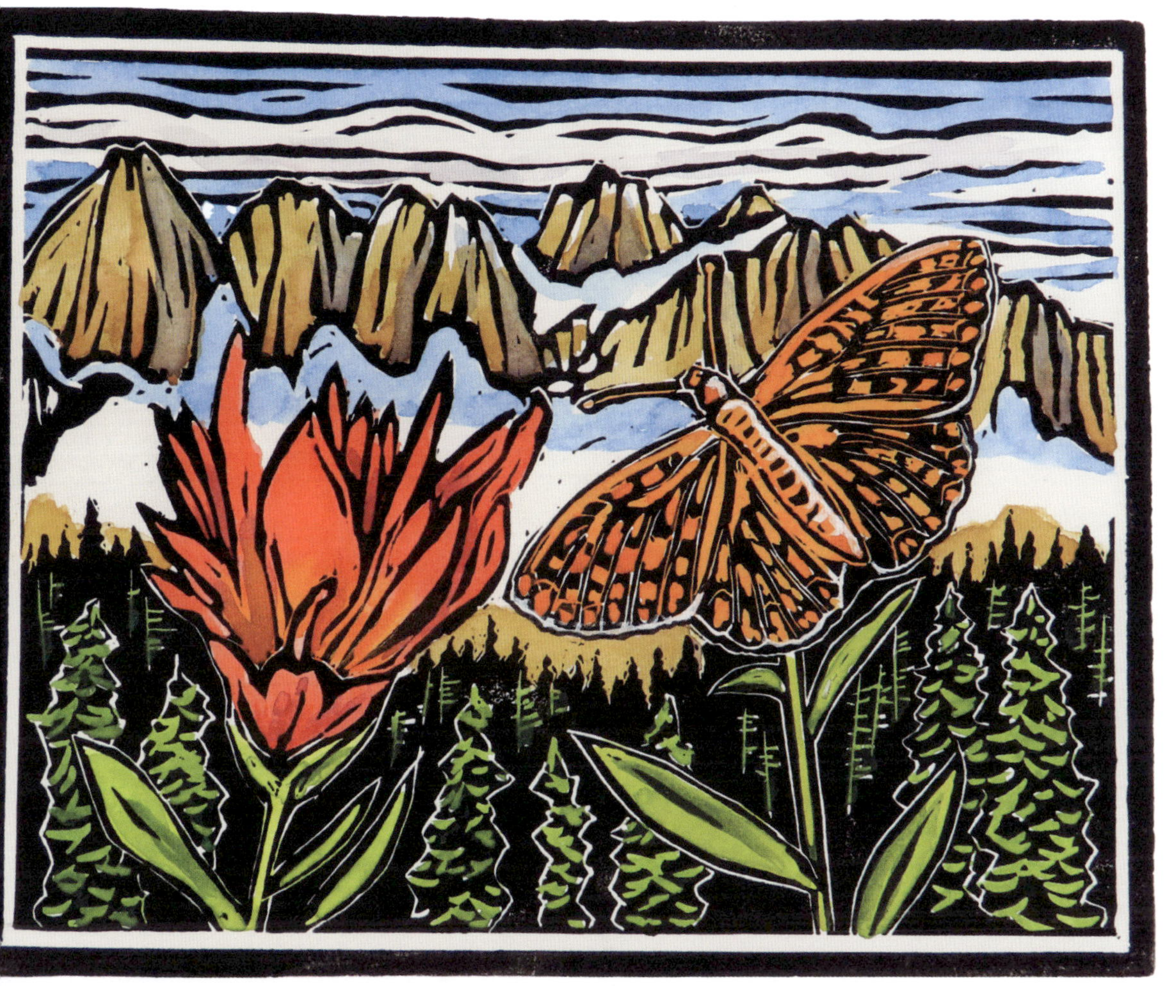

Alpine harsh paintbrush (*Castilleja hispida*, SCROPHULARIACEAE)

The perennial harsh paintbrush, with its distinctive scarlet hues, grows at elevations from 1,000 to 5,000 feet and blooms from mid-spring to midsummer. It's common in grassy meadows and forest fringes in Washington and Oregon, both west and east of the Cascades. The stems are 8 to 24 inches tall, with small lower leaves; the upper leaves develop five to seven lobes. The bracts and some upper leaves carry the color, which can be red, orange, or even yellow, attracting pollinators and hummingbirds. Paintbrushes are hemiparasites, gathering nutrients from the roots of other plants. The woodblock print pictures a northwestern fritillary visiting a blooming plant near Washington Pass in the North Cascades. I imagined this meeting of pollinator and flower, finding in their hues a likely compatibility—the ochres, golds, and rust tints of the Golden Horn granite batholith, the seductive scarlet paintbrush, and the sienna butterfly.

Mountain pride
(*Penstemon newberryi,* SCROPHULARIACEAE)

This aptly named perennial penstemon, flowering in midsummer—and incidentally, John Muir's favorite flower—grows in southernmost Oregon and in California, in the northern coast ranges, the Cascades, and the Sierra Nevada. Its preferred habitat is rocky slopes and cliffs from 2,000 to 11,500 feet. It is quite shrubby but grows no taller than 12 inches, with a woody base and flower stems carrying basal, lance-shaped evergreen leaves. Narrow, tubular, two-lipped flowers, 1 to 1½ inches long, are clustered at the top of each stem in hues from cherry red to violet-rose.

A trip up the Tioga Road with my students from Yosemite Conservancy was a highlight of the class I taught there one June. We walked a short distance up the granite slabs from Olmsted Point and were astonished at the variety of flowers blooming. It was not only the marvelous views but also the plant life growing right out of the cracks in the rocks that made this one of the most precious adventures I've ever had. I made a watercolor sketch on-site, and later, back in the studio, I felt that it needed more definition, so I added some pen lines.

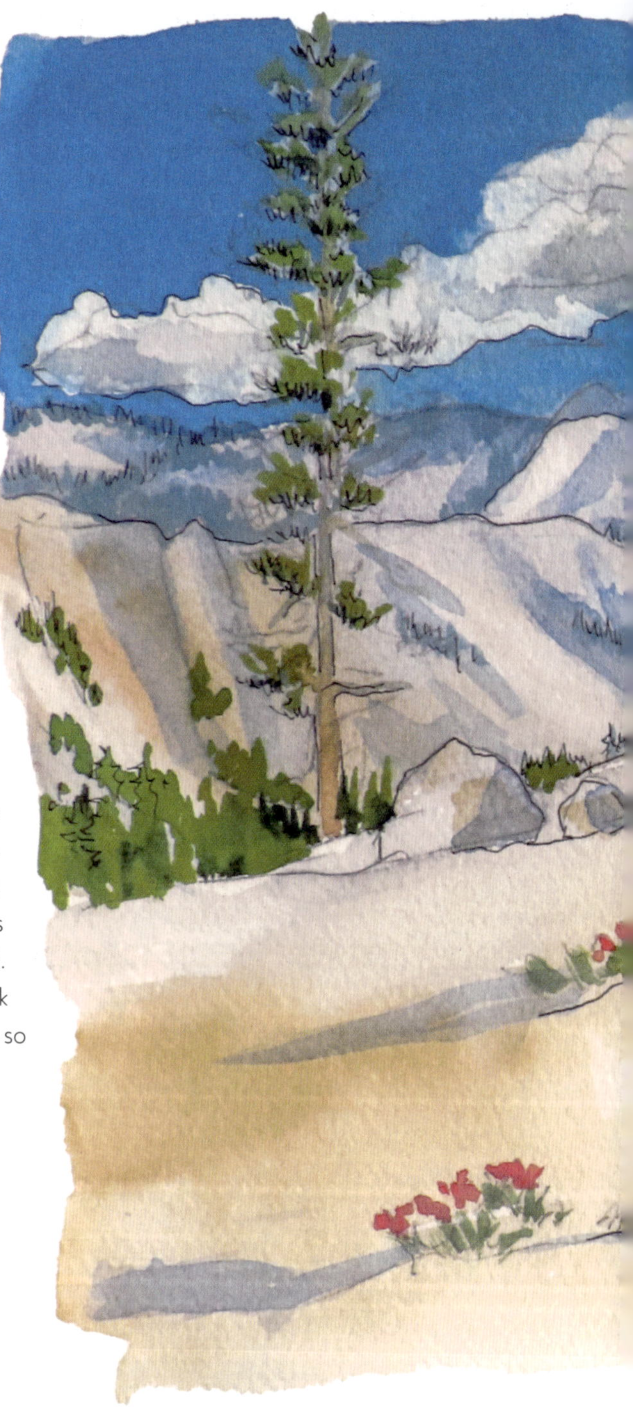

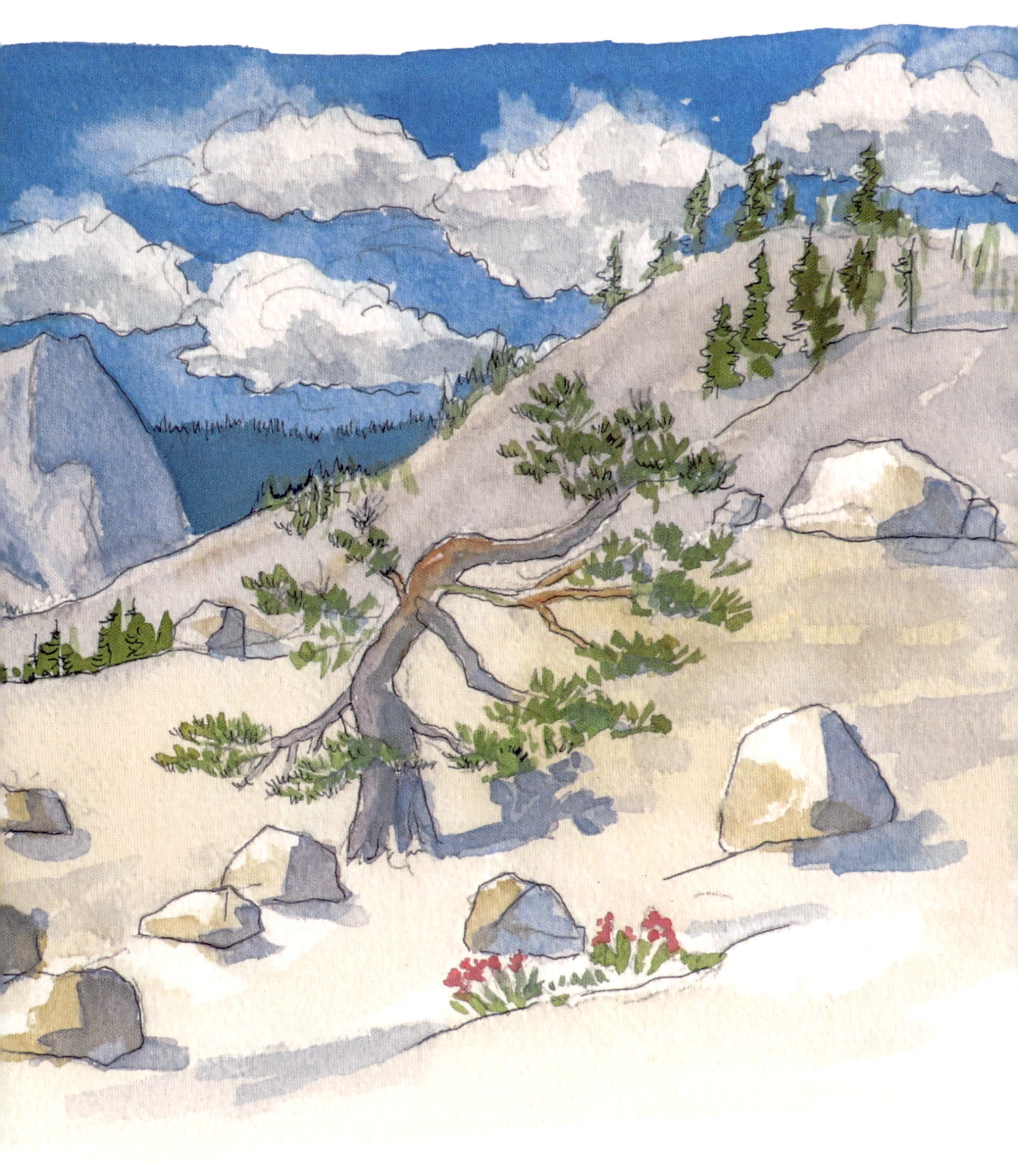

Shrubby cinquefoil (*Potentilla fruticosa*, ROSACEAE)

The perennial shrubby cinquefoil, also known as *Dasiphora floribunda*, is common in the western Washington Cascades as well as in eastern Oregon. A related plant, the fan-leaf cinquefoil, grows in the California Cascades and the Sierra Nevada. This 2-to-4-foot-tall woody shrub has tiny oval leaves less than 1 inch long. One or more yellow flowers grow at the end of each twig, with five or more petals surrounding a central disk. Masses of the flowery shrubs make an impressive display at Mount Rainier National Park in late summer, although it can bloom all summer long in the lower elevations of its range—it is found from 5,000 to 11,000 feet, depending on latitude. I painted this watercolor view of imposing Mount Rainier with cheerful cinquefoil flowering in the foreground from the Wonderland Trail near Berkeley Park. Cinquefoil is a popular garden plant, and I grow it in my backyard, where it blooms from July until frost.

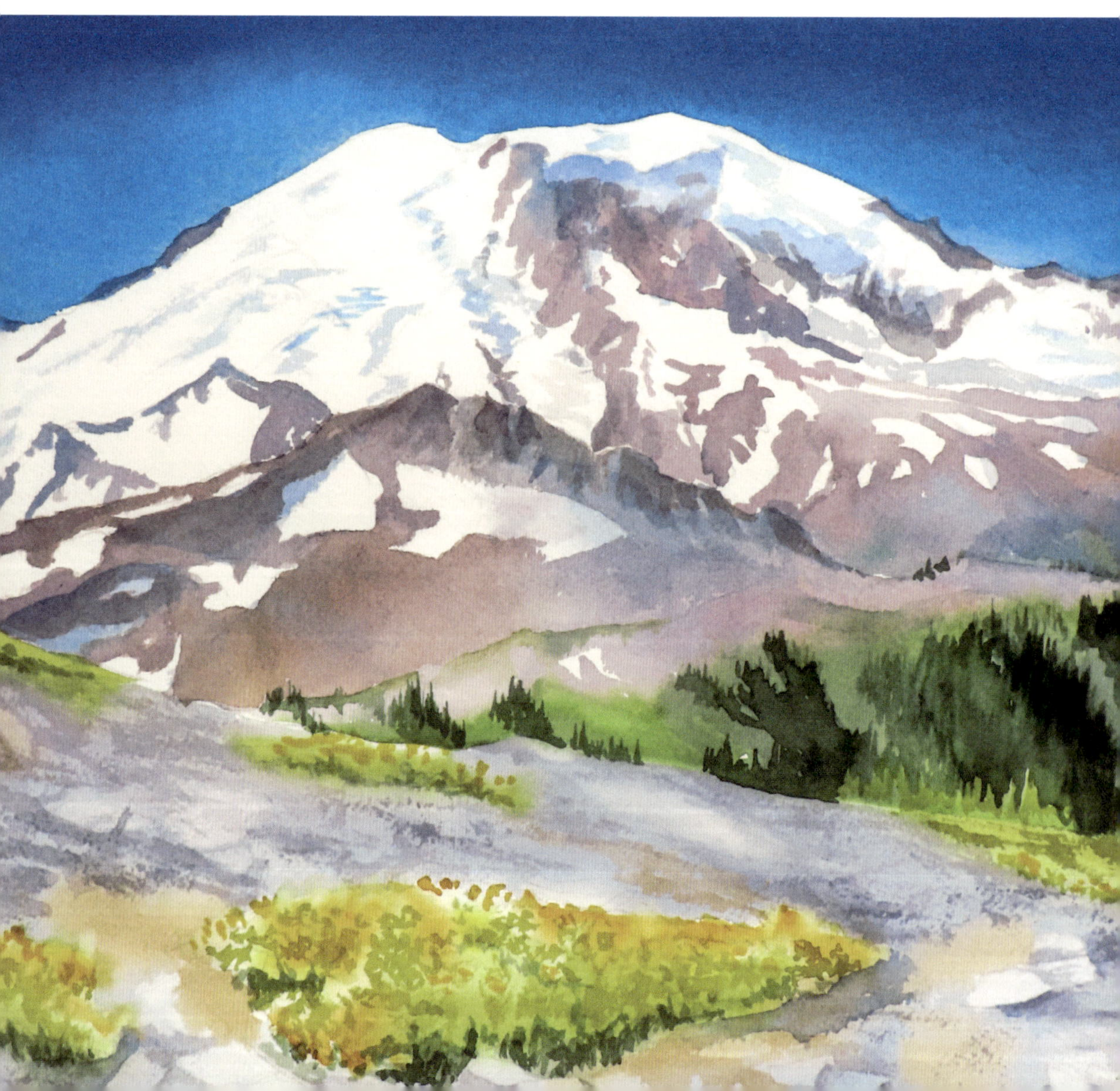

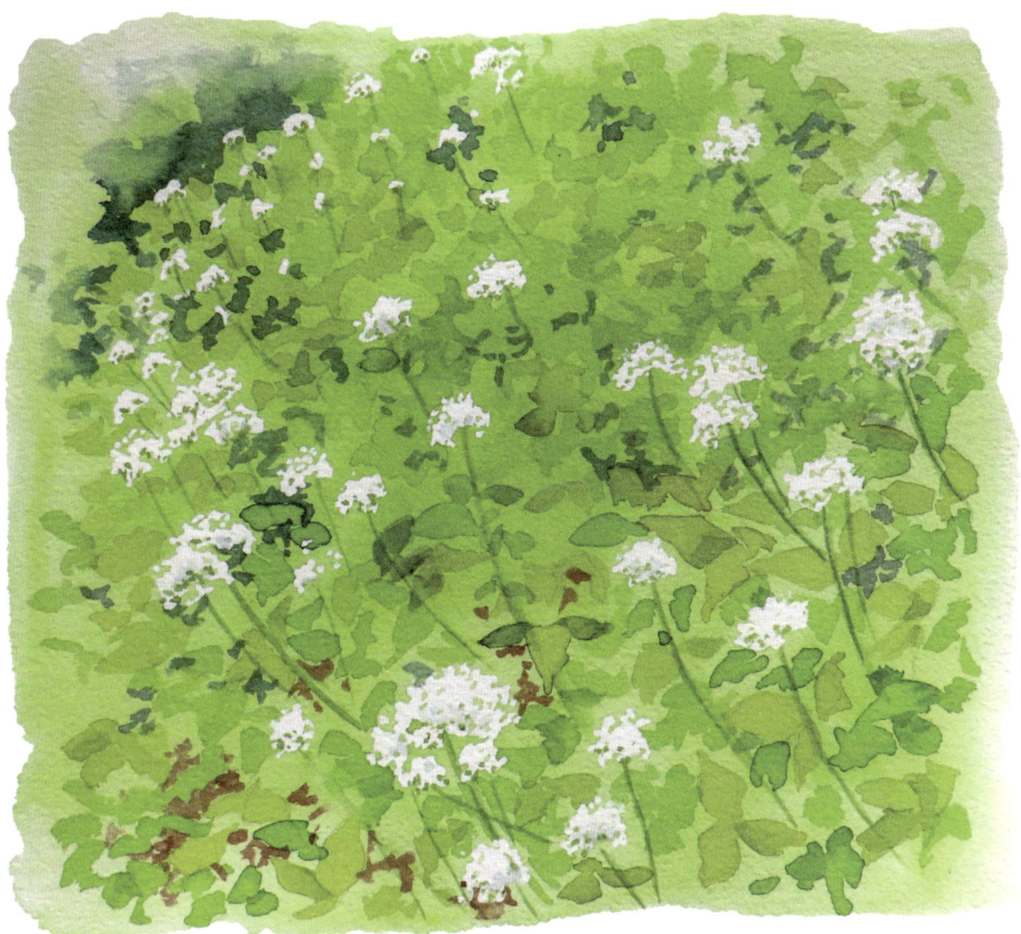

Sitka valerian (*Valeriana sitchensis*, VALERIANACEAE)

The perennial Sitka valerian is a delicate midsummer wildflower found in moist subalpine meadows, usually in airy white masses that give the meadows a feeling of purity and freshness. They are happiest in wet places, and I've seen them in the North Cascades at Stevens Pass, in the central Cascades, and most impressively, perhaps, at Mount Rainier National Park, where they filled an entire forest opening, growing upright even though the meadow took a dizzying 45-degree descent. The plants can grow up to 4 feet tall, with sturdy stems and leaves that are lobed or coarsely toothed. The compact flower heads are composed of many tiny flowers.

I painted this watercolor by sketching in the general shapes of the flowers, wetting the entire paper except the whites of the flowers, and then laying in various washes of green. I worked in stages, with the darker greens added last. The white flowers, seen as positive space, were defined by the negative space of green that surrounded them.

From my journal:

The meadows at Stevens Pass shelter a rich collection of wildflowers throughout the summer—a surprising and fortunate consequence of the deforestation that accompanied the development of the ski resort there. I hiked at the pass, on the Pacific Crest Trail, on an overcast day in early July just before mountain biking season got under way. There were few travelers since it was far too early for the PCT hikers, who show up in August and September after hiking northward from the Sierra and southern Cascades. Without a doubt it is a locale of compromised beauty, with the sprawling ski area and its array of chairs, bull wheels, poles, and cables; who wants a selfie in front of a disused ski area in summertime?

In any other year I would have postponed the outing, thinking that without sun there would be few pollinators, colors might be subdued, I could be cold, and the gloom could be overwhelming, as it often is high in the mountains with fog wreathing dark hemlocks and gray talus slopes. But because of family illness it had been months since I'd gone up to the mountains, and I missed them sorely. Also, prime summer hiking season has been shortened lately by wildfire season, which now may begin in June and last through September. I told myself it's now or never.

In the open forest just above the parking lot, Sitka valerian was blooming, with its tall stalks and airy sprays, and as the way opened to full light, there were luxurious drifts of them everywhere on each side of the trail. Just around the corner on open, sunbathed slopes, hundreds of lupine grew in startling diagonals. Next, I saw mountain asters, and then a small collection of columbine, beloved flower of hummingbirds. I photographed one bloom that was dramatically staged with a backdrop of white granite. Somehow everything was even more beautiful in the soft gray light, all of it a joyful reclaiming of everything that I have loved most in my life.

Colorado columbine
(*Aquilegia coerulea*, RANUNCULACEAE)

The perennial Colorado columbine deserves its designation as the state's official flower, with spectacular blooms up to 3 inches across. The five sepals are blue to lavender, with five scoop-shaped white petals that trail blue spurs. Yellow stamens decorate the inner base of the flowers. The plant can grow up to 3 feet tall and has mostly basal leaves, bluish green underneath and with rounded lobes. This columbine is most commonly found in the moist soil of willow thickets, aspen groves, and forest openings in Idaho, Montana, New Mexico, South Dakota, Utah, and Wyoming, as well as in its namesake Colorado. Bloom time is June to August. I painted the flower without a background, allowing its stunning shape and color to speak for itself.

Western pasqueflower
(*Pulsatilla occidentalis*, RANUNCULACEAE)

At Mount Rainier National Park, the perennial western pasqueflower, also known as the western anemone, appears from early June through autumn in all stages of growth. You may see the pristine 1-to-2-inch white flowers near a recently melted patch of snow in a shaded area, or perhaps you'll encounter an entire sunny meadow that melted out quite early brimming with the curious seedheads, which follow the briefly blooming flowers and can last up to two months. The seeds are attached to countless silky filaments that look like hair. As the plant ages further, the filaments fly away with the seeds attached, so it's no wonder meadows are full of them. In his classic book *A Year in Paradise*, Floyd Schmoe, an early Rainier park ranger, Quaker activist, and naturalist, describes them as "troops of little gray monkeys." Other names include moptop, towhead baby, and old man of the mountain. The nineteenth-century Washington botanist C. V. Piper wrote that the anemone "always excites attention, their plumed heads reminding one irresistibly of the caps worn by grenadiers."

Just outside the Sunrise Visitor Center, on the northeast side of the park, there is a display of wildflowers with signs identifying them. The pasqueflower seedhead is probably the most striking of all. I first noticed the display many years ago on a brief stop at the center after a hike. That small but meaningful Park Service education encouraged me (and, no doubt, many others) to begin recording, photographing, and painting all the flowering marvels I saw on my hikes and adventures. I hope this book spurs you to do the same.

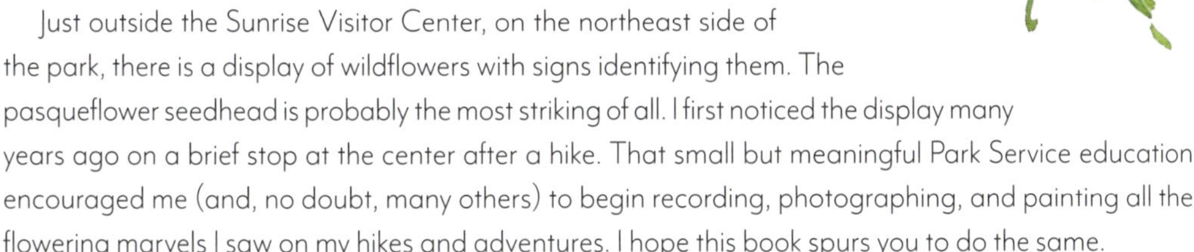

Pasqueflower

Mt. Rainier National Park, Skyline Ridge loop trail above Paradise

High up on Mazama Ridge,
a black bear sits in the background,
he's a creature that does not name
but appears all the same to enjoy
what lies in the open meadow before him,
as many pasqueflowers as stars in the sky,
the blooms reborn each year
after a snow-bound winter sleep
as deep and dreamless as his own.

—Jane Graham George

Explorer's gentian (*Gentiana calycosa*, GENTIANACEAE)

This perennial, also known as bog gentian, is one of the most beautiful plants of the wet alpine habitat and is more deeply appreciated because it is a late flower, seen in early autumn. The plant is 8 to 20 inches tall, sometimes growing prostrate, with round or egg-shaped green leaves. The elegant blooms, deep blue in color, face upward in the form of bells.

On a September day in Mount Rainier National Park, I encountered the most spectacular group of gentians I've ever seen, growing very close to the lower Sluiskin Falls of the Paradise River. The gentians were thriving in that moist location, creating a luxurious splash of blue-violet, a color like the zenith of Rainier's sky. I created both a block print and a pen and watercolor sketch of the gentians. For the block print, I decided to position the flowers on the edge of one of the Reflection Lakes, a few miles southeast of Paradise (see the "Mount Rainier National Park" sidebar, page 128). I so identify the flowers with Rainier that I wanted to show them in this much-photographed location, where the mountain is mirrored in the lake, surrounded by moist subalpine meadows. In the sketch, my goal was simply to reproduce the profusion of flowers.

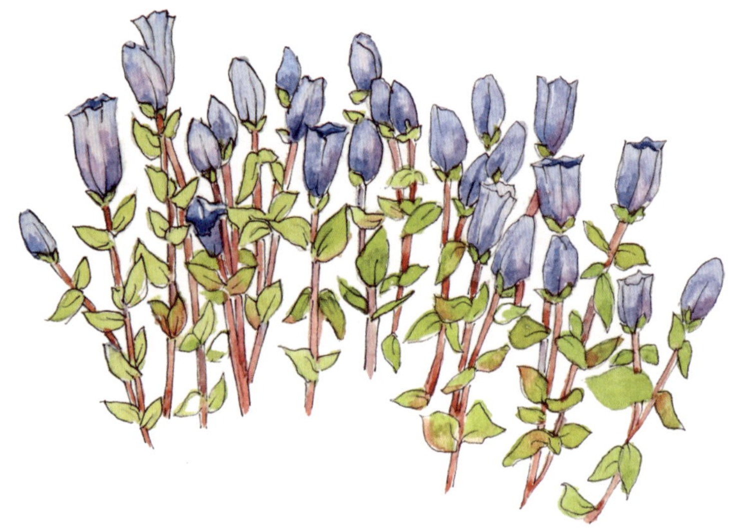

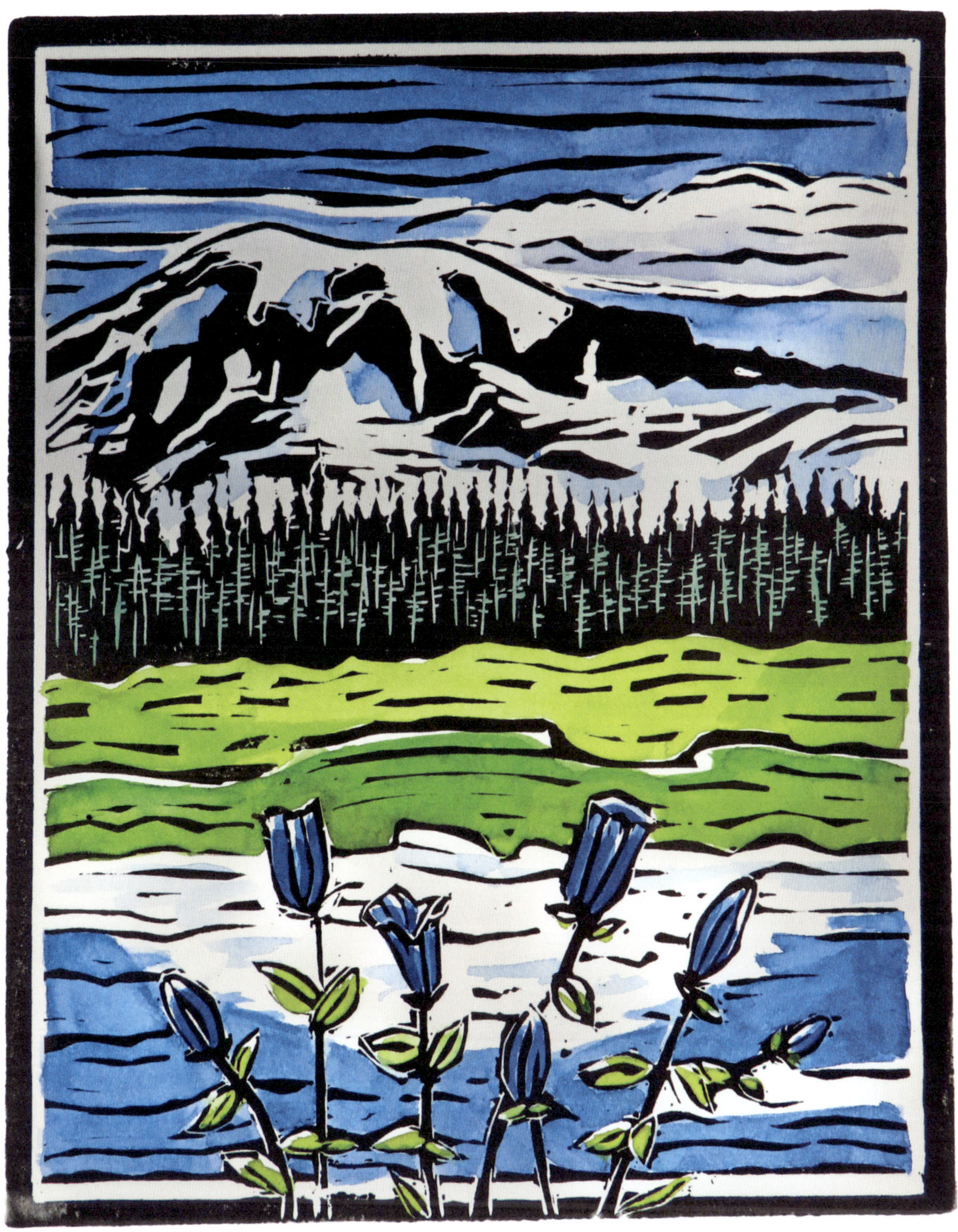

Deserts

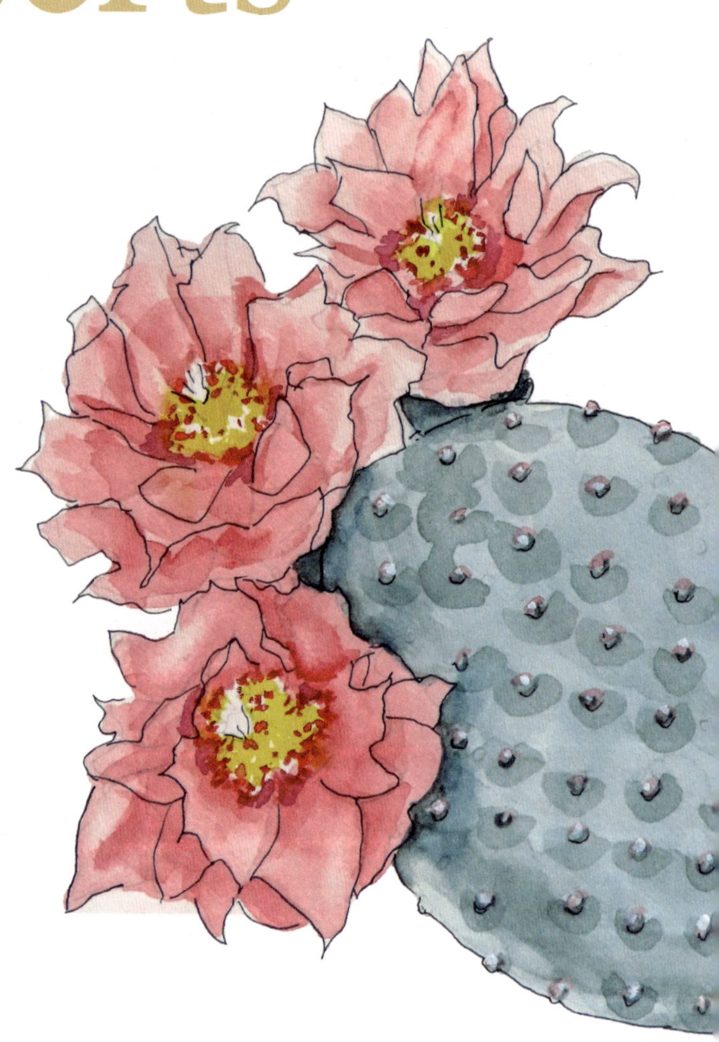

There are four major deserts in the United States: the Great Basin, the Mojave, the Sonoran, and the Chihuahuan. The Great Basin is a cold desert, with frigid winter temperatures, whereas the other three are classified as hot deserts, with extreme temperatures in summer. Each desert can be further divided into many subcategories, depending on the soil type and the major plant groups that live there. The "hot" deserts can put on spectacular wildflower shows, depending on the amount of rain that falls in winter.

The Great Basin has the most limited plant life, with only 800 species; it is located mostly in Nevada and Utah, although there are small sections in southern Idaho and eastern Oregon, eastern California and northernmost Arizona, and southwest Wyoming. The Mojave, found in Nevada and California, has greater diversity, with 1,700 to 2,000 plant species. The Sonoran Desert, largely in Arizona, is extremely plant-rich, with up to 2,000 species. The Chihuahuan Desert, most of which lies in Mexico—although there are small parts of it in eastern Arizona, New Mexico, and Trans-Pecos Texas—is considered not only the most diverse desert in the Western Hemisphere (and the largest in North America) but also one of the most diverse arid regions in the world, with almost 3,500 plant species, including more than 500 of the world's nearly 2,000 species of cactus.

The Sonoran and Chihuahuan Deserts have what is known as a "bimodal precipitation" pattern, with frequent, low-intensity rains in December and January, as in the Mojave (while at the same time, snow is falling in the Great Basin Desert), but with the addition of summer monsoons, weather systems that travel up from Mexico. This pattern supports both warm- and cool-season flora and fauna.

Desert wildflowers are mostly annuals, meaning that they germinate, flower, and set seed all in one season. They might be described as "avoiders." They evade the dry periods by virtually disappearing, spending most of the year (or sometimes many years) as seeds, thus buying a future for themselves. One study in the Sonoran Desert estimated the density of the seeds littering the desert floor to be between five thousand and ten thousand seeds per square meter. During a wet year, wildflowers can display huge mats of color in the desert as thousands of seeds burst into bloom (see the "Superblooms" sidebar in the Introduction).

Soil moisture levels must be ample, and daytime temperatures must be relatively cool, for the winter annuals to germinate, grow, and reproduce. Germination typically takes place in fall in the hot deserts. During this window, there must be a soaking rain of at least 1 inch to induce mass germination. Just 1 inch of rain provides enough soil moisture to allow seedlings to mature and produce seed, even if no more rain falls in that season. If rainfall is low, the plants remain small and may produce only a single flower and a few seeds, but that's adequate to ensure a future generation. Many people think that spring rain causes the wildflower display, but it is rain in the previous fall that precipitates growth.

Often, the hot-desert wildflowers produce two seed leaves during germination while they establish healthy root systems; then they may produce a rosette of leaves that lie flat on the ground, which allows them to receive maximum daytime warmth in winter, while also reducing water loss from the leaves. As spring approaches, these plants produce their flowers, frequently large and brilliantly colored.

Great Basin Desert

The Great Basin Desert, the largest desert in the United States at 209,000 square miles, is found in eastern Oregon, eastern California, southern Idaho, most of Nevada, western Utah, northernmost Arizona, and southwestern Wyoming. Rugged mountain ranges with peaks up to 10,000 feet parallel broad basins with desert scrub at elevations of about 4,000 feet. The desert's boundaries are often defined by the flow of water: within what is known as the Hydrographic Great Basin, precipitation evaporates, sinks underground, or flows into saline lakes; there is no flow to the Pacific Ocean or to the Gulf of Mexico. The Great Basin is classified as a cold desert, with frigid winters. The climate is partially the result of the basin being in the rain shadow of the Cascade Range in the north and the Sierra Nevada in the south.

Vegetation in the Great Basin is mostly limited to low-growing, small-leafed shrubs like greasewood and big sagebrush. Some areas of the Columbia Plateau in Washington might also be categorized as a cold desert; although the plant life there is a bit more diverse, the region is home to many of the same species found farther south.

The Colorado Plateau, another cold desert, is sometimes included in the Great Basin Desert region, even though its rivers flow into the Pacific and the Gulf of Mexico. When the plateau is more precisely designated a floristic province, defined by its taxonomic relationships, it is clear that the plant life there is related to the flora of the Great Basin and, in some cases, the Mojave. Encompassing eastern Utah, southwestern Colorado, northwestern New Mexico, and the northeast quarter of Arizona, the Colorado Plateau holds some of our most spectacular national parks and monuments, including Grand Canyon, Bryce Canyon, Arches, and Canyonlands. Zion and Grand Staircase–Escalante lie in and along the edge of the plateau. Because the region is surrounded by mountains, it is relatively geographically isolated, which has allowed for the evolution of many endemic species. Among the most interesting are the plants of the hanging gardens of the red rock (or slickrock) canyons (see the "Hanging Gardens of the Red Rock Canyons" sidebar, page 144).

Plains prickly pear cactus (*Opuntia polyacantha*, CACTACEAE)

The plains prickly pear cactus is widespread, growing as far north as Canada. It's a very common perennial plant of the Great Basin Desert, becoming more prevalent the farther south you go. I remember being surprised by the number I saw growing on the cliffs above the Upper Missouri River in north-central Montana. Its height is from 4 to 12 inches, and the flattened stems, or pads, can be up to 4 inches across and 5 inches long. The cactus forms clumps that can be several yards wide. In addition to the spines—the typical long needles growing from the areoles—there are also glochids, which are small bristles or barbs, more troublesome to step on or touch than the spines themselves. (Some people carry tweezers in prickly pear country in case they encounter a glochid!) Prickly pears bloom in May and June, producing 2-to-3-inch-wide blossoms, typically cream to yellow in color, but red is not uncommon. Often, multiple colors appear on a single plant. I started this illustration with watercolor on the flowers, then added colored pencil to the cactus pads, and completed the sketch with a black fine-point pen to indicate the spines.

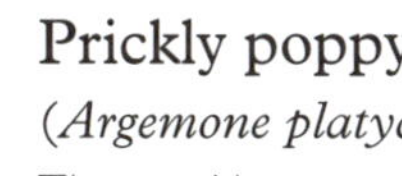

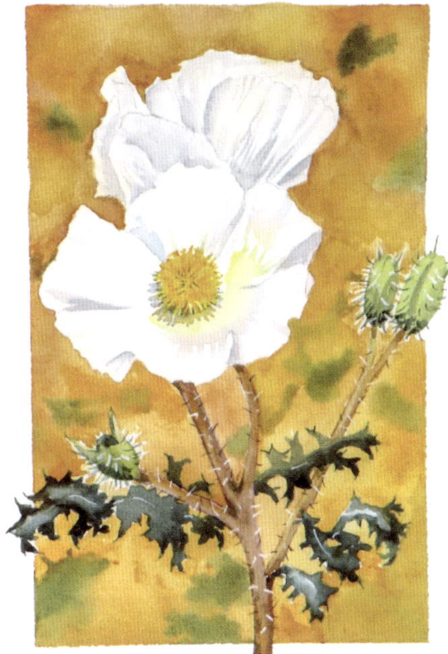

Prickly poppy

(*Argemone platyceras*, PAPAVERACEAE)

The prickly poppy is found throughout the Great Basin Desert; related species live in the deserts of California and Arizona, commonly in overgrazed and disturbed habitats, including along roadsides. The blue-gray leaves and stems look like those of a thistle, with spines and coarse bristles covering the stems and branches, but the flowers are quite different—delicate, crinkled, and white, with up to six 2-to-3-inch petals surrounding a large golden-stamen-filled center. The bloom time varies widely depending on location—as early as March and as late as November. The prickly poppy was once commonly and aptly known as cowboy's fried egg. I anchored the flower illustration in a yellow-ochre and sage-green watercolor wash, imagining this hue would be indicative of its desert environment.

Hanging Gardens of the Red Rock Canyons

Hanging gardens are one of the most unique features of the red rock canyons of the Colorado Plateau. Ranging from small and seasonal patches with very little vegetation to lush alcoves with many plants, hanging gardens develop where highly permeable sandstones and less permeable layers meet. These moist environments can support rare species—for example, at Utah's Arches National Park, where 8 to 9 percent of the Colorado Plateau's endemic plants grow. Scientists are monitoring the health of the hanging gardens there, specifically the endemics, to see what effects prolonged drought and climate change are having on the number and distribution of several of these species, among them alcove columbine, alcove bog orchid, cave primrose, and Eastwood's monkeyflower.

A notable named hanging garden is Weeping Rock in Zion National Park, also in Utah. The water (called "fossil water" by scientists) that drips from Weeping Rock is more than one thousand years old. It fell as snow or rain on the porous and permeable Navajo Sandstone formation above, slowly percolated down, and finally, above Weeping Rock, encountered a very hard rock layer called the Kayenta Formation. At that point it had nowhere to go and was forced to seep out horizontally along cracks, where alcoves and ledges allowed for the formation of both small and large hanging gardens.

The rock monoliths in Zion shelter many alcoves, including the one painted here, which I saw on the Riverside Walk to the Temple of Sinawava. The spring day was overcast with intermittent rain, and it made all the greens of the newly leafing cottonwoods and perennials appear almost neon in hue. Small flowers were blooming there, including alcove columbines and shooting stars, reminding me of the fresh flowers placed on church altars.

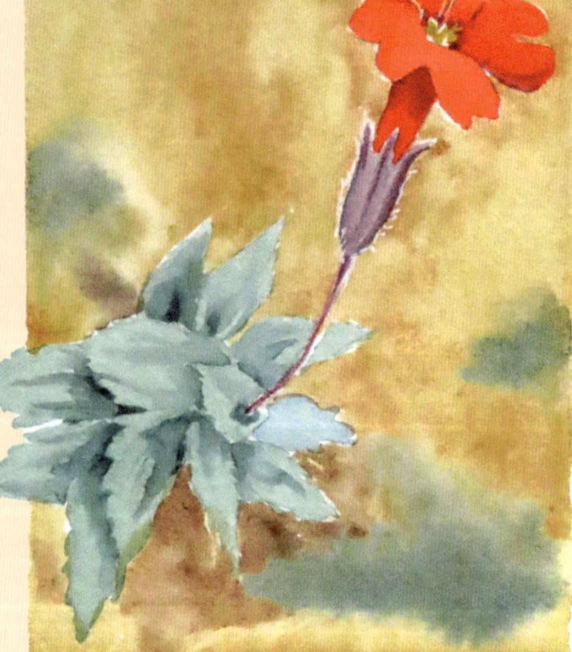

EASTWOOD'S MONKEYFLOWER

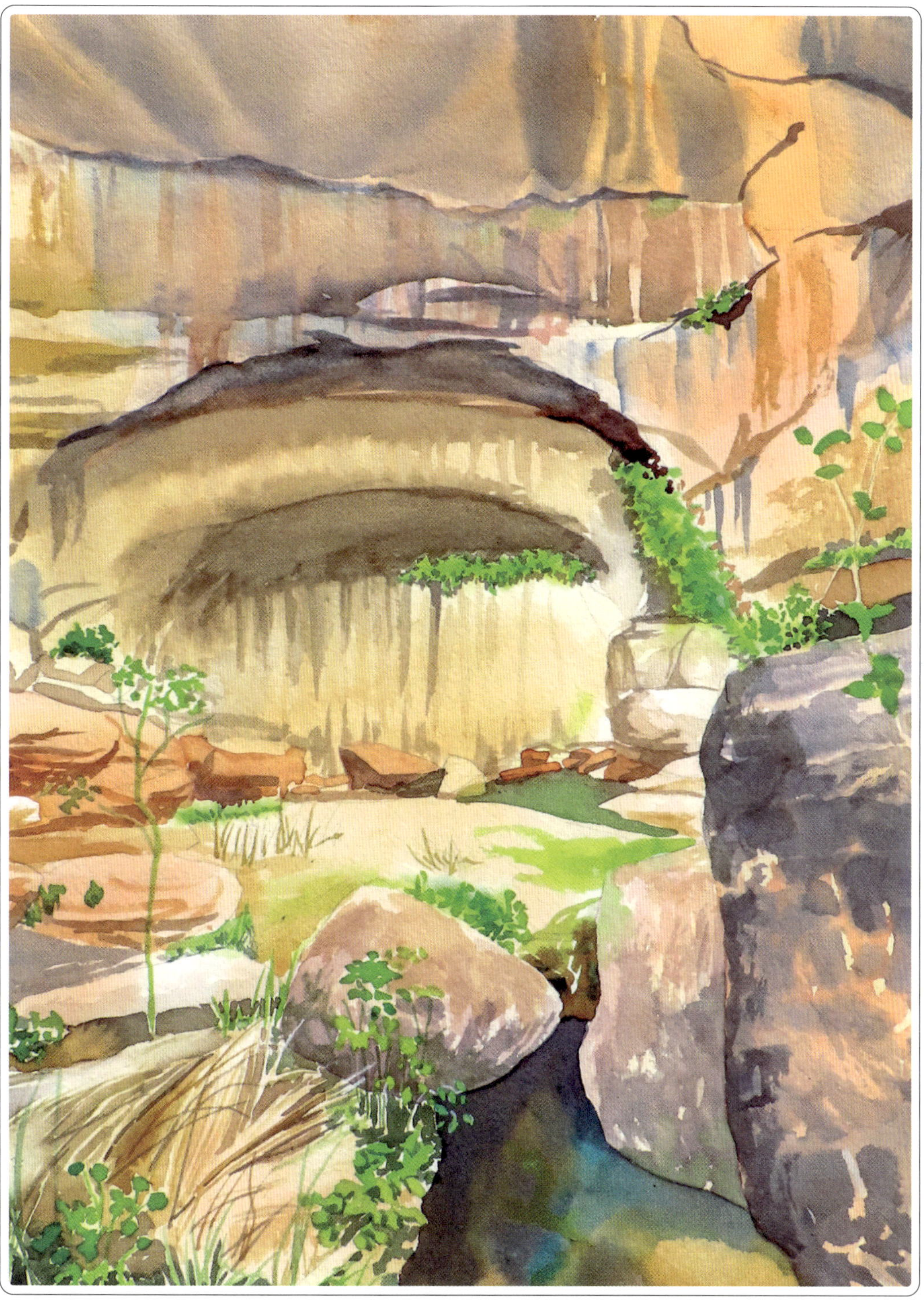

Alcove columbine (*Aquilegia micrantha*, RANUNCULACEAE)

The perennial alcove columbine is endemic to the red rock canyons of the Colorado Plateau—in Utah, in Colorado north to the Wyoming border, and as far south as Arizona. The plant thrives in hanging gardens, where it grows in niches and cracks and on ledges you wouldn't believe capable of supporting lush spring flowers like columbine and shooting stars. The stems can be up to 28 inches tall, but as with the one I illustrated, they often hang semiprostrate. The green leaves are basal and pinnately divided into three lobes. The flowers are white and yellow, sometimes tinged with pink or blue, with five petals and tubes that point backward, as well as five petallike sepals. At least thirteen species of columbine are recognized in Utah, and hybrids develop where ranges overlap, yielding other colors like blue and white, or red.

As I approached a red rock arch on a visit to Zion National Park, I noticed a ledge beneath it and saw the flowering columbine depicted here. It appeared very tiny from where I stood, so I used the zoom feature on my camera to get a closer view. The surrounding rock walls were so magnificent that I decided to do a watercolor to show the habitat (see the sidebar, page 144) and then a smaller, more detailed pen-and-wash illustration of the plant. When painting yellow or white flowers, it's difficult to make them stand out unless you paint a dark background around them or use pen. For this flower of the red rock canyons, I chose to use pen, since a dark watercolor behind it would not have very accurately represented its sandstone habitat.

Two-grooved milkvetch (*Astragalus bisulcatus*, FABACEAE)

Although appealing with its attractive foliage and flowers, the perennial two-grooved milkvetch, also known as locoweed, is poisonous to livestock. It sequesters the toxic chemical selenium, which in excessive amounts is also dangerous to humans, even though it is an essential mineral in our bodies. This milkvetch can be found on the Colorado Plateau and in Great Basin habitats, as well as in Idaho, Montana, and Wyoming. The plant stems are 18 to 28 inches tall and erect, with rows of pinnate leaves that help to identify it as a member of the pea family. Each stem can hold from twenty-five to eighty white, pealike flowers. The pods that develop contain two longitudinal grooves, thus its name.

When I saw two-grooved milkvetch at Utah's Kodachrome Basin State Park in mid-April, it was the sole bloomer. Profusely carpeting the shale canyons and flats of the park, putting on a silvery show, it reminded me of the snow that was still gripping the higher elevations we'd driven through to get there. The bees were as drawn to it as we were, the only game in town! The day we arrived was cold and cloudy and did not show off the splashy colors of the basin. I found the place rather austere and forbidding—until encountering the flowers and the bees.

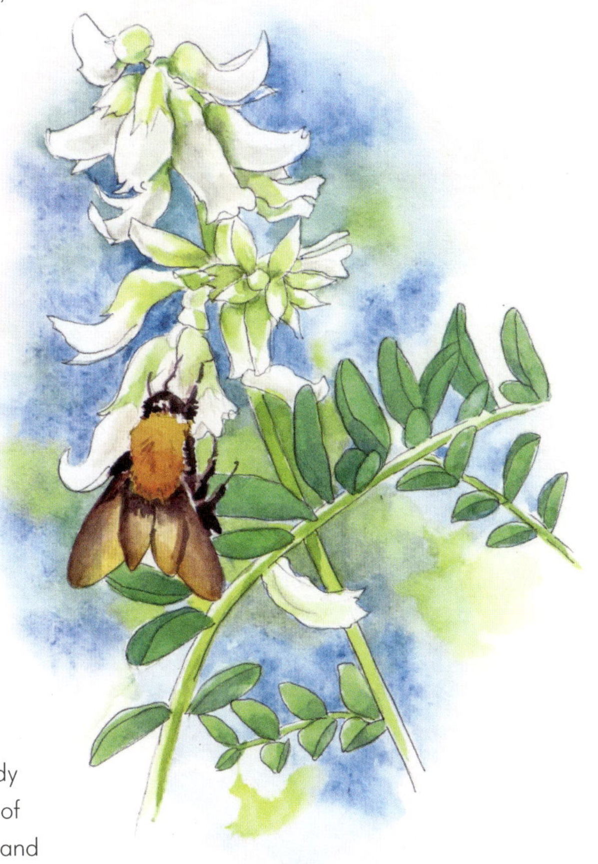

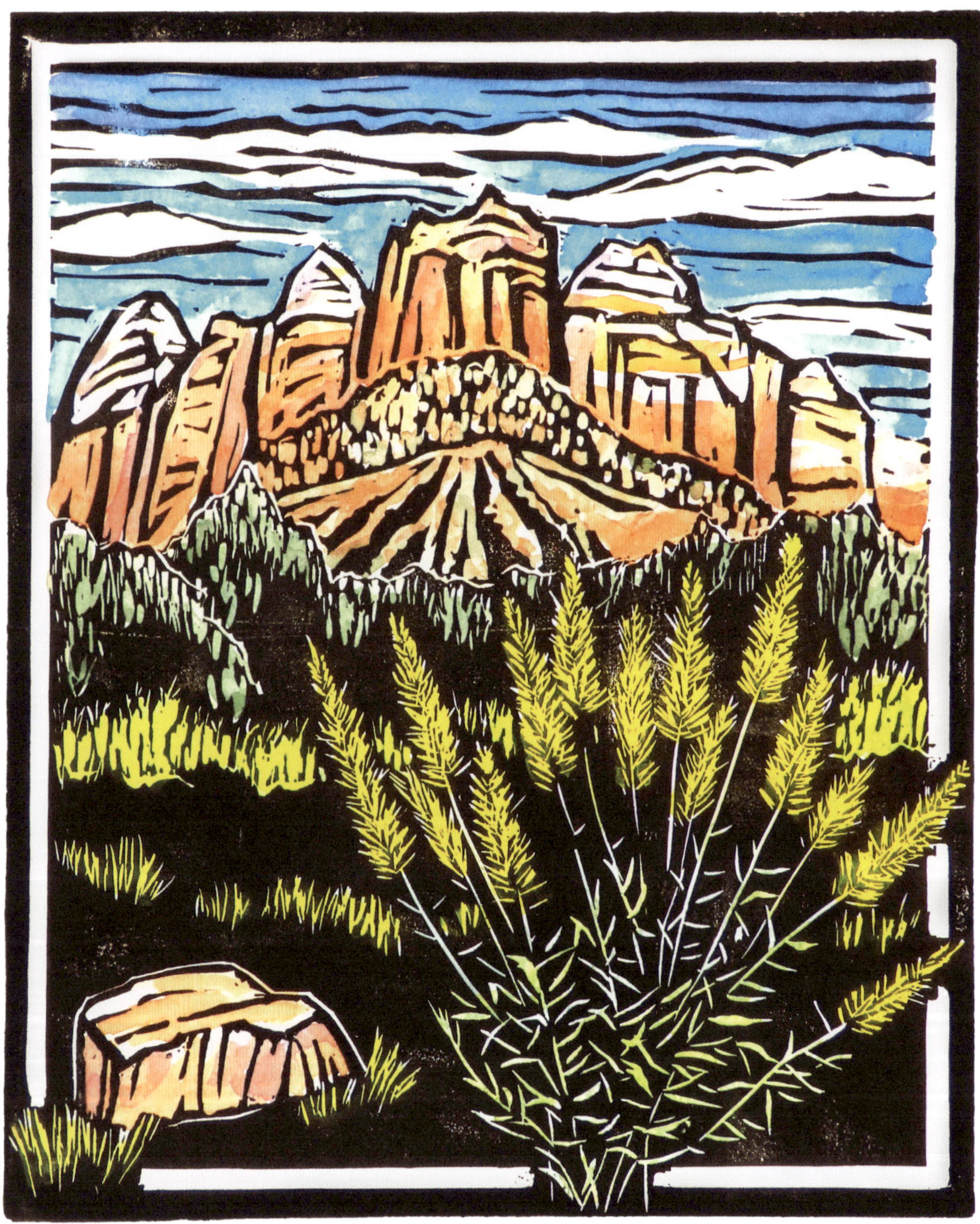

Prince's plume (*Stanleya pinnata*, BRASSICACEAE)

Prince's plume is a perennial plant of the mustard family that prefers clayey or silty soil, often growing on rocky outcrops and in pinyon pine or sagebrush communities. It can be found from Montana south to California and on the Colorado Plateau. Like milkvetch (see Two-Grooved Milkvetch), it accumulates selenium, a mineral that is toxic in higher doses. *Spring Wildflowers of Utah's Red Rock Desert*, by Peter Lesica and Walter Fertig, describes the selenium odor that the crushed leaves give off as "rotten egg stored in a dirty gym sock." I didn't notice the smell myself, maybe because I was so surprised by its tall beauty as I waited in the lineup of cars outside the south entrance to Zion National Park. It blooms in April on branches that are up to 4 feet high, with leaves close to the base, 2 to 6 inches long. The flowers have four yellow petals, each ½ inch long, and stamens twice that length, which give the plant a very airy and elegant silhouette.

Mojave Desert

The Mojave Desert is located in Southern California, extreme southern Nevada, and the lower elevations of northwestern Arizona, as well as in southwestern Utah. Altitudes range from 2,000 to 5,000 feet. It has a winter rainy season, when it can freeze, but not as often or as severely as in the Great Basin Desert. With the conspicuous exception of the Joshua tree (a larger treelike plant), plant life in the Mojave consists largely of low-growing shrubs. The creosote bush, also known as greasewood, grows widely throughout the Mojave. Many wildflowers of the aster family are present as well. Death Valley National Park is the most well-known Mojave domain.

From my journal:

> I had planned to make a trip to the desert Southwest to see the wildflowers in a season that offered the chance to experience a superbloom after a year of unprecedented heavy rain. The snowpack in the mountains of California set fifty-year records, and photos sent by friends in March showed the San Jacinto Mountains covered with snow as they loomed above the Coachella Valley near Palm Desert.

> My worry over a family member's serious case of Covid prevented me from making the desert trip. Meanwhile, I was taking a Zoom class on desert plants from Larry DeBuhr, a retired professor of botany and biology who now lives in Palm Desert. From Larry I learned all about desert plant adaptations and heard weekly reports about the superbloom—over the six weeks of class, students who were local went for hikes in the Coachella Valley and into the foothills and marveled at what they saw. It gave me a serious case of FOMO.

> On the other hand, the superbloom caused a rush to experience it, creating an amusement park atmosphere, and I wasn't at all sorry to miss out on that. But firsthand visual, sensory contact with the desert is exciting—I'm thinking of the scents of sagebrush and creosote bush, the ocotillo's unlikely scarlet blooms, the fluffy-looking teddy-bear cholla, and the enjoyment of walking up

Beavertail cactus (*Opuntia basilaris*, CACTACEAE)

The beavertail is a small perennial cactus that grows to just 1½ feet tall. Its spines are almost nonexistent;
its small, reddish-brown bristles on the flat, paddle-like pads make it a favorite of cactus gardeners. The
bright pink flowers, up to 3 inches across, bloom from March to June, depending on location. I felt that
the sculptural shape of the beavertail's cactus pads, combined with its intensely colored blooms, made it
a perfect subject for the bold look of a block print. In the pen and watercolor sketch, I took a closer look
at its flowers.

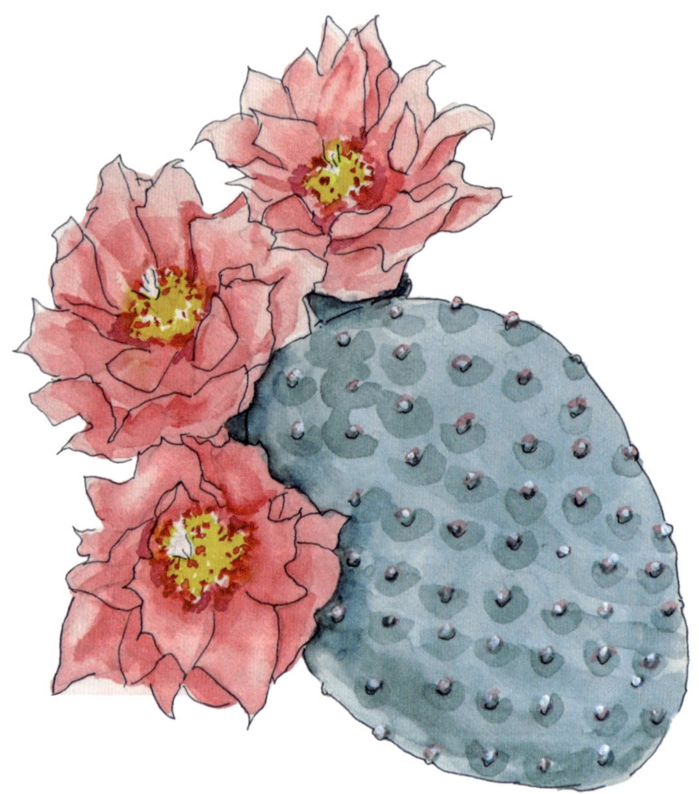

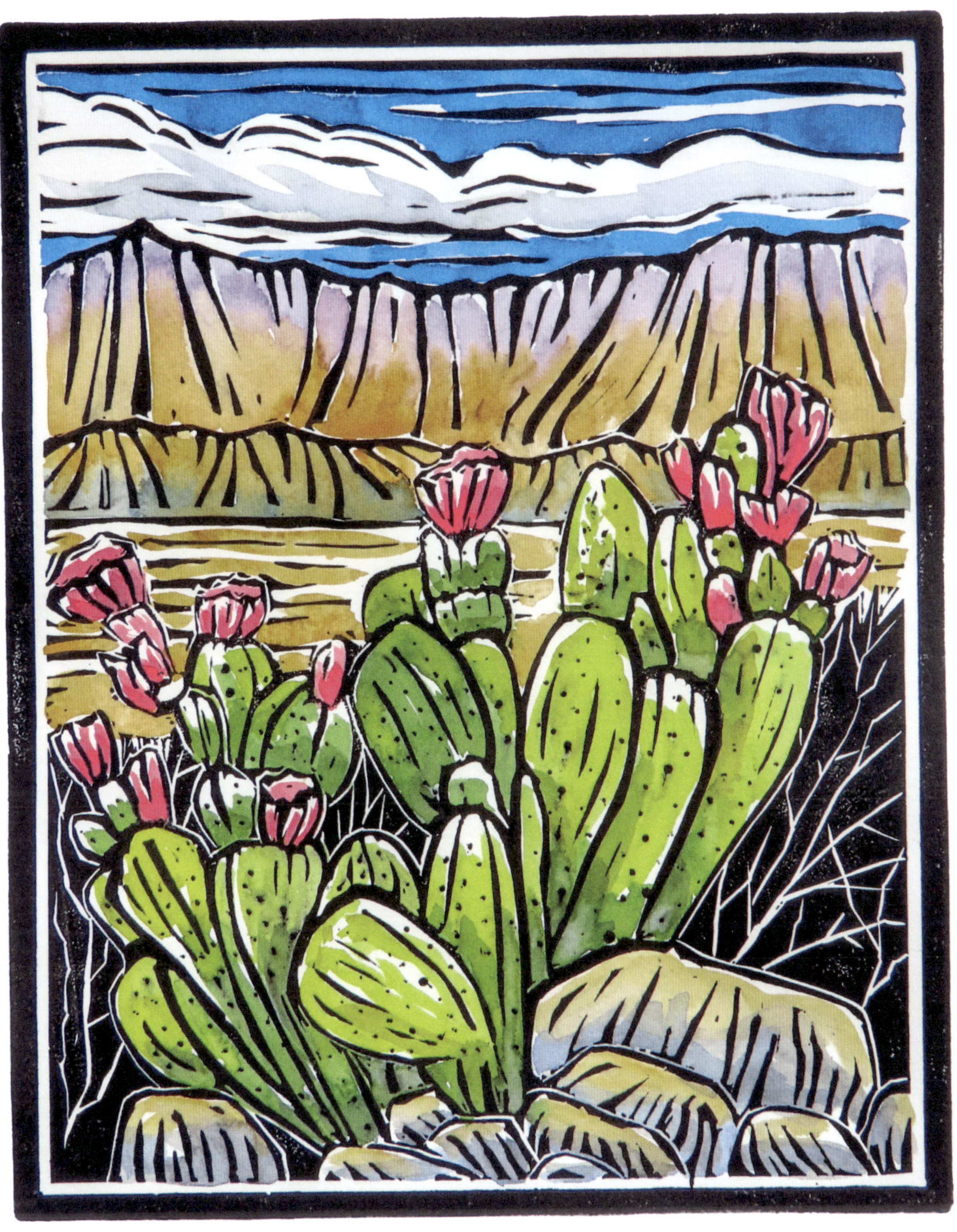

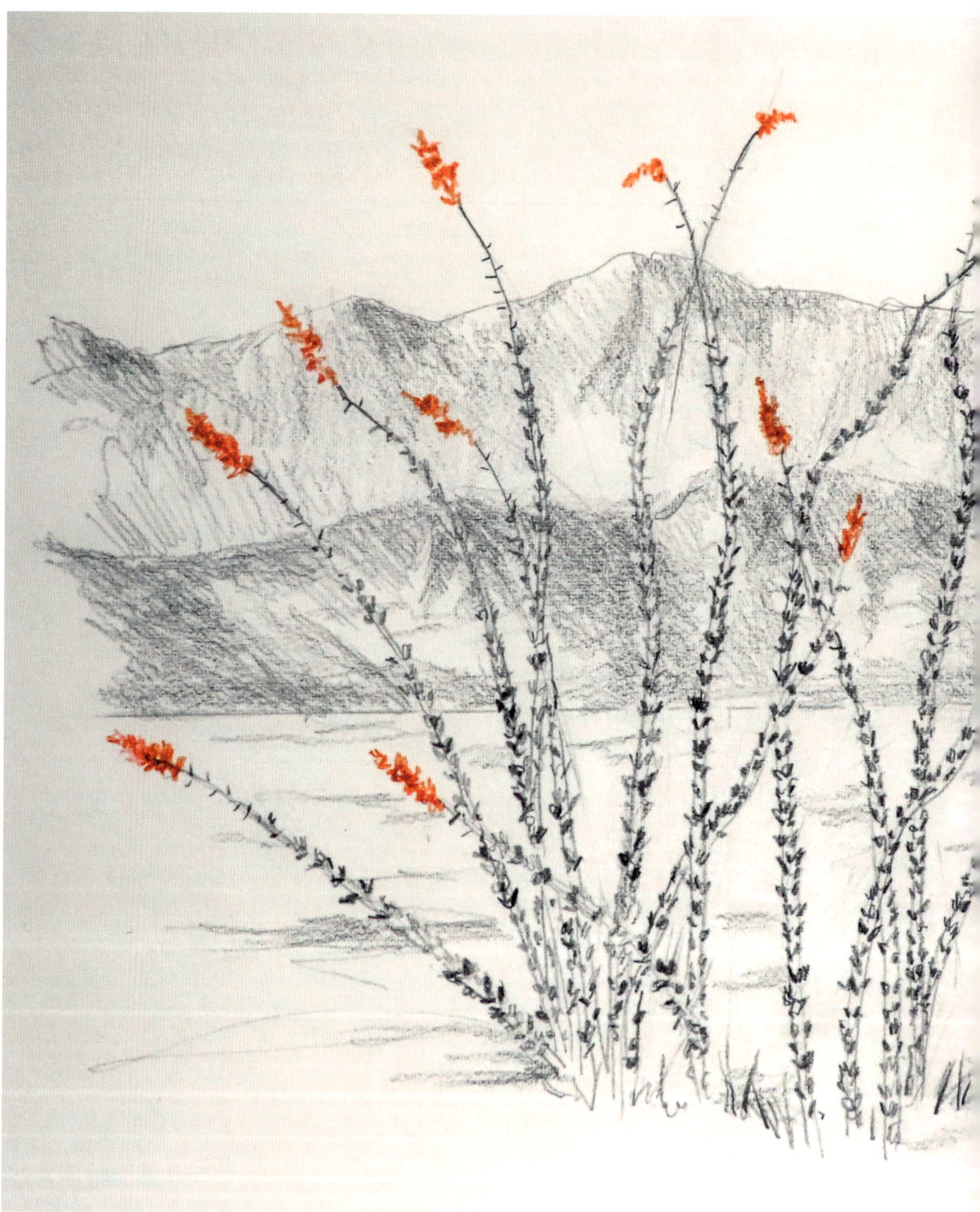

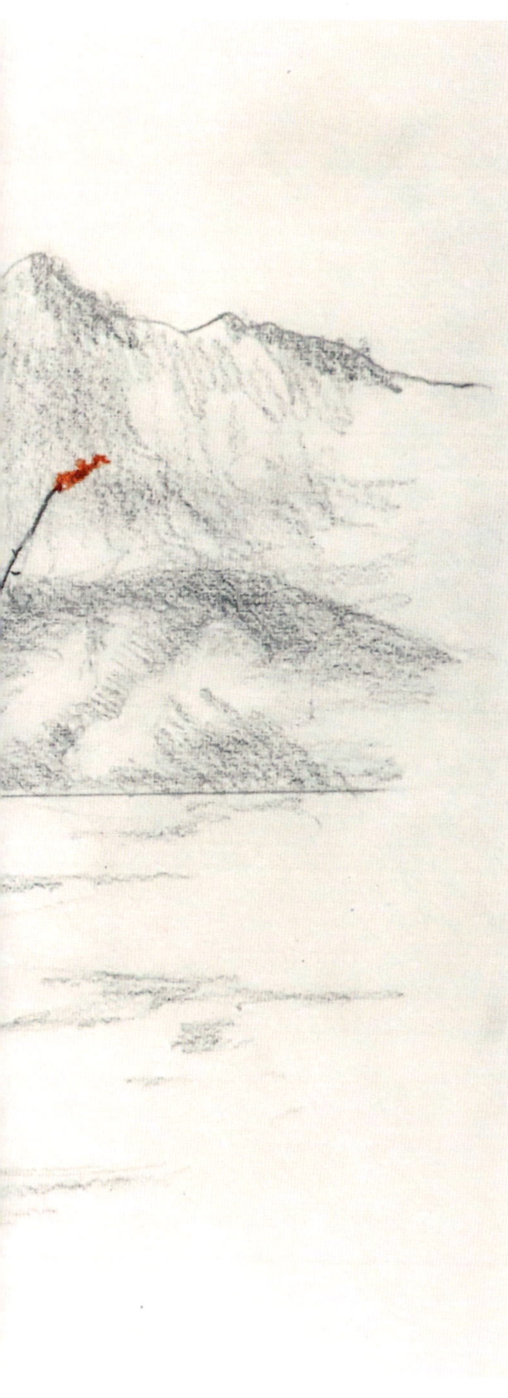

Ocotillo
(*Fouquieria splendens*, FOUQUIERIACEAE)

The perennial ocotillo (Spanish for "little torch") is one of the hallmark species of the desert, growing in all of the major deserts except the Great Basin. It ranges widely across rocky slopes below 4,500 feet, in grasslands as well as deserts. Its dry, thick, spiny stems can reach heights of 20 feet. Native peoples used these stems as a building material, weaving them into mats that they then overlaid with mud, used for roofing and walls. In winter the plants are very forbidding, with their dark, whiplike shapes reaching into the sky—in fact, one of its names is coachwhip. Other names include devil's walking stick, candlewood, and albarda. After a good rain, leaves emerge on the plants; once the soil dries out, the leaves will wither and drop, only to reappear following more rain—a cycle that can repeat several times in a year.

In spring, 1-inch scarlet flowers decorate the tips of the stems, coloring the desert landscape for a brief period of only one to two weeks—a bright display that attracts many hummingbirds to the tubular flowers. Bloom time overlaps with the hummingbird migration, which can begin in early March and go through May, giving the birds plenty of nectar for their northward migration. Anna's, black-chinned, broad-billed, broad-tailed, Costa's, and rufous hummingbirds all visit the ocotillo.

Appreciating the beauty of the flowers on such a forbidding plant structure, I decided to try a graphite pencil drawing of a desert landscape with a close-up of an ocotillo, using color only on the blooms. Desert landscapes often appear neutral in color, making desert flowers seem all the brighter.

Parry's phacelia (*Phacelia parryi*, BORAGINACEAE)

Parry's phacelia is an annual that grows in Southern California in various locales—coastal sagebrush scrub, chaparral, and open slopes, as well as in Mojave Desert environments. Stems can grow to 1½ feet tall and are thick and hairy, with broad, irregular leaves and stunning blue-violet flowers that bloom from March to June. It's easy to confuse this phacelia with *Phacelia minor* since they grow in the same areas, but in flower, they do look distinct: Parry's has shallow, bowl-shaped flowers, and *Phacelia minor*'s are more tubular. I used a combination of cobalt blue and carbazole violet to try to achieve the phacelia's remarkable blue—I wish there were a single blue tube paint that resembled it. Paint manufacturers have probably produced more blues than any other color, yet it is difficult to find just the right ones for the many subtle blues of the floral world. I decided to picture the wildflower growing in a talus field, its luxurious color to be appreciated all the more among the duller-hued rocks.

PARRY'S PHACELIA

Desert five-spot
(*Eremalche rotundifolia*, MALVACEAE)

The desert five-spot is a very conspicuous annual wildflower of lower elevations, common in the Mojave Desert and other desert areas below 3,800 feet. The flowers form a perfect globe, opening to five rounded pink petals with five bright red spots at their bases. The stems are 2 to 24 inches tall and bear rounded purple leaves. The flowers close at night; bloom time is April and May. I chose to surround my watercolor of the five-spot with a dark indigo backdrop, feeling that the dark blue would bring out the drama of the flower's globular shape and intense color.

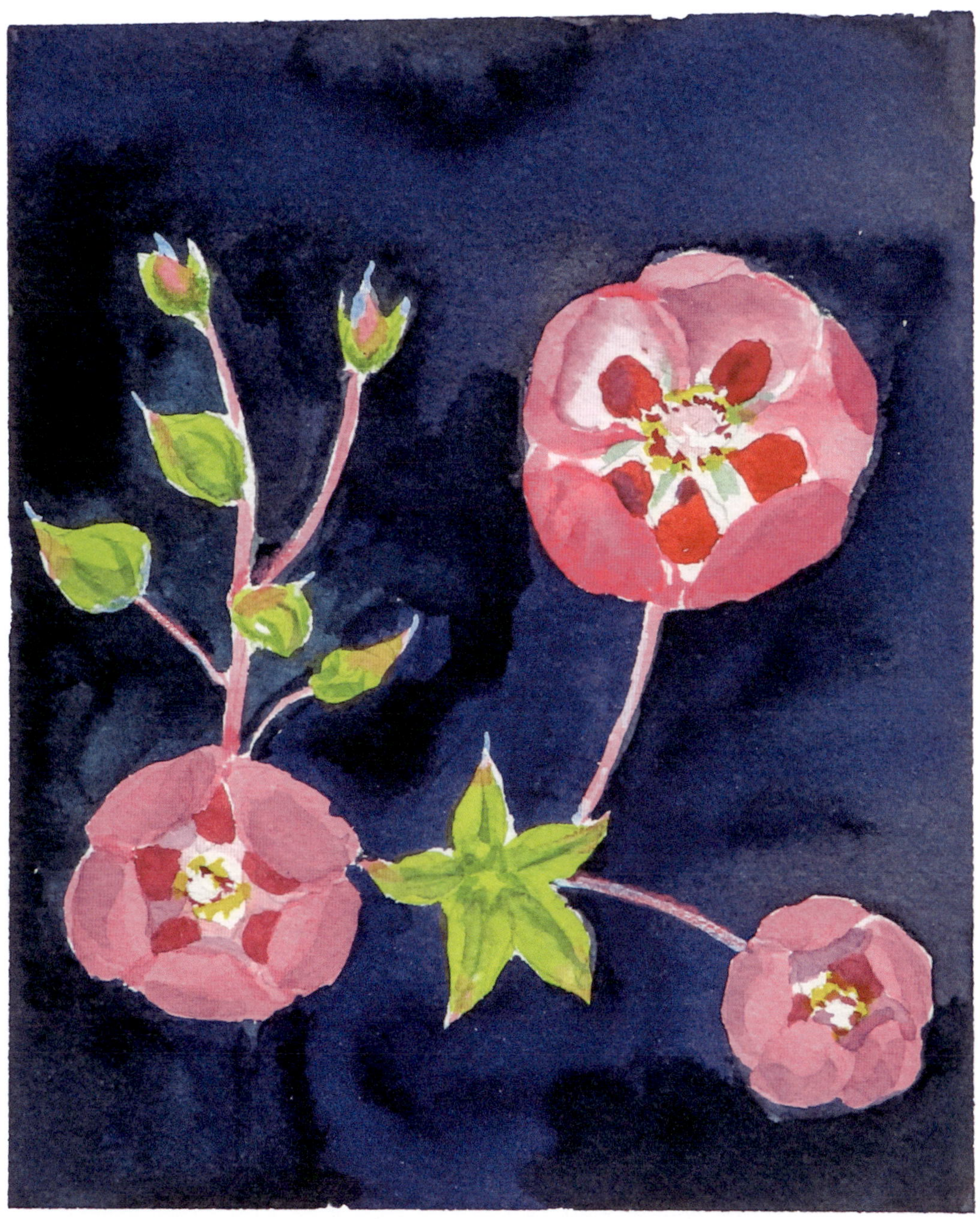

DESERT FIVE-SPOT

Teddy-bear cholla (*Cylindropuntia bigelovii*, CACTACEAE)

The teddy-bear cholla is not as cuddly as its name suggests. Its profusely white-spined branches appear fluffy like a teddy bear's fur from a distance but are painful if you come in contact with them. Its other common name is jumping cholla, because of the readiness of the barbed spines to inflict damage. This large perennial cactus can grow from 6 to 15 feet and blooms anytime from March through August,

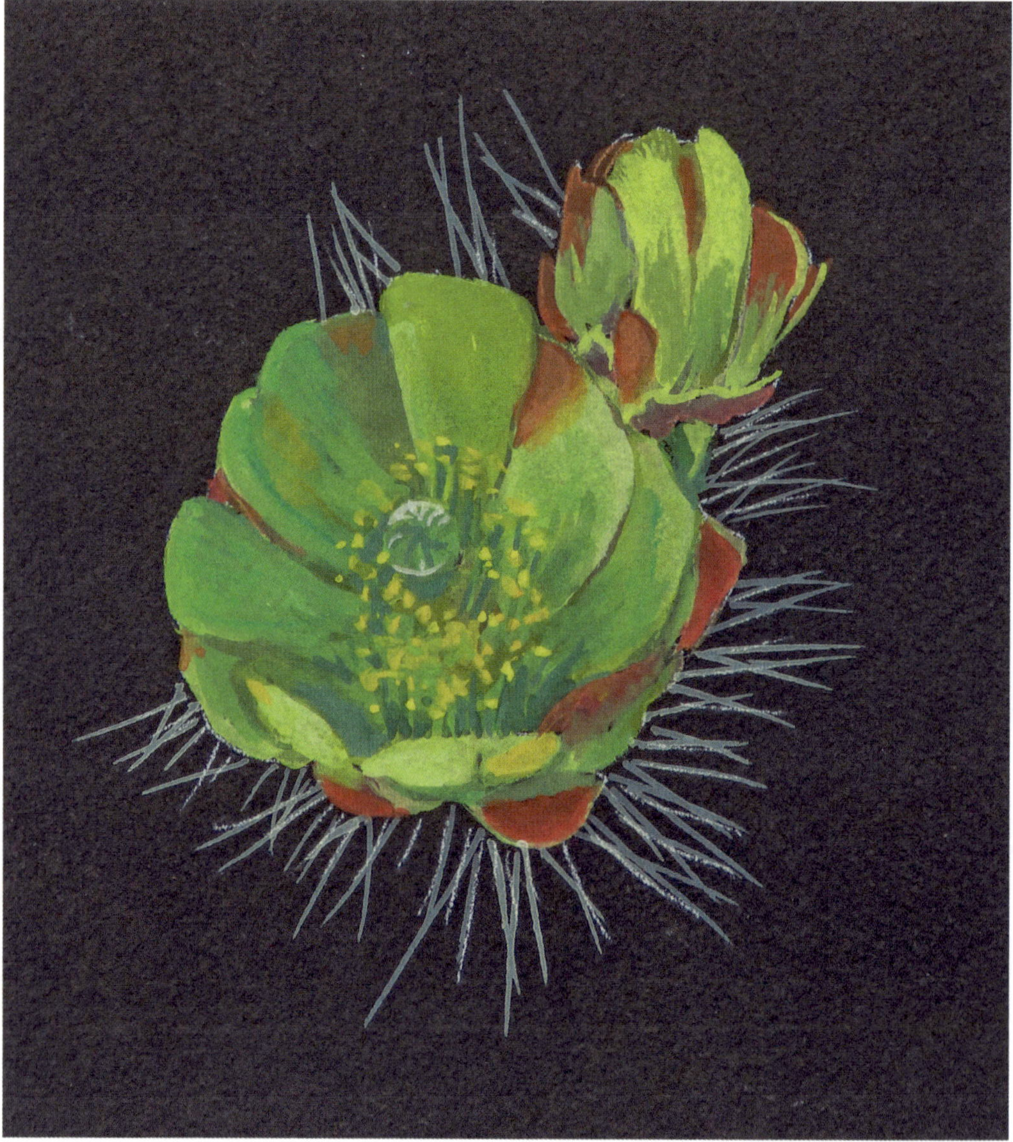

TEDDY-BEAR CHOLLA BLOOM

depending on location, with individual blooms lasting two to three days. When I visited Joshua Tree National Park one February, I stopped midway through my drive to see the otherworldly multiacre Cholla Cactus Garden in Pinto Basin. The teddy-bear cacti were aglow, their spines backlit by the afternoon sun. The greenish-yellow (and sometimes red-tipped) blooms weren't in flower at the time, but the small yellow fruits, which can remain on the cholla for years, almost looked like flowers.

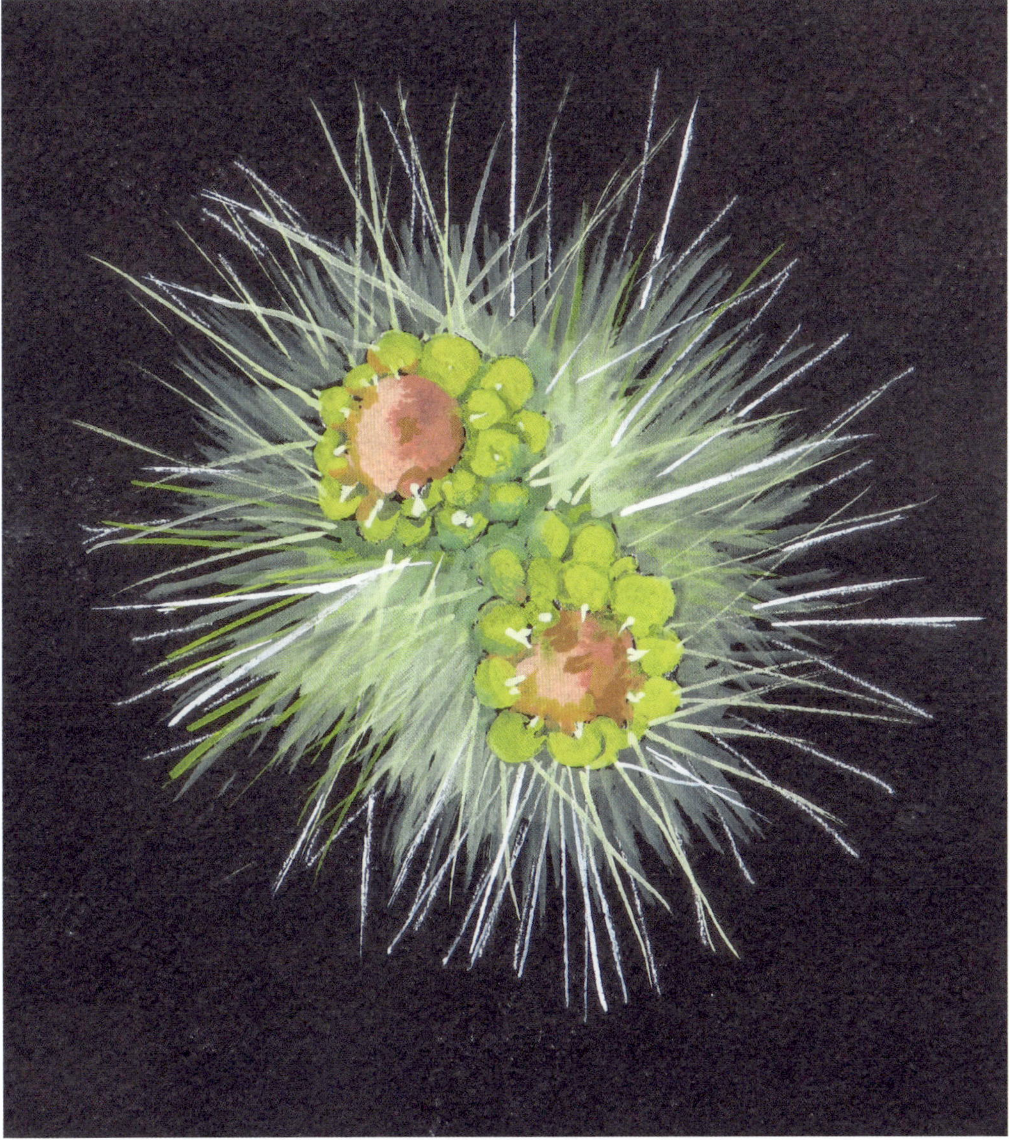

TEDDY-BEAR CHOLLA FRUIT

Desert mariposa lily (*Calochortus kennedyi*, LILIACEAE)

The perennial desert mariposa lily might be mistaken for the California poppy because of its cup-shaped orange petals, but the delicate, grasslike leaves help identify it as a member of the lily family. The plant can be erect or twisted, up to 8 inches tall, and it produces one to six flowers per stem. It grows in both creosote bush scrub and pinyon-juniper woodlands from 2,000 to 6,500 feet. In the western Mojave Desert, the petals are red; in the eastern Mojave, orange; and in the Panamint Range of Death Valley, the blooms are yellow. In addition to California, the lily blooms in Arizona, Nevada, and Utah. Flowering time is April to June, depending on elevation.

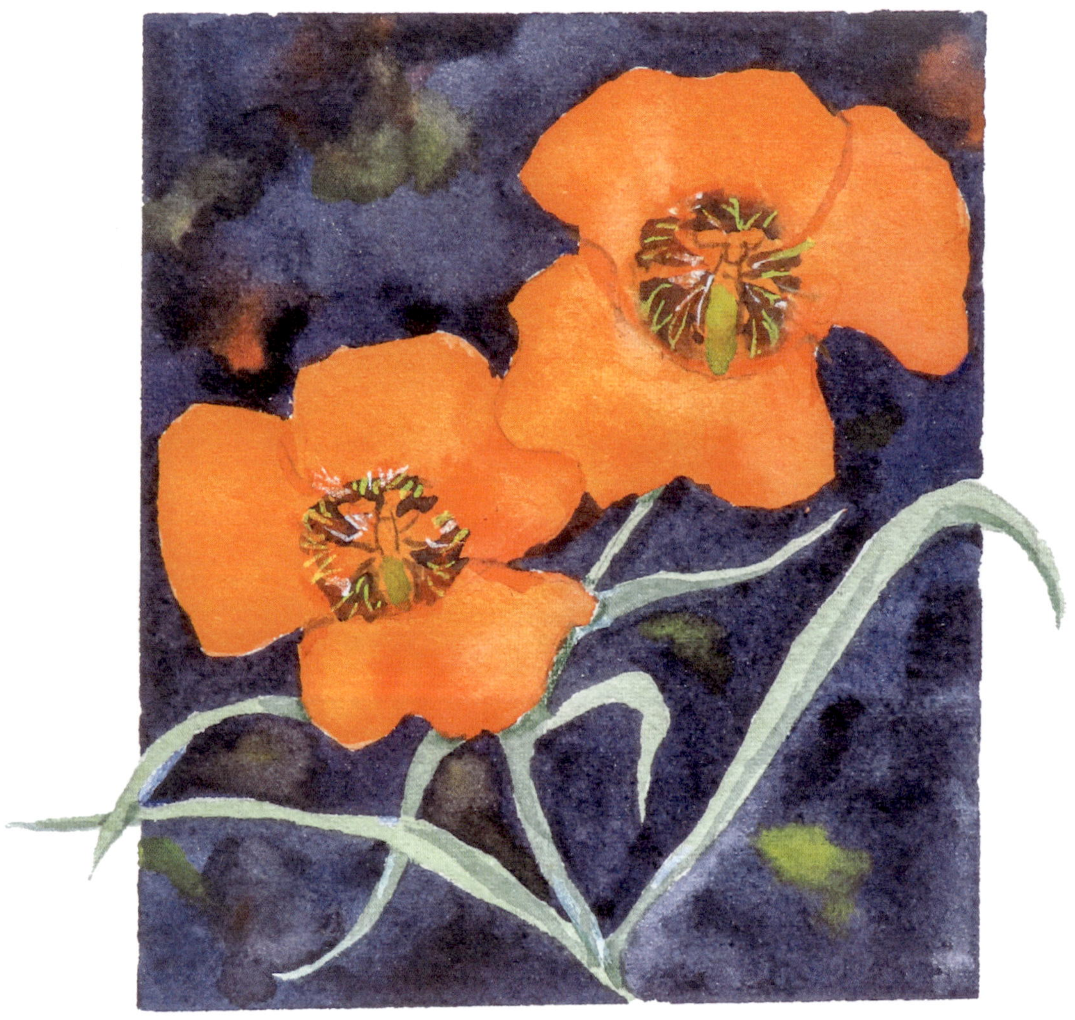

Eaton's firecracker penstemon (*Penstemon eatonii*, SCROPHULARIACEAE)

Eaton's firecracker penstemon is a common spring perennial that is widespread in the Southwest, from Colorado and Utah to California, Arizona, and New Mexico. It can be found in fields, on roadsides and dry rocky slopes, and atop mesas, all at lower elevations. In the Mojave, it grows in creosote and sagebrush scrub and in pinyon-juniper woodlands. The tubular red flowers are clustered on long stems, 1 to 3 feet tall, with pointed leaves up to 4 inches long. The flowers, not surprisingly, are hummingbird favorites.

Before sketching the plant, I wetted the paper and tinted it with a very weak wash of yellow ochre, a color well suited to expressing the dry landscape of the Mojave. After the wash dried, I sketched and painted the leaves and flowers, confident that the scarlet color would sit well atop the warm, pale glaze of ochre.

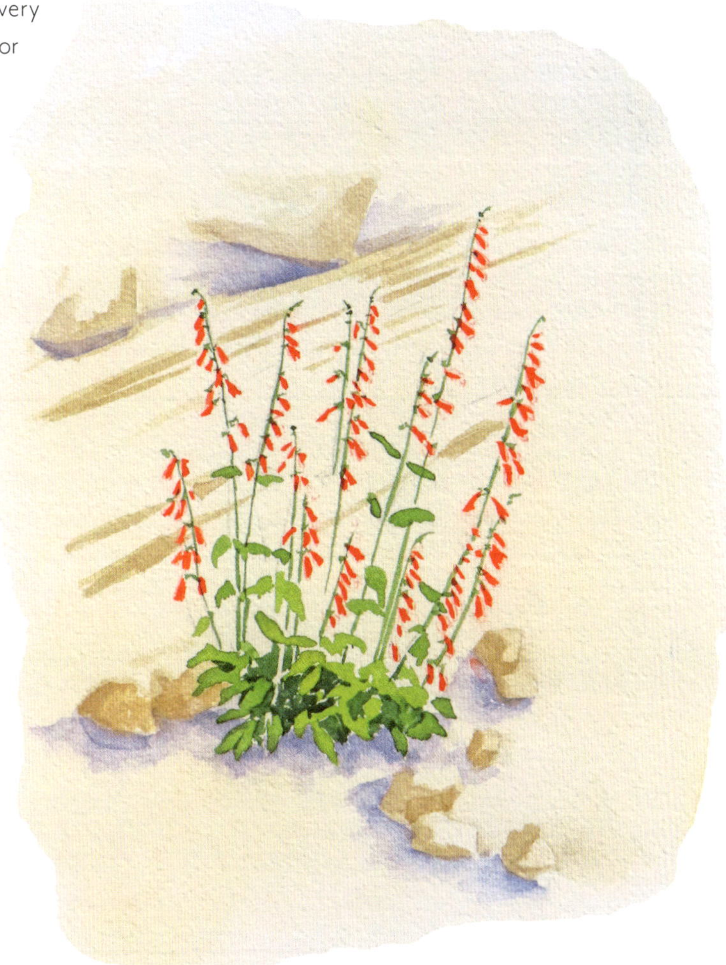

Death Valley National Park

Death Valley National Park encompasses more than 3.4 million acres, of which 93 percent is designated wilderness. A land of extremes, it is the largest US national park outside Alaska and it claims the lowest elevation in North America, at Badwater Basin. In addition to the basin's salt flats, Death Valley embraces high ranges, canyons, sand dunes, alluvial fans, and even oases.

The plant community of the desert floor is called alkali sink scrub, because of its salinity. The main shrubs have fleshy leaves and stems and include saltbush, greasewood, pickleweed, creosote bush, and iodine bush. Carpeting the floor beneath the larger plants are annual wildflowers, not visible in most years because of the lack of rainfall—typically less than 2 inches annually, and in some years, none at all. Death Valley is famous for its blasting summer heat, with temperatures as high as 120 degrees in July, so spring comes early, from late March to early April, as do the wildflowers. By May, summer has arrived, and many wildflowers, almost all of them annuals, have completed their cycle of bloom and seed-spreading.

Rain is crucial for a rich display of wildflowers. It needs to be spaced out through fall, winter, and spring. The first rainfall of ½ inch or more washes the protective coating off wildflower seeds, allowing them to sprout. Then more rainstorms are essential in the winter and spring. The finest springtime blooms happen when a rainstorm arrives in September or October and then El Niño–type weather, which allows for above-average rainfall, occurs over the following months. The plants remain small and hug the ground until the spring sun warms the soil; meanwhile, the roots are extending and growing beneath the desert surface.

When warmth arrives, the aboveground plants grow and bloom. If spring brings harsh winds, the plants won't develop, or if they have, they will dry out and blooms will disappear. No matter what conditions occur, the annual wildflowers disperse so many seeds that they will survive until a more auspicious year. An interesting symbiosis exists between Death Valley ants and wildflower seeds. In carrying the seeds into their underground nests and storing them for present and future consumption, ants in the very saline valley floor end up essentially burying and protecting the seeds from the driest, saltiest conditions, thus giving the seeds a chance for future germination.

The peak bloom times for the valley floor and alluvial fans is mid-February to mid-April. At mid-elevations of 2,000 to 5,000 feet, blooms occur in early April to early May. Above 5,000 feet, blooming periods are from late April to early June. Common flowers are desert golds, desert marigolds, evening primroses, and mariposa lilies. Massive, striking displays can include purple sand verbena, tall stalks of desert lilies, and prickly poppies.

In 2023, after years of drought so severe that even the indestructible creosote bush was dying in the park, Hurricane Hilary arrived in August and resulted in the wettest day in Death Valley history. Then storms followed throughout the fall and winter, filling Badwater Basin with a lake that tourists were able to kayak! Lake Manly, a depression formed during the Pleistocene epoch, fills very rarely (and briefly), only when winter rains are extremely heavy. The result was that 2024 became a superbloom year when tens of thousands of acres bloomed simultaneously.

Patrick Donnelly, the Great Basin director for the Center for Biological Diversity, who frequently collaborates with Naomi Fraga, director of conservation programs at the California Botanic Garden (see the "Superblooms" sidebar in the Introduction), was quoted in the *Washington Post* about the superbloom in April 2024: "With my job, I have a sense of impending doom 24/7," he said, referring to the years of drought. "So I'm going to enjoy this. . . . I love flowers in the desert, it's the thing that makes me happiest in the world, you get addicted to it. So I'll just take it and try to drink it all up while I can."

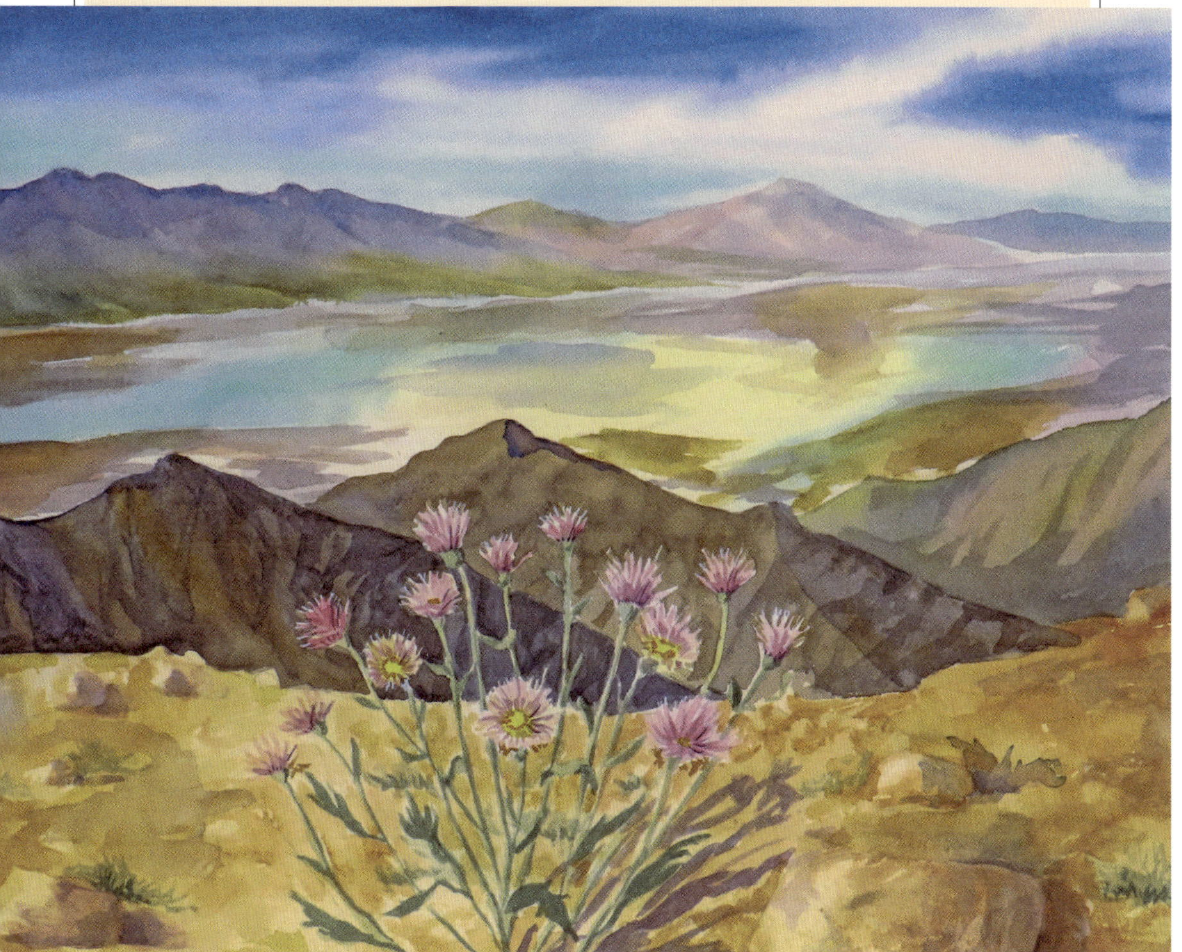

MOJAVE ASTER AND BADWATER BASIN

Sonoran Desert

*The desert . . . is made like an old-fashioned museum. Each object is
an individual specimen, standing on its own solitary pedestal.*

—William T. Hornaday, from *Camp-Fires on Desert and Lava*

The Sonoran Desert extends from southeast California into Baja California and covers much of central and southern Arizona, encompassing mountains that range from 3,000 to 10,000 feet. It is the most recognizably desertlike of the four major US deserts and is home to the saguaro and the organ pipe cactus. From December to March, the Pacific weather system brings rain to the desert. From July to mid-September, summer monsoons arrive from Mexico, with brief periods of wet tropical rain and frequent thunderstorms. In the Sonoran Desert, spring and summer come earlier than in other parts of the United States, arriving in most years in February and May, respectively.

Bladderpod (*Peritoma arborea*, CAPPARACEAE)

The perennial bladderpod is a native shrub of the West that can be found in many different habitats, including coastal bluffs, desert washes, and sandy plains, at elevations below 4,300 feet. Its leaves are narrow and about an inch long, with densely clustered tubular yellow flowers attractive to pollinators. Each flower cluster contains both unopened flower buds at the tips and opened flowers, as well as the fruits, almond-shaped pods that change from a peach color to brown when dried out. The shrub, which can grow up to 6 feet tall, blooms most of the year and can be a valuable garden plant, requiring very little water. Related to the culinary caper plant, it has a scent that some describe as sulfurous, like burned popcorn; others describe it as a green pepper smell.

I observed several bees visiting the open flowers I illustrated here. I used pen and watercolor since I find that yellow flowers often require more definition when they are not surrounded by darker washes.

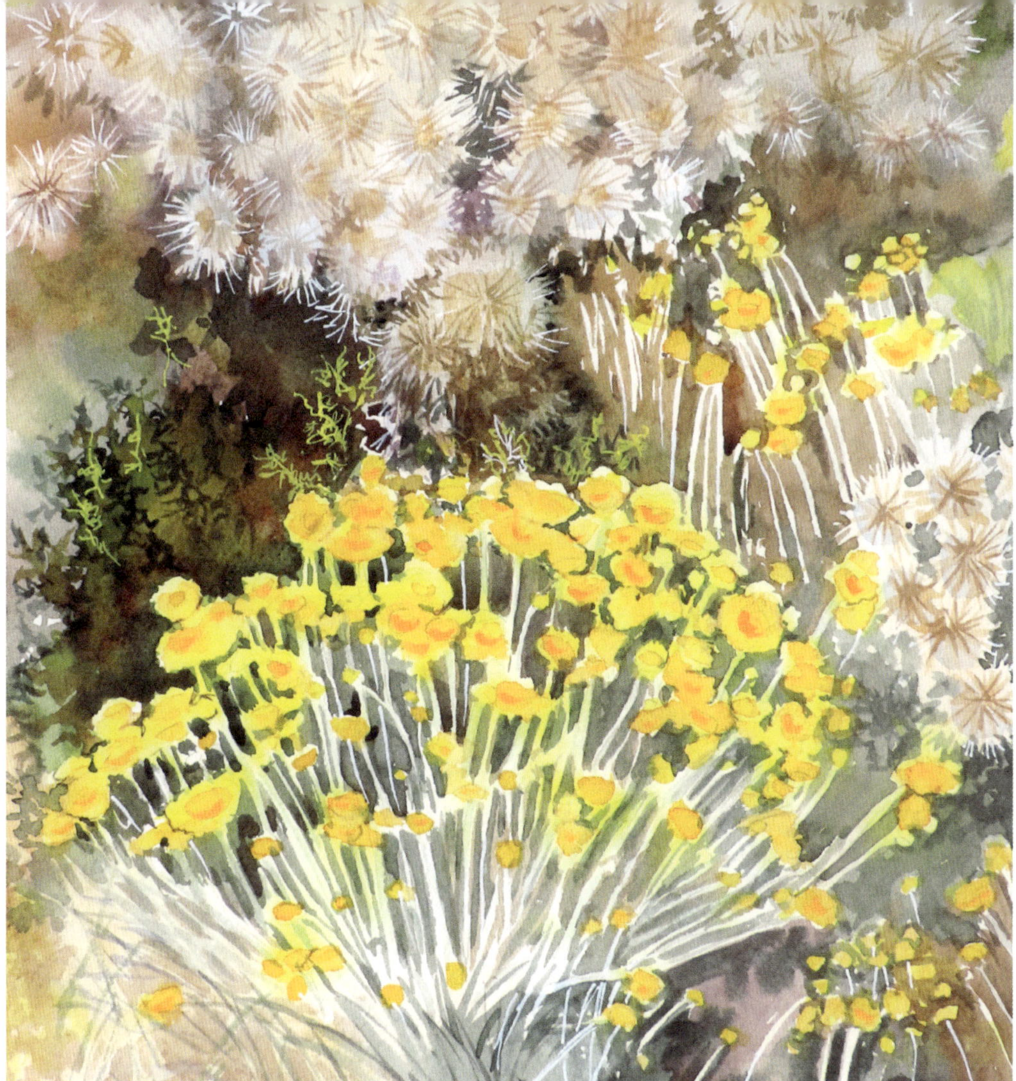

Desert marigold (*Baileya multiradiata*, ASTERACEAE)

The desert marigold is very bright and floriferous, growing as either a biennial or a short-lived perennial. It thrives in poor soils, sandy plains, and rocky slopes and grows from 8 to 20 inches tall. Bright yellow, daisy-like flowers, 2 inches wide, perch playfully on almost leafless stems above mounds of woolly gray foliage. Plants bloom sporadically over a long period, though the lushest period of flowering is from early March to May. The flowers turn papery with age, which gives them their other name, paper daisy. Dense swaths of desert marigolds line many roadways in Arizona.

Once again, I relied on gouache in this illustration (see the "Watercolor and Gouache for a Field of Flowers" sidebar, page 165). I knew that the cholla cactus spines would be difficult to represent against the dark watercolor background, especially if I relied only on saving tiny areas of paper that could easily and accidentally get filled in by the dark watercolor. So, atop the dry dark wash, I used a combination of white gouache and a Posca pen to suggest the spines.

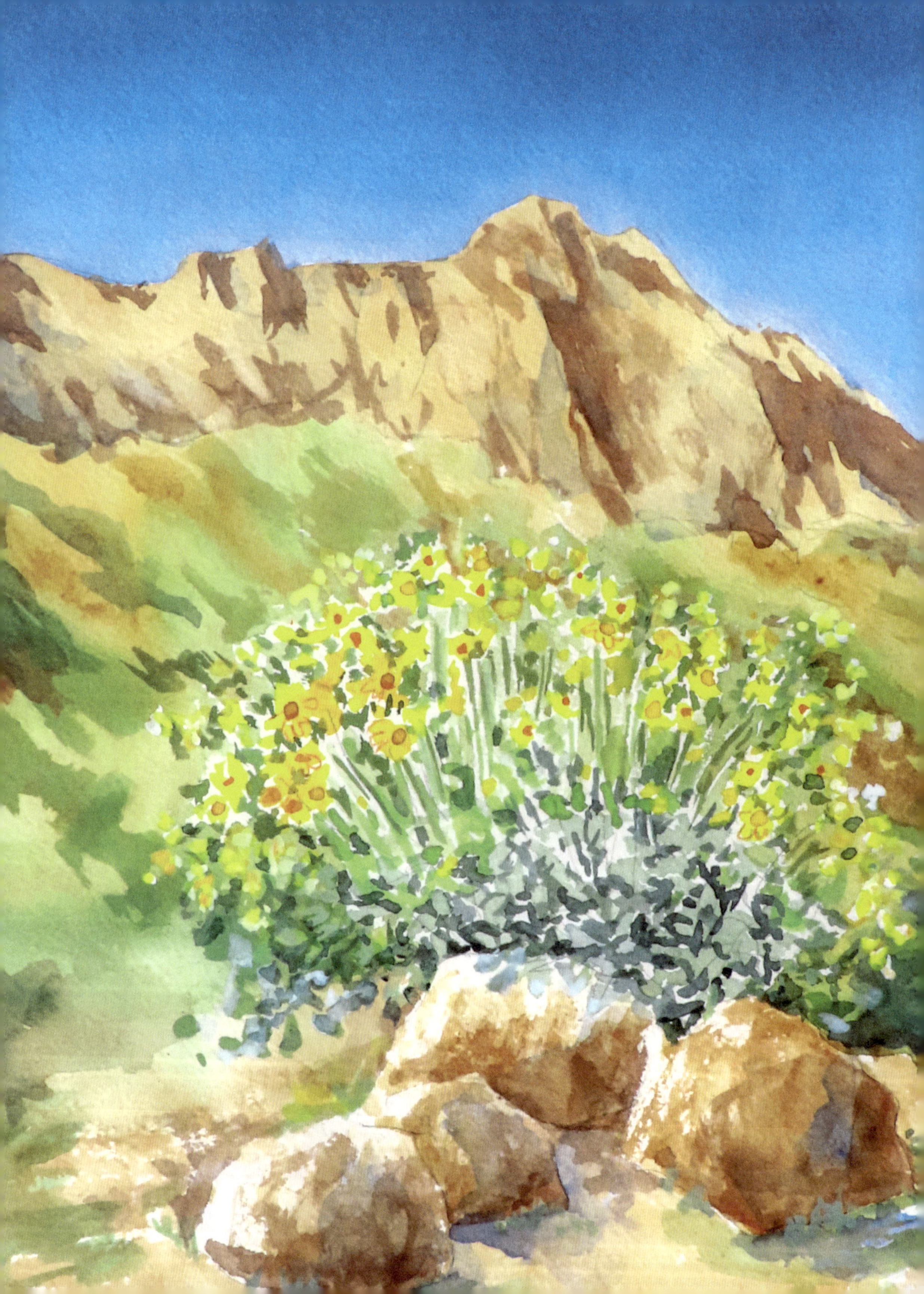

Brittlebush (*Encelia farinosa*, ASTERACEAE)

Brittlebush, a perennial, grows widely in the West—in California, into Nevada and Utah, and in much of Arizona (except for the eastern part of the state). It reaches up to 5 feet tall, forming a mounded shrub with attractive gray-green foliage, often several feet across. Bright yellow ray flowers with central gold-orange disks are borne atop tall, thin stems from March to May, and at times as early as February, making this a very long bloomer, often spectacular in wild Southwest landscapes. I painted this brittlebush with dry Arizona peaks in the background (see the sidebar).

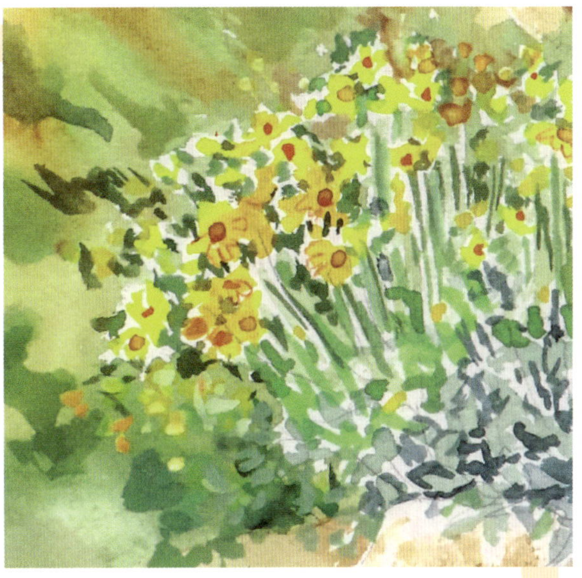

Watercolor and Gouache for a Field of Flowers

Gouache is a French word for a paint that has been made opaque, unlike transparent watercolors. It comes from the Italian word *guazzo*, which means "mud," and the consistency can sometimes resemble that. It has been used for many centuries; Persian miniatures were created with this medium. Gouache is also called "body color," and to create it, dry white pigment is added to the colored pigments, which allows for painting lighter colors over darker colors, a method much more like acrylic or oil painting.

I painted this landscape of brittlebush with a background of Arizona peaks using mostly watercolor. When there are brightly colored or white flowers in a landscape, it can be difficult to rely completely on watercolor to represent the dappled appearance of a mass of flowers. That's when I turn to gouache. I began with the watercolor, painting the flowers first and then working around them with broader washes. Next, I mixed Hansa yellow medium with permanent white gouache, which creates a much more opaque paint mixture, and I dabbed that on to extend the range of the yellow flowers. I also used it, mixed with green, for a few areas of leaves in order to show their profusion. With brush markers, I sketched in some leaf shapes and darker greens to strengthen the contrast between the foliage, the flowers, and the dusty backdrop.

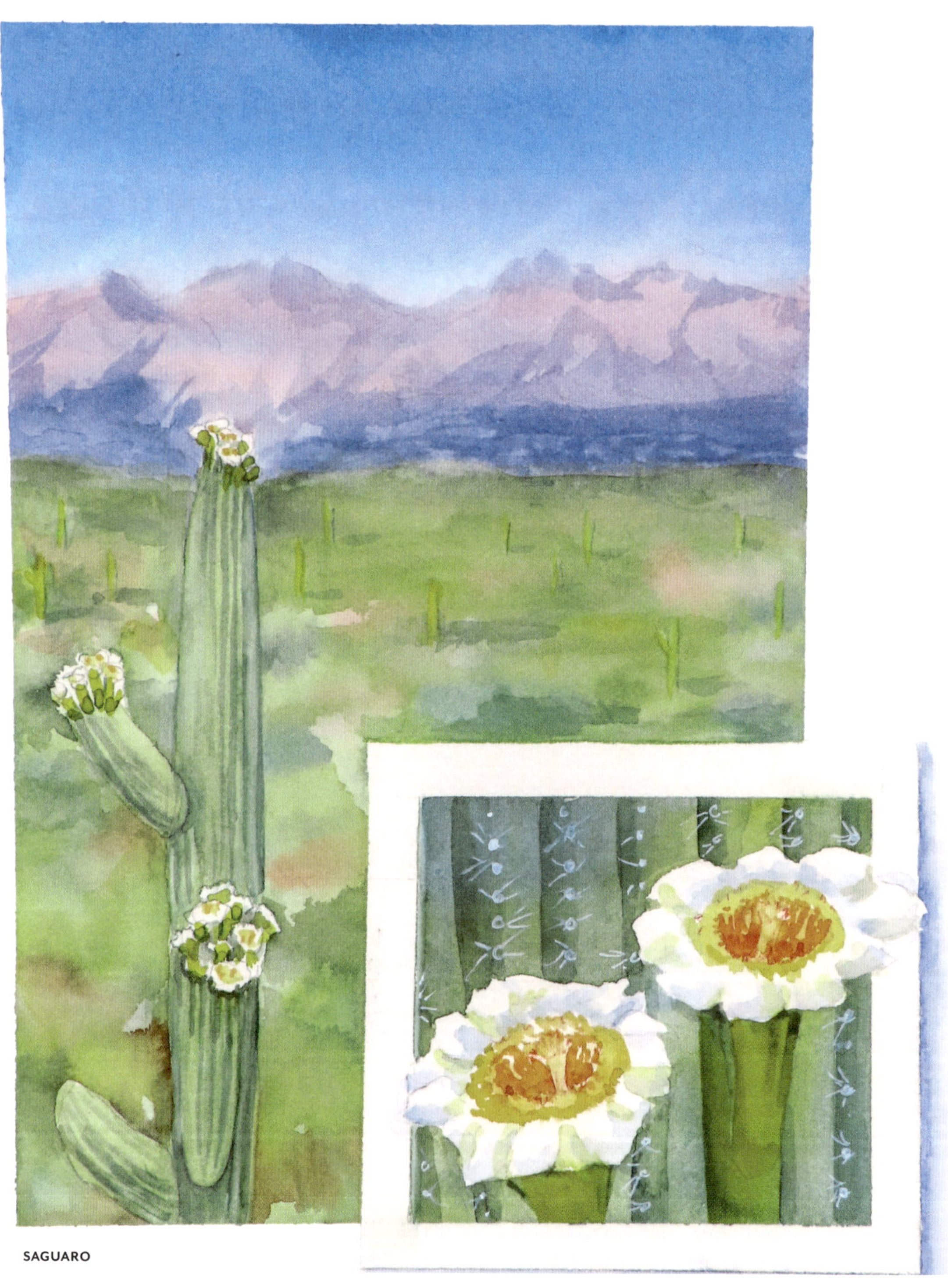

SAGUARO

Saguaro (*Carnegiea gigantea*, CACTACEAE)

The saguaro cactus can grow up to 60 feet tall and can develop multiple arms. In the United States, it lives only in the Sonoran Desert, where its need for both winter and summer moisture is met. The saguaro is a symbol of the Southwest and has been featured in many films and artworks. Edward Abbey called these cacti "planted people." On a recent trip, as I drove on Interstate 10 from California to Arizona, the saguaro seemed to magically appear off the freeway as soon as I crossed the state line. I knew I was encountering one of the strangest individuals of the plant world and couldn't wait to see more of them at the Desert Botanical Garden in Phoenix and in the wild at Saguaro National Park.

Saguaros can live up to 150 years, and it takes a very long time for them to develop their characteristic arms—up to 75 to 100 years. Some individuals never grow arms, whereas one was found that had seventy-eight! The arms, as well as the top, help the plant to reproduce, as the ends of each develop flowers and fruit. The saguaro has evolved to absorb and store rainwater, and you can see it expand as it takes in water. It is a keystone species, providing food and habitat for many other species. Cactus wrens, Gila woodpeckers, and owls make use of holes for nests, and bats and other birds feed on the fruit. Indigenous peoples, including the Tohono O'odham and Pima, have also used the cactus in a variety of ways for millennia. The ribs, when dried out, look a lot like wood and were used as building materials. Seeds were ground to make bread. The fruit is sweet and is harvested to make syrup, jams, and candies.

The saguaro's 3-inch white flowers grow in clusters, with each one opening after sunset and lasting only one day. A single plant can often have buds, flowers, and shriveled blooms occurring all at once, since the flowering season goes on for more than a month, from the end of April into the beginning of June. The flowers are pollinated at night by long-nosed bats, and by day by Gila woodpeckers, white-winged doves, hooded orioles, and finches, as well as by honeybees.

I decided to do a watercolor that shows the desert habitat near Tucson, in the eastern section of Saguaro National Park, with the Rincon Mountains as a backdrop; I inset a close-up of the saguaro's flowers.

Purple owl's clover
(*Castilleja exserta*, SCROPHULARIACEAE)

The annual purple owl's clover is called *escobita* in Spanish, meaning "little broom," which the flowers resemble; its hot pink to red-violet spikes grow up to 15 inches tall in vast meadows during wet springs. I found an old out-of-print book with an almost

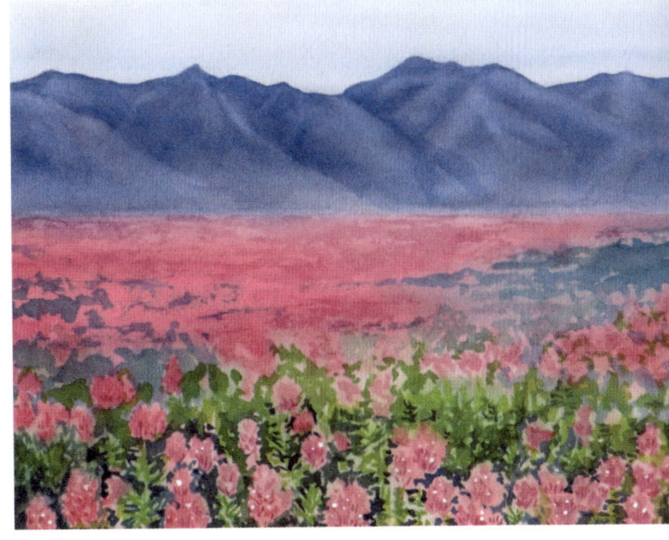

PURPLE OWL'S CLOVER

unbelievable photo that I took some license with and interpreted as a watercolor. My hope is to someday see this unique phenomenon in person! April is the best time to see the blooms, when they carpet plains, mesas, and the slopes of deserts and grasslands in unusually wet years, between 1,500 and 4,500 feet. The plant also grows in the Mojave. As with most paintbrushes, or plants of the *Castilleja* genus, the color is in the sepals as well as the petals. The "owl" name may have come from the way the corollas peer from the bracts like the head of an owl hidden in foliage.

Desert globe mallow (*Sphaeralcea ambigua*, MALVACEAE)

The desert globe mallow is an adaptable perennial that grows in desert areas and even along stream banks, ranging from southern Nevada into Southern California, western Arizona, and southwest Utah. It can reach up to 36 inches in height and has gray-green leaves that are small and somewhat triangular. When it's in bloom, dozens of bright orange flowers—each 1 inch across and composed of five heart-shaped petals—grow on spikes. The whole is reminiscent of the hollyhock, an old cottage garden favorite that is also a member of the malva tribe. Globe mallows can bloom any time of the year, depending on location. The plants often form huge colonies—a blazingly beautiful sight, especially in red rock areas, like the scene illustrated here at Snow Canyon State Park in Utah. I came across another colony in an undeveloped lot across the street from the hotel I stayed at in St. George, Utah. It was such a welcome glimpse of wild nature creating its own special kind of beauty in an unexpected place—beside the manicured grounds of a hotel! But signs posted everywhere advised of a future large-scale development there. Like in so many places in the West, the wild tends to lose out when up against moneyed interests.

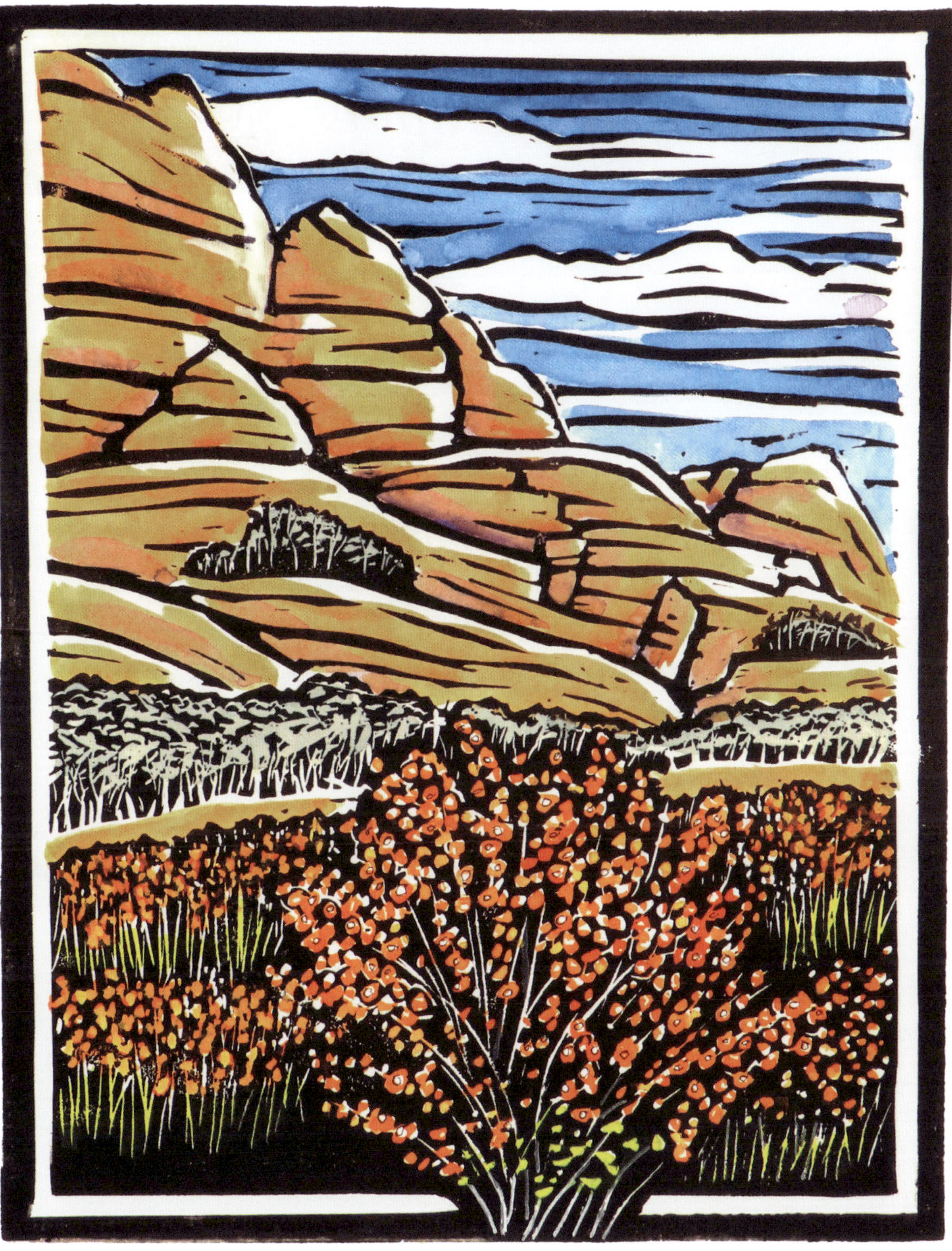

Cactus: The Xerophile

I've been growing cactus plants ever since I moved into my first apartment; they are entertaining housemates, even if they do inflict pain now and then. Cacti are both strange and beautiful, their sculpted forms unlike any other plants, and they are among the most interesting of the family of xerophytes, plants adapted to living in environments with little water. *Xerophile* describes an organism that can thrive in extremely dry conditions (in Greek, *xeros* means "dry" and *philos* means "loving"). The word can also refer to the people who love these plants, and there are many. In his essay titled "Cactus Teaching," Michael Crichton describes a small cactus he finds in a garden as "dignified, silent, stoic." How can a plant be assigned so much personality? Perhaps it's because we admire any living thing that has figured out how to survive in a very harsh and forbidding environment.

I like to picture the evolution of this plant over geological time, imagining one of those implausible time-lapse videos. It begins its life on Earth as a normal angiosperm, with barbless lush green leaves in the warm and rainy Eocene epoch. Next, during the Pleistocene, as the climate gets colder and summer rainfall begins to disappear along the Pacific coast, the great mountains of the Sierra Nevada and the Cascades rear up, and deserts appear in the mountains' eastern rain shadows. The cacti adapt and evolve, little by little forced to shed delicate leaves and grow thick skins—protections against heat, lack of water, and water loss—as well as spiny armor to fend off desperate predators. And to ensure pollination in this new climate, the plants put on the most outrageous flower shows, often with giant shapes, huge numbers of stamens, and gaudy colors that bees, hummingbirds, bats, and other pollinators find irresistible.

Cacti are found throughout the West, although in the northwestern states they are mostly limited to the prickly pear, or *Opuntia*, genus. Farther south, the number of species increases dramatically. In Nevada there are twenty-six; in California, thirty-five; in Arizona, eighty-three; and in New Mexico, fifty-six. Some of the most common western genera are *Opuntia*, which includes chollas and prickly pears; *Carnegiea*, which includes the saguaro; *Echinocereus*, which includes the hedgehog cactus; and *Mammillaria*, which includes the pincushion species.

Cacti are characterized by succulence, a fleshy surface that protects inner soft, watery tissue. Although many nondesert plants and species other than cacti are succulent, cacti alone evolved a thick and waxy surface covering, called the cuticle, and eliminated most leaves and stems, instead developing spines, which are essentially the replacement for leaves (though some cactus species have small leaves that are shed as the plant matures). Spines emerge from areoles—clearly marked areas above the normal position for a leaf. This is the most distinctive feature that appears in some form throughout the cactus family, and in no other. Chollas and prickly pears have additional spines, minute bristles called glochids.

Some cactus species have developed downward-facing spines, especially in juvenile individuals. These "drip-tips" capture rainwater, so that even a very light rain can be collected into large droplets that fall to the soil and moisten the cactus's roots; because most roots are quite shallow, even a small amount of water will reach them. As a prickly pear or saguaro cactus matures, when it is about 5 or 6 feet in height, its spines are no longer downward facing—the joints or arms take over and collect water into large drops, and sometimes even small streams. Saguaros, like others in the *Carnegiea* genus, are an exception to the shallow-root habit of cacti; instead, they have a deep underground tuberous root system that stores water and food.

Cacti are perennials and require more than one season to mature and flower. They produce some of the most beautiful flowers in the plant kingdom, in colors ranging from white, pink, red, and yellow to orange and even bicolor combinations. Sepals, petals, and stamens issue from a floral tube, and beneath the tube is the ovary, which develops the fruit. There can be many colorful sepals and petals and hundreds of stamens. It is this profusion of rich colors and petals and stamens that has made cactus flowers one of my favorite blooms to paint and draw.

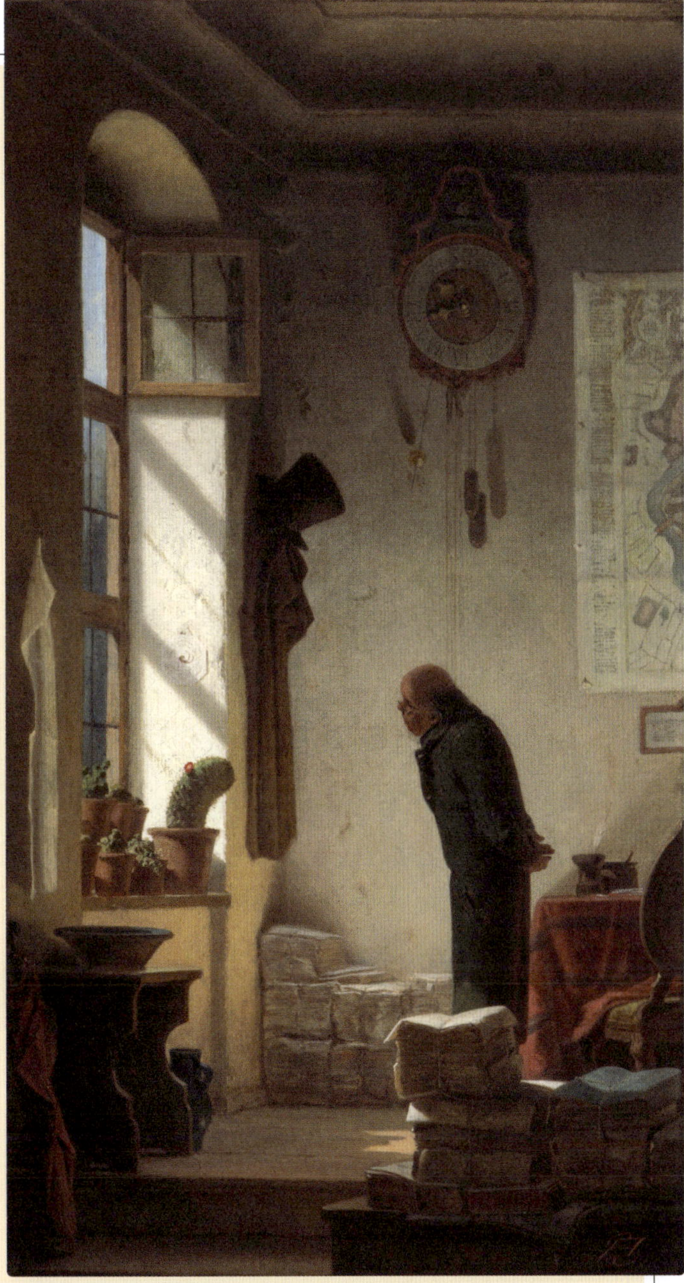

THE CACTUS LOVER, CARL SPITZWEG (GROHMANN MUSEUM COLLECTION AT MILWAUKEE SCHOOL OF ENGINEERING, MILWAUKEE, WISCONSIN)

Chihuahuan Desert

The Chihuahuan Desert is the southernmost of the United States deserts, ranging from New Mexico to Texas at a relatively high elevation, from 3,000 to 5,000 feet. It also extends into northern Mexico. Winter can be cold, and there are winter freezes, but even so, this desert supports a wide range of plant life, with shrubs, leaf succulents, and cacti (see the sidebar) among the larger species. Bear grass, yucca, and agave are also common.

Mexican hat (*Ratibida columnifera*, ASTERACEAE)

The perennial Mexican hat, also known as prairie coneflower, grows throughout the Southwest east of California and Nevada, blooming anytime between May and November, depending on available moisture. It ranges from 1½ to 3 feet tall, with leaves on the lower portion of the stem that are feathery and deeply cleft. The flower petals vary from dark red and yellow to all red or all yellow. A dramatic central disc protrudes ½ to 2 inches above the drooping petals, making the flower look very much like the tall, broad-brimmed sombreros worn during Mexican fiestas.

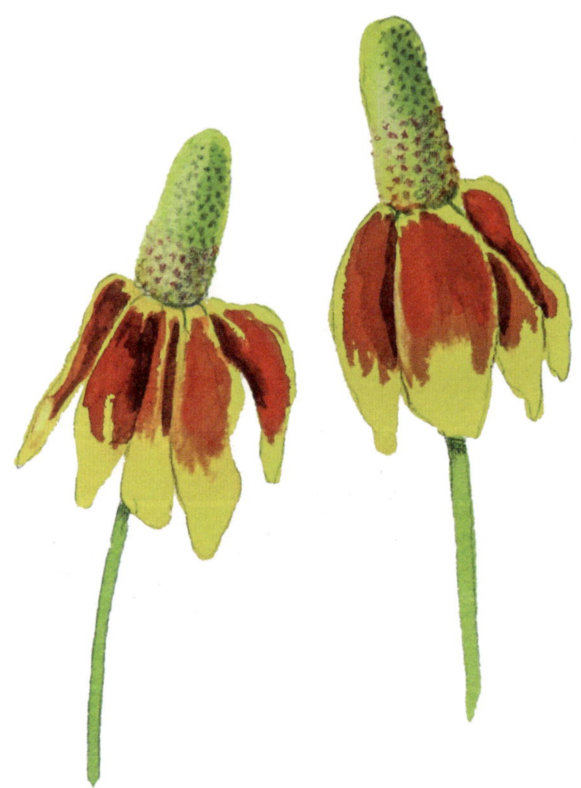

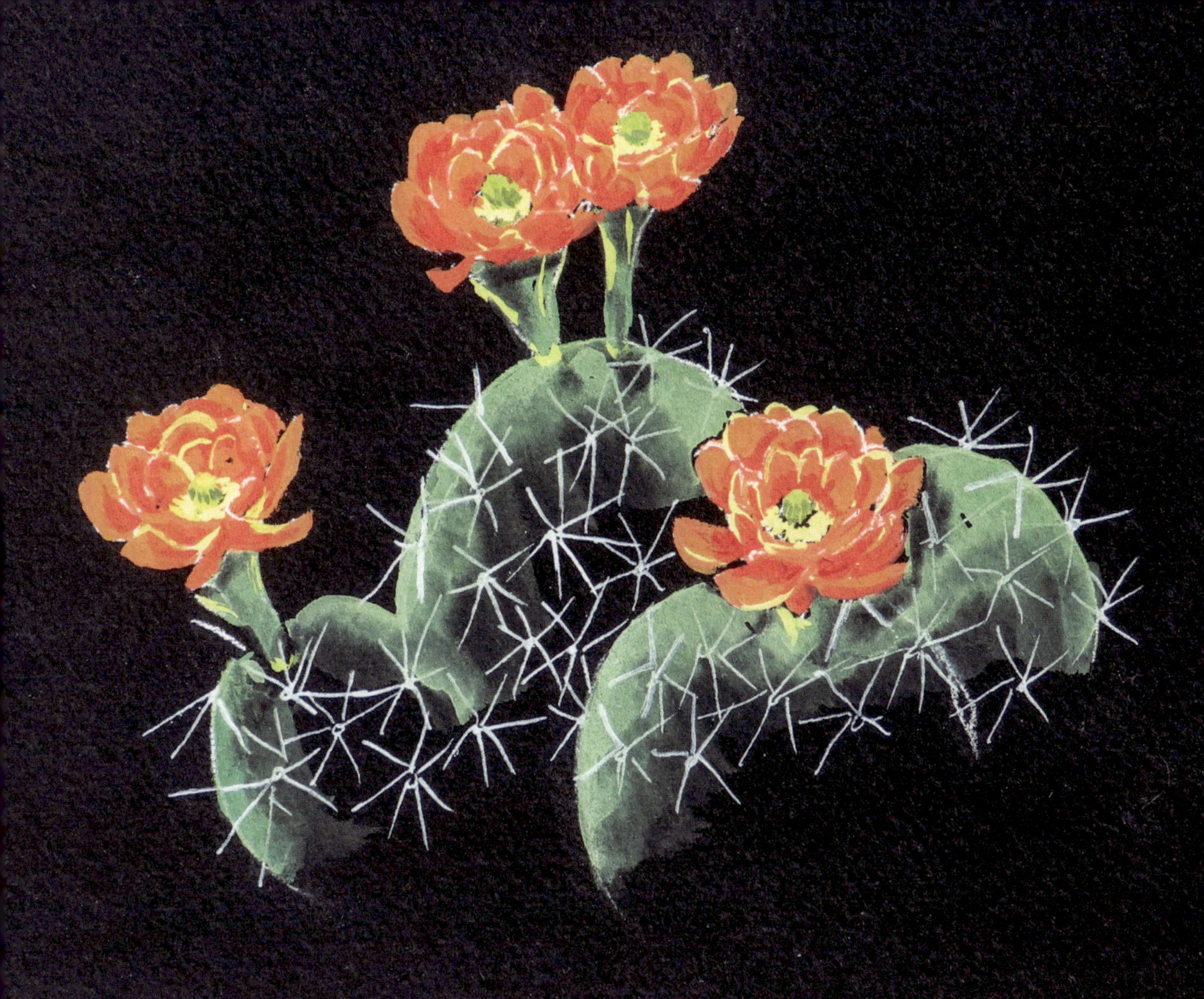

Claret cup hedgehog cactus (*Echinocereus triglochidiatus*, CACTACEAE)

Although only 16 inches tall, the perennial claret cup hedgehog cactus, also called the kingcup or strawberry hedgehog cactus, grows in clumps that can reach 3 to 4 feet across or more. It can escape notice when it isn't flowering, but in April and May, when it's covered in mounds of red-orange flowers, a color somewhat rare among Southwest desert cacti, you can't miss it. The flowers grow only at the top of the cactus and are mostly at the same height, so that all of them are visible at once. The bloom period is usually abbreviated, ending in May in most locations, but if temperatures are cooler or the weather is moist, it may persist through June. This cactus is most common in rocky areas and on cliff faces throughout the Southwest; in New Mexico, look for them in the Guadalupe Mountains, Carlsbad Caverns National Park, and White Sands National Park. I painted this vignette on black watercolor paper, using watercolor, gouache, and Posca acrylic pens. You can create shaded areas when you add less paint, allowing the black paper to show through.

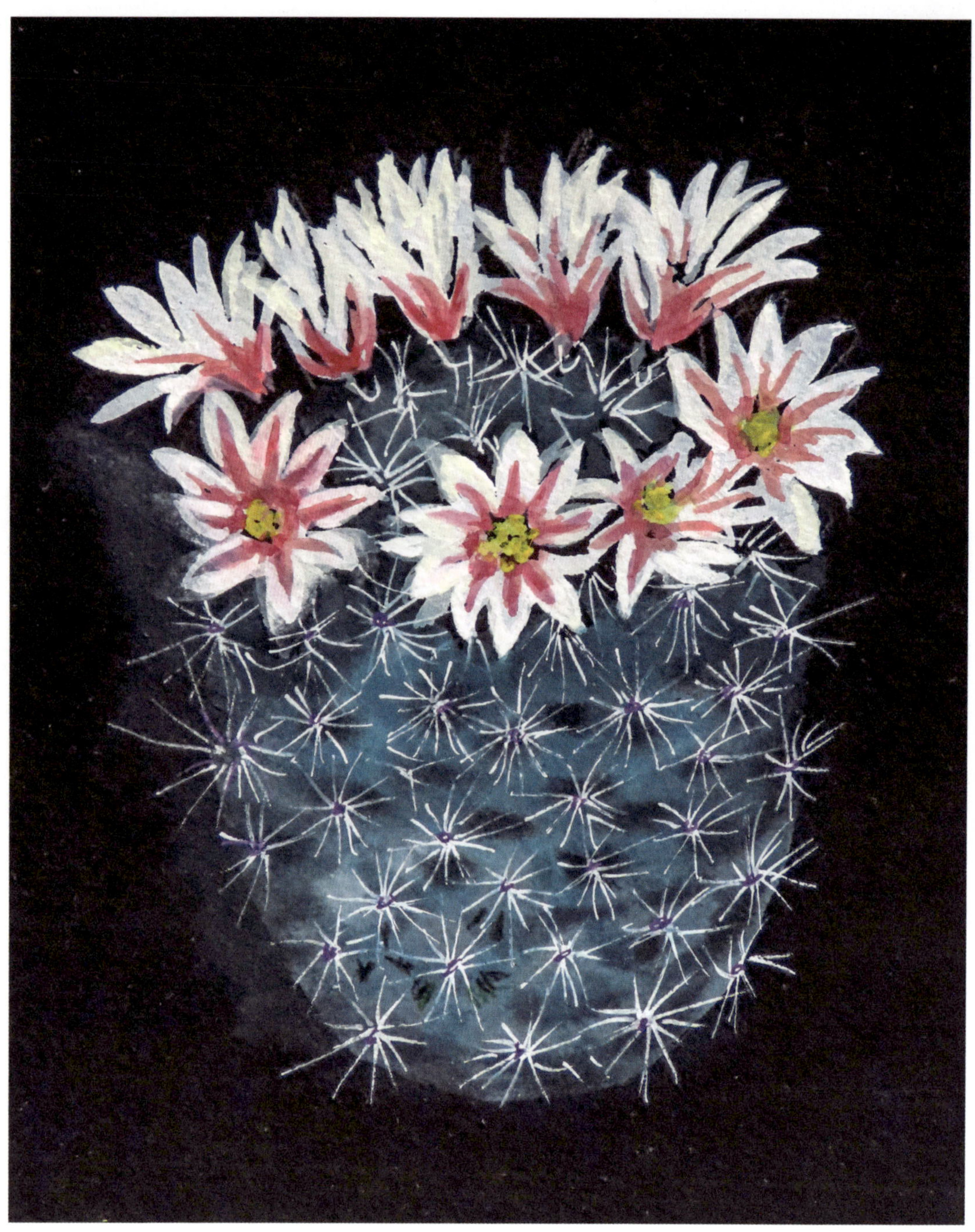

ARIZONA FISHHOOK PINCUSHION CACTUS FLOWERS

Arizona fishhook pincushion cactus (*Mammillaria grahamii*, CACTACEAE)

Like other fishhook cacti, the perennial Arizona pincushion has small, hooked, downward-facing central spines, called drip-tips, that protect it against desert browsers and aid in collecting moisture (see the "Cactus: The Xerophile" sidebar, page 170). It has the added advantage of growing beneath teddy-bear cholla, whose protective spines also help to fend off trampling grazers. The pincushion grows in deserts and grasslands, favoring rocky slopes and plains below 4,500 feet. It flowers from mid-April through early September, the blooms triggered by summer rains. Five to seven days after a soaking, flowers up to 1½ inches wide appear, in colors of pink to lavender with white margins. They are pollinated by bees. The scarlet, berrylike fruit is as colorful as the flowers, and the block print here was inspired by that.

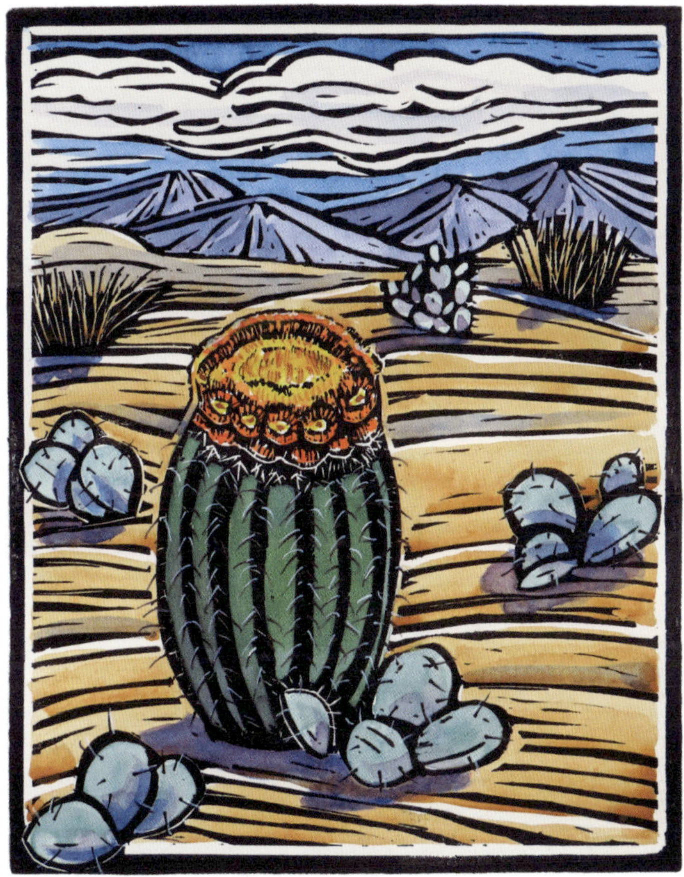

ARIZONA FISHHOOK PINCUSHION CACTUS FRUIT

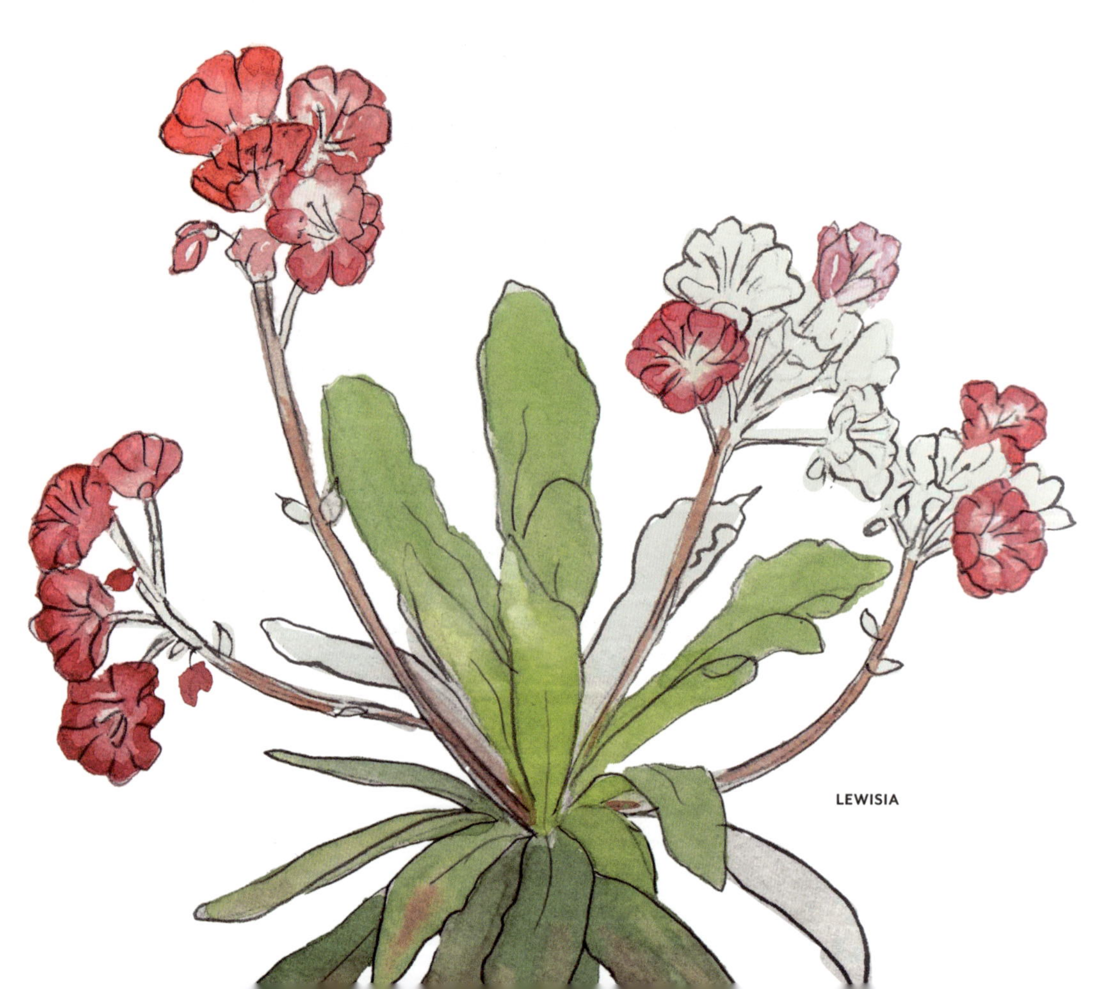
LEWISIA

Acknowledgments

I offer thanks to my family and friends, who've accompanied me on so many of my outdoor excursions: Tom, Rose, David, Jane, Julie, Gerry, Dave, Kendall, Ilona, and Martin.

To Paul Kasprzyk: partner, fellow wildflower seeker, and careful first reader and editor whose joie de vivre inspires me daily.

To everyone who has assisted me in publishing: my agent, Anne Depue, whose long and wise experience has supported me through five books; Mountaineers Books editor in chief Kate Rogers, for careful guidance and wonderful ideas; developmental editor Linda Gunnarson, who created order from chaos, with warm support always; Mountaineers Books managing editor Janet Kimball, whose serious attention and care for my book made working with her a pleasure; copyeditor Laura Larson, whose excellent research skills kept me accurate, and whose invaluable suggestions refined my prose; Mountaineers Books senior publicist Marissa Litak, who finds the perfect venues and bookstores, where I have the pleasure of meeting my readers; book designer Kate Basart, whose artistry makes my books beautiful; and to the Mountaineers Books sales and marketing staff and the warehouse crew: without your hard work there would be no readers. My thanks to Art Freeman and Bill Rogers for providing photos as inspiration. Thanks also to Pomegranate owners, Katie and Tom Burke, editors Cory Mimms and Alyssa Flynn, and the rest of the Pomegranate staff; and Cary Cartmill of Digital Canvas Northwest.

To the poets: John Daniel and Kim Stafford of Oregon; Tim McNulty and Saul Weisberg of Washington; and Jane Graham George of New Zealand.

To my colleagues at the outdoor institutes where I teach: Christian Martin of North Cascades Institute; Katie Roloson of the Yellowstone Forever Institute; Lora Spielman–Dell Isola of Yosemite Conservancy; and Maria Elting and the staff at the Sitka Center for Art and Ecology.

To the librarians and staff at the Elisabeth C. Miller Library, University of Washington Botanic Gardens: Brian Thompson, Rebecca, Nick, Lena, and Laura. And to Larry De Buhr, retired professor of botany, who enlightened me about desert plants.

To Wynne Brown for sharing Sara Plummer Lemmon's art, for our conversations about it, and for her wonderful book, *The Forgotten Botanist: Sara Plummer Lemmon's Life of Science and Art.*

To my printmaking teachers and friends: first teacher, Jocelyn Curry, who introduced me to the joy of printmaking; Roberta Long; Virginia Hungate-Hawk; and Charlie Spitzack.

To my many students: you continue to inspire me.

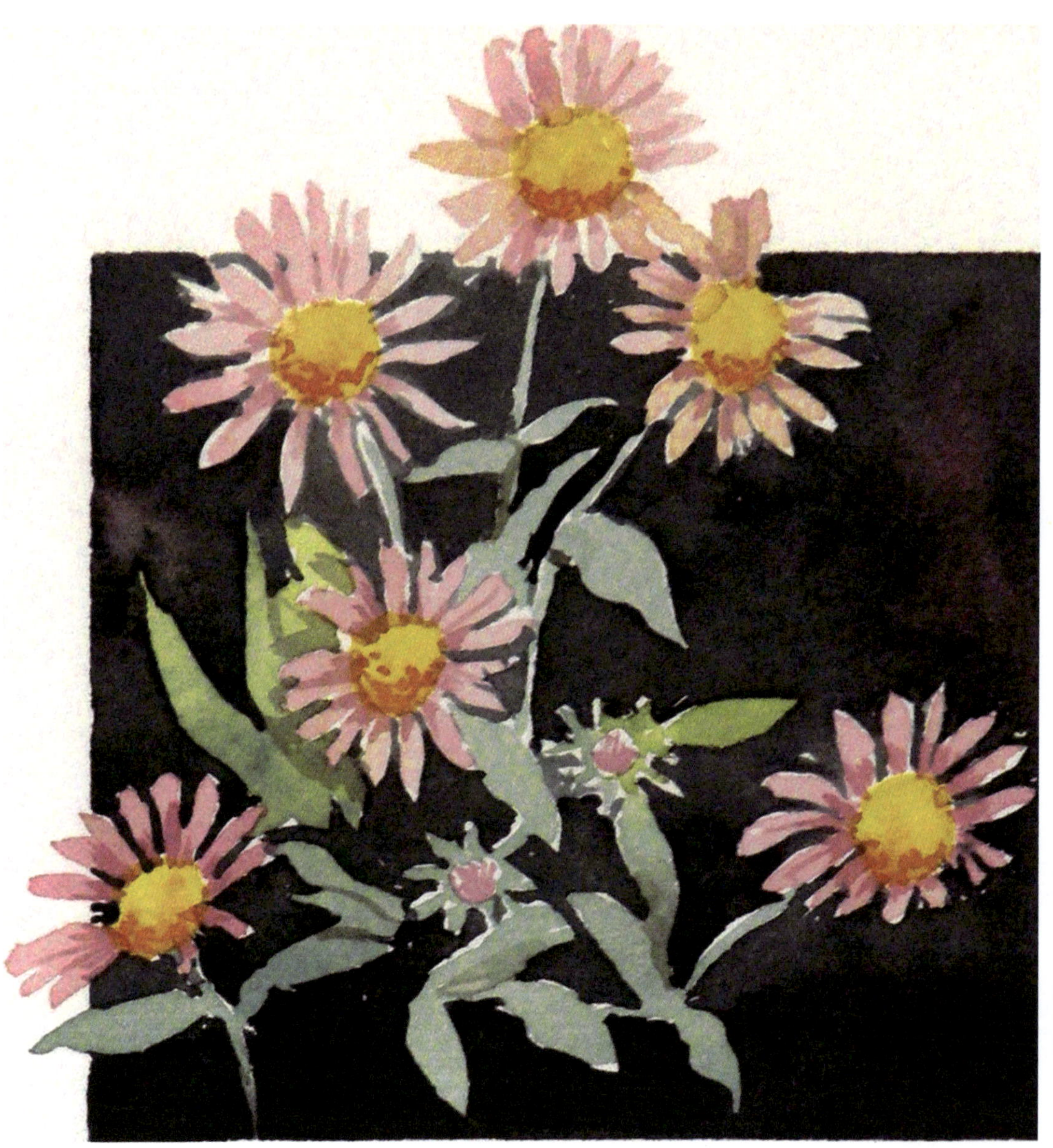

MOUNTAIN DAISY

Glossary

alternate: Growing at alternate intervals on a stem or branch

annual: A plant that lives one year

anther: The flower organ that produces pollen

areole: A small space or interstice, such as an area bounded by small veins in a leaf; in cacti, a sharply defined small area bearing spines and sometimes glochids

banner: The upper, upright petal of a pea-type flower; also called the standard

basal: Pertaining to or forming a base

biennial: A plant that lives two years

bract: A modified leaf below a flower or inflorescence

calyx: Collective term for the sepals of a flower

composite: Made up of distinct components; compound

corm: A thick, vertical, underground stem

corolla: Collective term for the petals of a flower

cuticle: A waxlike, water-repellent surface covering some plants

filament: The stalk supporting the anthers

floret: Small individual flowers within the larger flower head, as in sunflowers

glochid: A fine barbed bristle in the areole of a cholla or prickly pear cactus, different from the larger spines

inflorescence: Collective term for the flowers on a stem; a cluster of flowers

lanceolate: Shaped like the head of a lance or spear

node: The point on a stem where branches or leaves arise

opposite: Branching in pairs

palmate: Spreading like the fingers of a hand

panicle: A much-branched inflorescence of stalked flowers

pedicel: A flower stalk

perennial: A plant that lives three years or longer

petiole: The stalk part of the leaf that is attached to the stem

pinnate: Feather-like

pistil: The seed-bearing organ of a flower, including the stigma, style, and ovary

raceme: An inflorescence of stalked flowers along a stem

ray flower: The outer flower of a composite flower head (used with the aster family)

rhizome: An underground stem

rosette: A ring or cluster of bracts or leaves; also called a basal leaf cluster

sepal: One of the segments, usually green, forming the calyx of the flower

sessile: Without a stalk or petiole

spadix: A central spike crowded with small flowers

spathe: The large bract just below and enclosing a spadix

spike: An inflorescence with stalkless flowers along a stem

spur: A hollow projection from a petal or sepal that contains nectar

stamen: The male organ of a flower, consisting of the filament and anthers

stigma: The apex of the pistil of a flower, where pollen is deposited at pollination

stolon: A horizontal shoot that puts down roots; also called a runner

succulence: Fleshy, soft, watery tissue

tendril: A slender, clasping appendage that attaches a plant to something else

tepals: Sepals and petals that are indistinguishable from one another

umbel: A flower cluster whose stalks radiate from a common center

whorled: Coiled, curled, or having convolutions

wing: In many plants of the pea family, either of the two lateral petals

Further Reading & Resources

FIELD GUIDES

California Field Guides

Benson, Lyman. *The Native Cacti of California.*
Stanford, CA: Stanford University Press, 1969.

Blackwell, Laird R. *Wildflowers of California: A
Month-by-Month Guide.* Berkeley: University of
California Press, 2012.

——*Wildflowers of the Sierra Nevada and the Central
Valley.* Edmonton, AB: Lone Pine Publishing, 1999.

Faber, Phyllis M., ed. *California's Wild Gardens: A Guide
to Favorite Botanical Sites.* Berkeley: University of
California Press, 1997.

Laws, John Muir. *Sierra Wildflowers: A Hiker's Guide.*
Berkeley, CA: Heyday, 2019.

Munz, Philip A. *Introduction to California Desert
Wildflowers.* Edited by Diane L. Renshaw and Phyllis
M. Faber. Rev. ed. Berkeley: University of California
Press, 2004.

——*Introduction to California Spring Wildflowers.*
Edited by Diane Lake and Phyllis M. Faber. Rev. ed.
Berkeley: University of California Press, 2004.

Ornduff, Robert. *Introduction to California Plant Life.*
Revised by Phyllis M. Faber and Todd Keeler-Wolf.
Rev. ed. Berkeley: University of California Press, 2003.

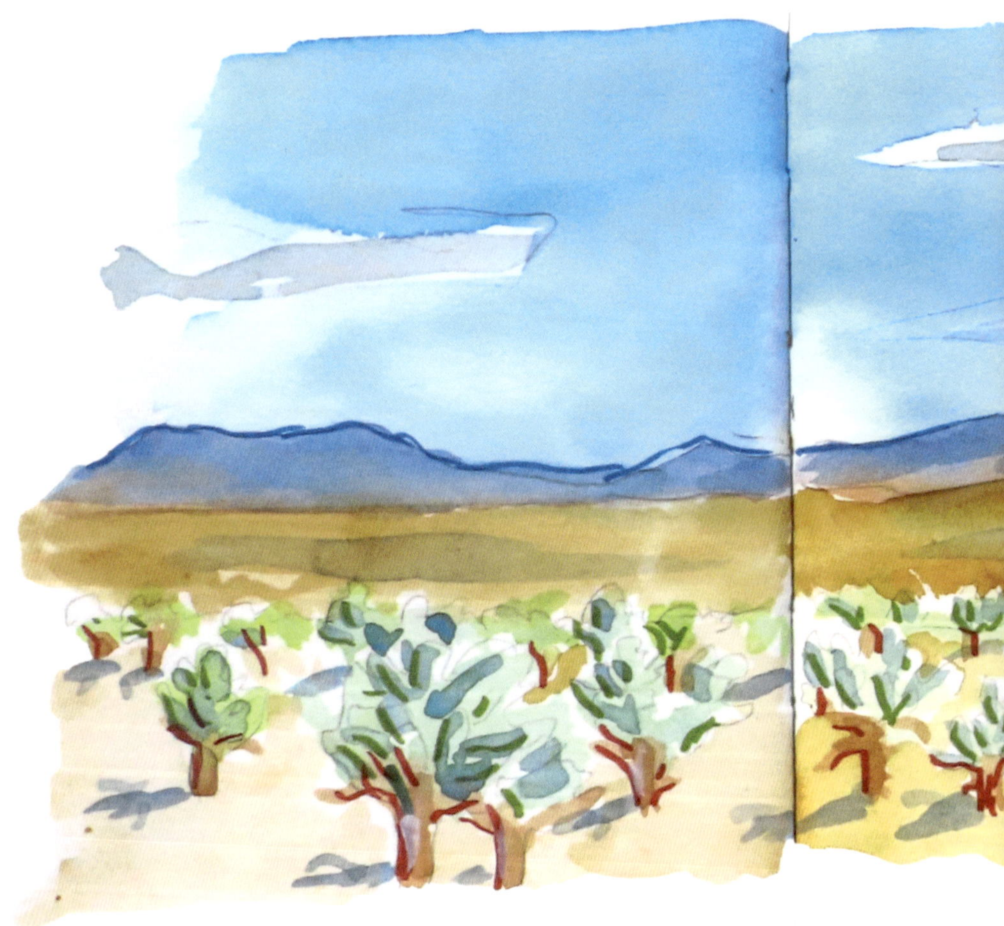

TEDDY-BEAR CHOLLA GARDEN, JOSHUA TREE NATIONAL PARK

Quinn, Ronald D., and Sterling C. Keeley. *Introduction to California Chaparral*. Berkeley: University of California Press, 2006.

Rundell, Philip W., and Robert Gustafson. *Introduction to the Plant Life of Southern California: Coast to Foothills*. Berkeley: University of California Press, 2005.

Wilson, Lynn, Jim Wilson, and Jeff Nicholas. *Wildflowers of Yosemite*. Mariposa, CA: Sierra Press, 2005.

Pacific Coast Field Guides

Blackwell, Laird R. *Wildflowers of Mount Rainier*. Edmonton, AB: Lone Pine Publishing, 2000.

Jolley, Russ. *Wildflowers of the Columbia Gorge: A Comprehensive Field Guide*. Portland: Oregon Historical Society Press, 1988.

Niehaus, Theodore F. *A Field Guide to Pacific States Wildflowers: Washington, Oregon, California and Adjacent Areas*. Peterson Field Guides. Boston: Houghton Mifflin, 1976.

Strickler, Dee. *Northwest Penstemons: 80 Species of Penstemon Native to the Pacific Northwest*. Columbia Falls, MT: The Flower Press, 1997.

———*Wayside Wildflowers of the Pacific Northwest*. Columbia Falls, MT: The Flower Press, 1993.

Turner, Mark, and Phyllis Gustafson. *Wildflowers of the Pacific Northwest*. Portland, OR: Timber Press, 2006.

Whitney, Stephen, and Rob Sandelin. *Field Guide to the Cascades and Olympics*. 2nd ed. Seattle: Mountaineers Books, 2004.

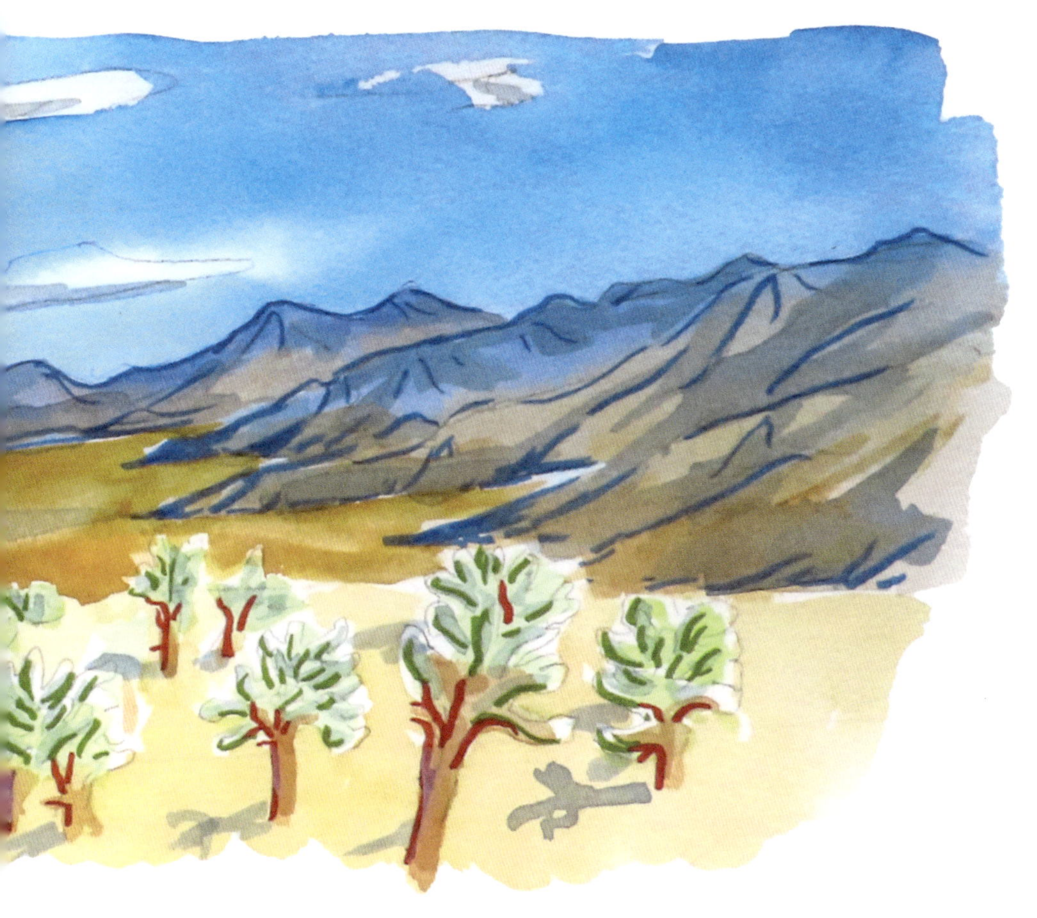

Rocky Mountain Field Guides

Denver Botanic Gardens and Butterfly Pavilion. *Pollinators of the American West.* Essex, CT: Falcon Guides, 2024.

Guennel, G. K. *Guide to Colorado Wildflowers.* Vol. 2, *Mountains.* 2nd ed. Englewood, CO: Westcliffe Publishers, 2004.

Nagy, Linda S. *Rocky Mountain Wildflowers: Field Guide.* 3rd ed. Fairplay, CO: High Country Artworks, 2019.

Strickler, Dee. *Alpine Wildflowers: Showy Wildflowers of the Alpine and Subalpine Areas of the Northern Rocky Mountain States.* Columbia Falls, MT: The Flower Press, 1990.

——*Forest Wildflowers: Showy Wildflowers of the Woods, Mountains and Forests of the Northern Rocky Mountain States.* Columbia Falls, MT: The Flower Press, 1988.

——*Prairie Wildflowers: Showy Wildflowers of the Plains, Valleys and Foothills in the Northern Rocky Mountain States.* Columbia Falls, MT: The Flower Press, 1986.

Southwest Field Guides

Bowers, Janice Emily. *100 Roadside Flowers of Southwest Woodlands.* Tucson, AZ: Southwest Parks and Monuments Association, 1987.

Bowers, Nora Mays, Rick Bowers, and Stan Tekiela. *Wildflowers of Arizona: Field Guide.* 2nd ed. Cambridge, MN: Adventure Publications, 2024.

Desert Botanical Garden Staff. *Desert Wildflowers.* Phoenix: Arizona Highways Books, 1999.

Dodge, Natt N. *Flowers of the Southwest Deserts.* 9th ed. Globe, AZ: Southwest Parks and Monuments Association, 1976.

Lesica, Peter, and Walter Fertig. *Spring Wildflowers of Utah's Red Rock Desert.* Kalispell, MT: Trillium Press, 2017.

General Guides to Western Wildflowers

Stewart, Jon Mark. *Mojave Desert Wildflowers: A Field Guide to High Desert Wildflowers of California, Nevada and Arizona.* Albuquerque: Jon Stewart Photography, 1998.

Stokes, Donald, and Lillian Stokes. *The Wildflower Book: From the Rockies West; An Easy Guide to Growing and Identifying Wildflowers.* Boston: Little, Brown, 1993.

Taylor, Ronald J. *Sagebrush Country: A Wildflower Sanctuary.* Rev. ed. Missoula, MT: Mountain Press, 1992.

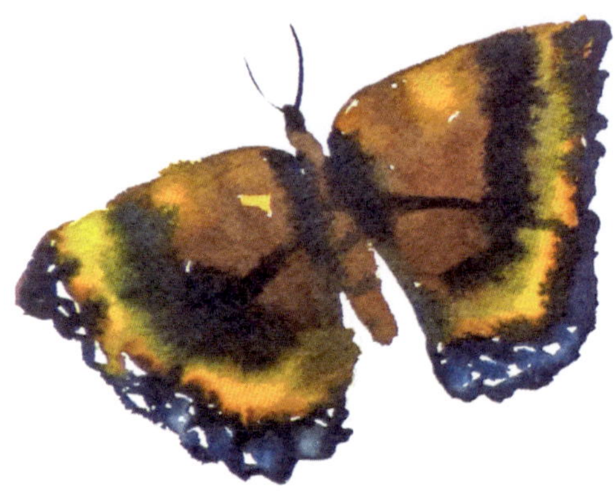

OTHER BOOKS

Brown, Wynne. *The Forgotten Botanist: Sara Plummer Lemmon's Life of Science and Art.* Lincoln: University of Nebraska Press, 2021.

Cactus Store, ed. *Xerophile: Cactus Photographs from Expeditions of the Obsessed.* Rev. ed. Berkeley, CA: Ten Speed Press, 2021.

Carr, Emily. *Wild Flowers.* Victoria: Royal BC Museum, 2006.

Kimmerer, Robin Wall. *Braiding Sweetgrass.* 2nd hardcover ed. Minneapolis: Milkweed Editions, 2020.

Mabey, Richard. *The Cabaret of Plants.* New York: W. W. Norton, 2017.

Munger, Susan H. *Common to This Country: Botanical Discoveries of Lewis and Clark.* New York: Artisan, 2003.

Musgrave, Toby, and Chris Gardner. *Wild Edens: The History and Habitat of Our Most-Loved Garden Plants.* London: Kyle Books, 2022.

Torre, Dan. *Cactus.* London: Reaktion Books, 2017.

ONLINE RESOURCES

Bloom Times

There are a variety of websites you can check to find out more about seasonal wildflower bloom times.

California

- Calscape: https://calscape.org/
- Theodore Payne Wildflower Hotline: 818-768-1802, ext. 7. You can listen to reports for Southern and central California, updated each Friday, March through June. https://theodorepayne.org/learn/wildflower-hotline/

Pacific Northwest
- Northwest Wildflowers: Details what is in bloom on any given day in specific locations. https://nwwildflowers.com/map/

Southwest
- Desert Botanical Garden: A map of seasonal blooms for Arizona; the information is not available online at all times of the year, so check in early spring. https://dbg.org/
- Lady Bird Johnson Wildflower Center, University of Texas at Austin: www.wildflower.org/whatsinseason/

Plant Identification
- iNaturalist: www.inaturalist.org/
- PictureThis: www.picturethisai.com/
- Pl@ntNet: https://plantnet.org/en/ (app) and https://identify.plantnet.org/ (website)
- USDA Plants Database: https://plants.usda.gov/home

GARDENS TO VISIT

Cactus Gardens

Arizona
- Arizona–Sonora Desert Museum (near Tucson): www.desertmuseum.org/
- Desert Botanical Garden (Phoenix): https://dbg.org/
- Tohono Chul (Tucson): https://tohonochul.org/

California
- Arizona Garden at Stanford University: https://facops.stanford.edu/arizona-garden
- Cactus Garden at the Getty Center (Los Angeles): www.getty.edu/visit/center/top-things-to-do/gardens/
- Deutsch Cactus Garden (Fresno): www.fresnodiscoverycenter.org/the-deutsch-cactus-garden
- Huntington Library Botanical Gardens (Huntington Beach): https://huntington.org/botanical-gardens
- Kate O. Sessions Cactus Garden at Balboa Park (San Diego): https://balboapark.org/parks-trails-gardens/kate-o-sessions-cactus-garden-balboa-park/
- Sunnylands (Rancho Mirage): https://sunnylands.org/

Botanical Gardens with Native Plants and Wildflowers

Arizona
- Desert Botanical Garden (Phoenix): https://dbg.org/
- Tucson Botanical Gardens: https://tucsonbotanical.org/

California
- California Botanic Garden (Claremont): www.calbg.org/
- Mendocino Coast Botanical Gardens (Fort Bragg): www.gardenbythesea.org/
- San Diego Botanic Garden (Encinitas): https://sdbg.org/
- San Francisco Botanical Garden in Golden Gate Park: https://gggp.org/san-francisco-botanical-garden/
- Santa Barbara Botanic Garden: https://sbbotanicgarden.org/
- UC Santa Cruz Arboretum and Botanic Garden: https://arboretum.ucsc.edu/

Colorado
- Betty Ford Alpine Gardens (Vail): https://bettyfordalpinegardens.org/
- Denver Botanic Gardens: www.botanicgardens.org/

Idaho
- Idaho Botanical Garden (Boise): www.idahobotanicalgarden.org/

New Mexico
- ABQ BioPark (Albuquerque): www.cabq.gov/artsculture/biopark
- Santa Fe Botanical Garden: www.visitsfbg.org

Oregon
- Hoyt Arboretum (Portland): www.hoytarboretum.org
- Leach Botanical Garden (Portland): www.leachgarden.org
- Mount Pisgah Arboretum (Eugene): https://mountpisgaharboretum.org/
- The Oregon Garden (Silverton): www.oregongarden.org

Utah
- Red Butte Garden (Salt Lake City): www.redbuttegarden.org
- Red Hills Desert Garden (St. George): www.redhillsdesertgarden.com

Washington

- Carkeek Park Demonstration Garden (Seattle): www.seattle.gov/parks/allparks/carkeek-park
- The Gifts Garden at the Evergreen State College (Olympia): www.evergreen.edu/longhouse /ethnobotanical-gifts-garden
- Kruckeberg Botanic Garden (Seattle): www.kruckeberg.org/
- Kul Kah Han Native Plant Garden in H. J. Carroll Park (Chimacum): www.nativeplantgarden.org/
- Northwest Native Plant Garden in Point Defiance Park (Tacoma): www.metroparkstacoma.org/ place/northwest-native-garden/
- Salal Native Plant Garden (Mount Vernon): www.wnps.org/salal-programs/garden
- Washington State University Extension of Benton and Franklin Counties Master Gardeners Demonstration Garden (Kennewick; shrub-steppe habitat): https://extension.wsu.edu/benton -franklin/mastergardeners/our-programs /demogarden/

SUPPLIES

The following list includes the materials that have performed best for me over the years.

Art Materials Stores

There are countless online resources and some fine, well-stocked retail outlets for art supplies. I recommend that you shop at retail art stores to get the best advice. The sales staffs are almost always artists and love helping you find just what you need.

- Artist and Craftsman Supply, retail and online: www.artistcraftsman.com
- Blick Art Materials, retail and online: www.dickblick.com
- John Neal Books, www.johnnealbooks.com
- McClain's Printmaking Supplies (online only): www.imcclains.com
- Paper and Ink Arts: www.paperinkarts.com/

Drawing Materials

- HB and 5B pencils
- A mechanical pencil (with 0.7 mm lead and an eraser), ideal for field sketches and general sketching
- Faber-Castell Albrecht Dürer watercolor pencils

- Caran d'Ache watercolor crayons
- Caran d'Ache oil-based pastel crayons (not water soluble)
- Staedtler white Mars plastic eraser
- Pilot G-Tec pen, 0.38 mm and 0.5 mm nib widths
- Stylist felt-tip pen; dissolves into a nice blue-black, excellent for quick sketches
- Staedtler brush pens, a variety of grays and browns
- Tombo or other brush markers, variety of colors
- Posca white pen, for small details on feathers and other highlights
- Winsor & Newton pens, variety of colors and nib widths
- Acrylic inks, variety of colors
- Scratchboard and tools

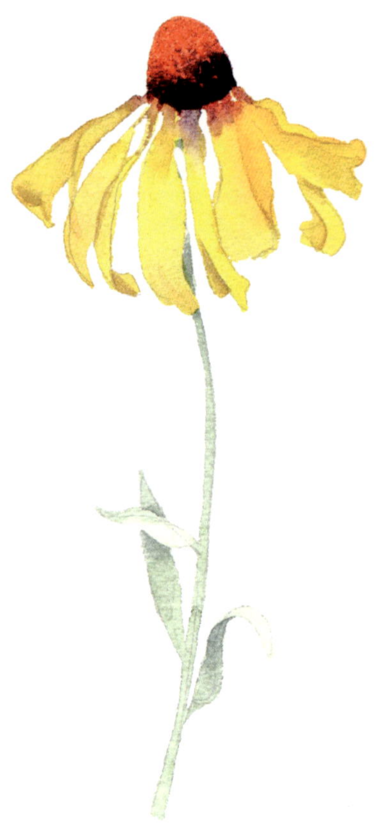

Sketchbooks

- Stillman & Birn archival-quality sketchbooks; available spiral-bound or softbound, in white, ivory, gray, and tan. The colored papers are ideal for making sketches on toned paper with white gouache.
- Hahnemühle sketchbooks with 100 percent cotton paper, assorted sizes
- Your own sketchbook with Arches 100 percent rag paper, spiral-bound at an office supply company

Watercolor Materials

- Watercolor papers: Arches 140-pound cold press; Fabriano Artistico 140-pound cold press; Lanaquarelle 140-pound cold press; Saunders Waterford 140-pound cold press and all of them also in hot press for a smooth surface; Twinrocker handmade paper in various tints and sizes; black Stonehenge Aqua cold press. You can have these papers cut and spiral-bound into a sketchbook at an office supply store or specialty binder.
- Bristol or other smooth drawing paper: 90-pound weight (minimum) so it can handle a light watercolor wash
- Brushes: Da Vinci Maestro sable rounds, numbers 2, 4, and 6, plus a ¾-inch flat sable brush and a ½-inch flat synthetic brush
- Palettes: John Pike Palette; San Francisco Slant Palette with multiple large wells for mixing washes
- Portable watercolor sets: Sennelier, Winsor & Newton, Van Gogh; alternatively, fill an empty portable travel palette with the paints listed below

Watercolor Tube Paints in Primary Colors (a Warm and Cool of Each)

I prefer Daniel Smith watercolors. Other high-quality manufacturers are Winsor & Newton, Old Holland, Schmincke, Sennelier, and M. Graham.

- Blue: phthalo blue (red shade), phthalo blue (green shade)
- Yellow: Hansa yellow deep, Hansa yellow medium
- Red: permanent alizarin crimson, pyrrol scarlet
- Other colors: Hansa yellow light, yellow ochre, quinacridone gold, quinacridone burnt orange, perylene red, quinacridone pink, quinacridone magenta, carbazole violet, phthalo green, perylene green, French ultramarine blue, cobalt blue, indanthrone blue, permanent white gouache

Printmaking Materials

- Safety-Kut carving blocks; available in various sizes, but cheapest if you buy the biggest and cut your own
- Speedball carving tools and handle: tools numbers 1–5 (U-gouge, big and small; V-gouge, big and small; square gouge)
- Charbonnel etching inks (which I use for relief printing): soft black, carbon black, and many other colors available
- Burnt plate oil for thinning ink
- Speedball water-soluble inks for proofing and colored prints
- Papers: Arches 140-pound hot press; Fabriano Artistico 140-pound hot press; Lanaquarelle 140-pound hot press; Kozo-shi Japanese washi paper for colored multiple block prints
- Shina plywood for carving wood blocks

Index

Page numbers in italics refer to illustrations

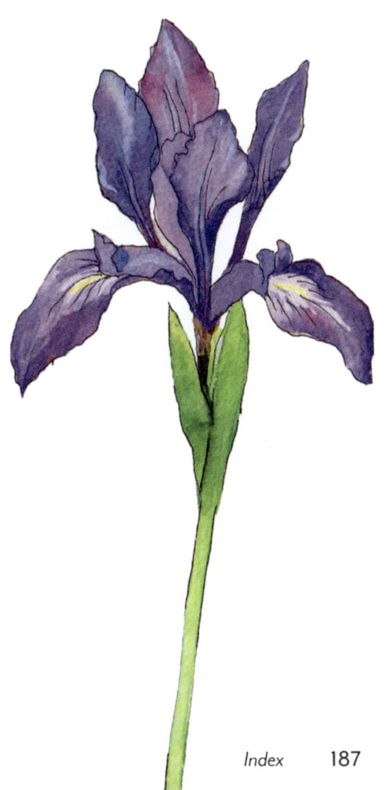

About the Author

MOLLY HASHIMOTO explores parks and wildlife refuges all over the West, finding inspiration for her artwork in the natural world all around us. Her work has appeared for more than thirty years on cards and calendars published by Pomegranate Communications, and her previous books under the Skipstone imprint include *Colors of the West, Birds of the West, Trees of the West,* and *Mount Rainier National Park: An Artist's Tour.*

Dedicated to connecting people with nature through hands-on art experiences, Molly Hashimoto teaches aspiring artists and has led plein air art workshops throughout the West, including at the North Cascades Institute, Yellowstone Forever Institute, Yosemite Conservancy, and Sitka Center for Art and Ecology. She lives in Seattle.

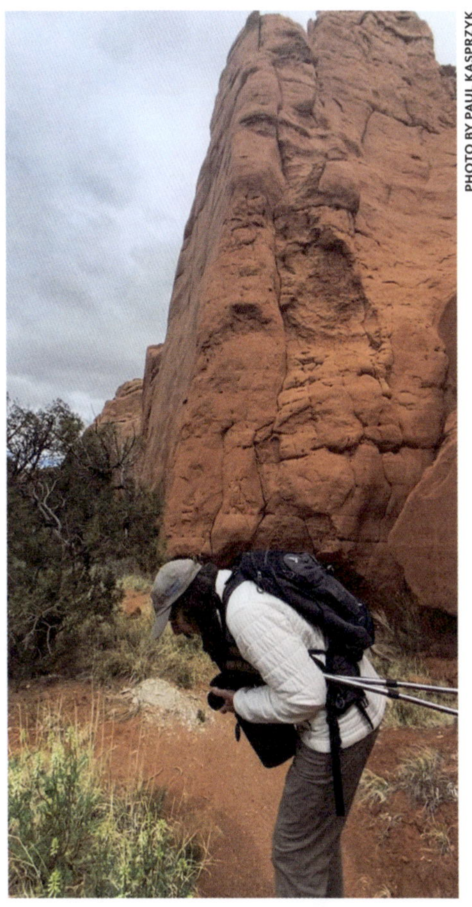

EXAMINING TWO-GROOVED MILKVETCH IN KODACHROME BASIN STATE PARK, UTAH

Also Available

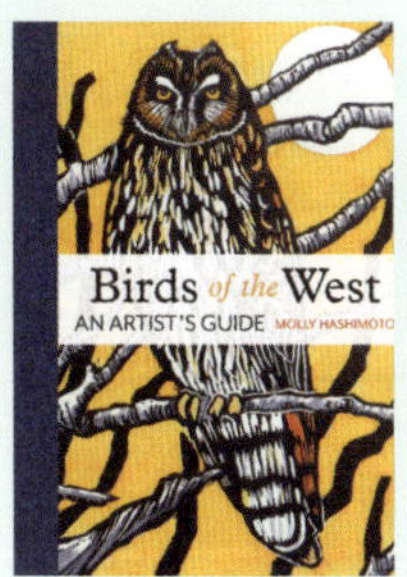

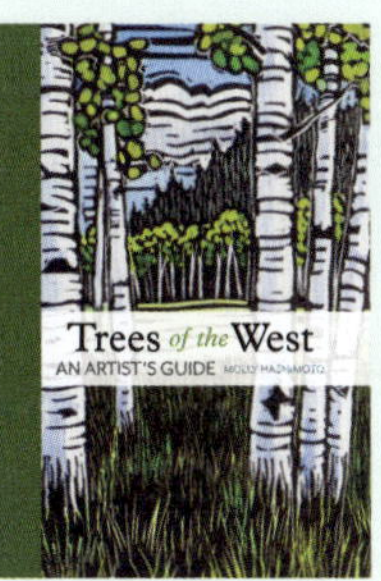

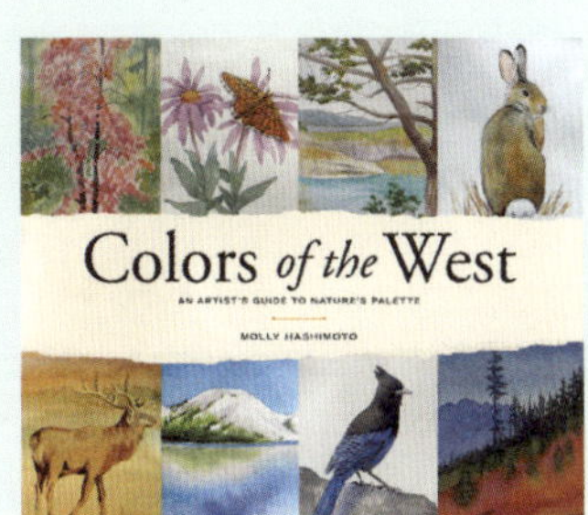

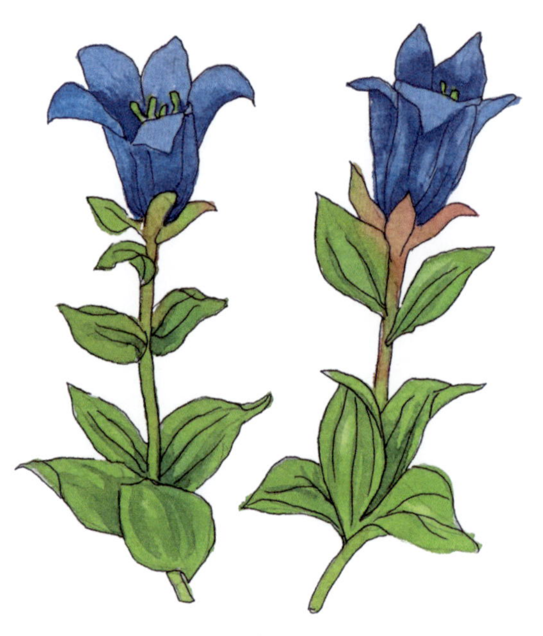